1 2 OCT 2021
30 APR 2024

Dig

Please return/renew this item
by the last date shown.

01473 351249 | help@suffolklibraries.co.uk

www.suffolklibraries.co.uk

Make a donation to support our work at
www.suffolklibraries.co.uk/donate

Every purchase of a Facet book helps to fund CILIP's advocacy, awareness and accreditation programmes for information professionals.

Digital Literacy Unpacked

Edited by

Katharine Reedy and Jo Parker

© This compilation: Katharine Reedy and Jo Parker 2018
The chapters: the contributors 2018

Published by Facet Publishing,
7 Ridgmount Street, London WC1E 7AE
www.facetpublishing.co.uk

Facet Publishing is wholly owned by CILIP: the Library and Information Association.

The editor and authors of the individual chapters assert their moral right to be identified as such in accordance with the terms of the Copyright, Designs and Patents Act 1988.

Except as otherwise permitted under the Copyright, Designs and Patents Act 1988 this publication may only be reproduced, stored or transmitted in any form or by any means, with the prior permission of the publisher, or, in the case of reprographic reproduction, in accordance with the terms of a licence issued by the Copyright Licensing Agency. Enquiries concerning reproduction outside those terms should be sent to Facet Publishing, 7 Ridgmount Street, London WC1E 7AE.

Every effort has been made to contact the holders of copyright material reproduced in this text, and thanks are due to them for permission to reproduce the material indicated. If there are any queries please contact the publisher.

British Library Cataloguing in Publication Data
A catalogue record for this book is available from the British Library.

ISBN 978-1-78330-197-3 (paperback)
ISBN 978-1-78330-198-0 (hardback)
ISBN 978-1-78330-199-7 (e-book)

First published 2018

Text printed on FSC accredited material

SUFFOLK LIBRARIES	
30127 08828127 9	
Askews & Holts	03-Aug-2021
025.04	

Typeset from editors' files by Flagholme Publishing Services in 11/14pt Revival565 and Frutiger
Printed and made in Great Britain by CPI Group (UK) Ltd, Croydon, CR0 4YY.

Contents

List of figures and case studies vii

Foreword ix
   Rosie Jones

Notes on contributors xi

Introduction xxi

Part I Approaching digital literacy 1

1 **The trouble with terminology: rehabilitating and rethinking**   3
   'digital literacy'
   Jane Secker

2 **Unpacking digital literacy: the potential contribution of central**   17
   services to enabling the development of staff and student
   digital literacies
   Joe Nicholls

3 **Collaboration and coaching: powerful strategies for developing**   29
   digital capabilities
   Clare Killen

Part II Learning in a digital world 45

4 **Digital literacy in UK and European schools: enhancing school**   47
   children's motivation to read for pleasure
   Geoff Walton, Mark Childs, Vedrana Vojković Estatiev, Janet Hetherington
   and Gordana Jugo

5 Digital games: providing unique digital literacy challenges in childhood   63
Dean Groom and Judy O'Connell

6 Students in the SADL: lessons from LSE's digital literacy programme   83
Jane Secker

7 Copyright and digital literacy: rules, risk and creativity   97
Chris Morrison

Part III Developing staff digital literacies   109

8 D4 curriculum design workshops: a model for developing digital literacy in practice   111
Liz Bennett and Sue Folley

9 #creativeHE: an animated Google Plus platform for challenging practitioners to think differently   123
Chrissi Nerantzi and Norman Jackson

10 Developing library staff digital literacies   139
Charles Inskip

Part IV Digital citizens and workers   153

11 Digital literacy and open educational practice: DigiLit Leicester   155
Josie Fraser with Katharine Reedy

12 Transforming the workplace through digital literacy   169
Bonnie Cheuk and Katharine Reedy

13 Critical digital literacy education in the 'fake news' era   179
Philip Seargeant and Caroline Tagg

14 Onwards! Why the movement for digital inclusion has never been more important   191
Adam Micklethwaite

Conclusion   203

Index   205

List of figures and case studies

Figures
1.1	Beetham and Sharpe's model of digital literacies, 2010	6
1.2	The wider literacies landscape	7
2.1	Learning literacies development framework (Jisc, 2013) adapted from Sharpe and Beetham (2010)	18
3.1	The six elements of the Jisc Digital Capabilities Framework (individual model)	31
3.2	All Aboard's digital skills in higher education metro map	31
7.1	The five elements of critical copyright literacy	99
8.1	A hierarchical model to depict learners developing effective strategies for learning with technology	113
8.2	The Appreciative Inquiry Model, the basis for D4 curriculum design workshops	114
8.3	Example of the Debate Jisc ViewPoint card used in the design stage	116
9.1	Model of scaffolded social learning in an online learning environment	124
9.2	Day 3 challenge for the #creativeHE course in January 2017	127
10.1	Comparison of the frequency of use of 'information literacy', 'digital literacy' and 'media literacy' as search terms, 2004–2017	140
11.1	DigiLit Framework Strands (DigiLit Leicester project, 2014, shared under Creative Commons Attribution 4.0 International License (CC by 4.0))	161
11.2	DigiLit Leicester survey results 2014, shared under Creative Commons Attribution 4.0 International License (CC by 4.0)	162

Case studies

2.1	Digital curation to develop digital literacies	25
2.2	Presentations and presenting to develop digital literacies	26
3.1	The University of Southampton: working in partnership with students	34
3.2	Faculty of Humanities: the Mission Employable Project	34
3.3	Salford City College: cascading skills through staff and student champions	34
3.4	University College London: modern variations on a radical tradition	35
3.5	The University of Lincoln: how digital are you?	35
3.6	Lancaster University: digital fluency for everyone	37
3.7	The University of Hertfordshire: Building digital capability through collaborative engagement	37
3.8	Derby Adult Learning Service: peer support tutor service leads to embedded use of technology in curriculum activities	39
3.9	South Eastern Regional College: a whole college approach to developing digital capabilities	40
3.10	Leicestershire Adult Learning Service: an integrated approach to staff development using supported experiments and coaching techniques	40

Foreword

I am delighted to be asked to introduce this book: its timing is key, given the rate of technological change and advances in our thinking around skills, and it contributes practice, theory and research to a topic that is important on a global scale. In fact, I would say more than 'important': digital literacy is a powerful subject, which supports inclusivity, social mobility and digital citizenship. Across all sectors, we can't avoid the digital agenda and this text provides a fabulous insight into digital literacy and learning. The contributors are thought leaders and experts in their fields: they are exactly who we should be listening to. Finally, I can't finish this foreword without mentioning the editors of the text. Jo and Katharine have done so much for digital literacy; they have promoted the topic, shared their knowledge in the sector, produced ground-breaking resources and along the way won awards. They really know what they are talking about – I have no doubt you will enjoy reading this book!

> Rosie Jones
> Director of Library Services,
> The Open University

Notes on contributors

Dr Liz Bennett is a university teaching fellow in the School of Education and Professional Development at the University of Huddersfield. Liz's role is to deliver strategic and operational development for the School's teaching portfolio. She has introduced approaches to self-regulated learning to the School and promoted the D4 curriculum design approach (see Chapter 8) to supporting the development of digital literacies in the curriculum. This initiative has had widespread take up with over 250 colleagues from across the University participating in the workshops. She is currently the principal investigator on a scoping project funded by the Society for Research in Higher Education entitled Students' Learning Responses to Feedback on Their Progress Using Learning Analytics Dashboards, and has published extensively on higher education practices and learning technology.

Dr Bonnie Cheuk is a strategic, hands-on, business-and-results-driven executive with strong expertise in digital transformation, web–digital channel management, information and knowledge management, collaboration, social media and Enterprise 2.0. Originally from Hong Kong, she has more than 20 years of international work experience with multinational corporations in Hong Kong, Singapore, the USA, the UK and Europe. Her expertise lies in blending her deep understanding of information and knowledge management, change management, communication and facilitation principles and practices with her knowledge of the latest technologies to deliver business solutions and drive change. She has led the successful roll out of social collaboration and knowledge sharing programmes for Euroclear, Citigroup, Environmental Resources Management (ERM) and the British Council. Bonnie is currently partnering with business and technology leaders to shape the future digital workplace experience for employees, and to refresh the web, social media and digital strategy to improve client experience for a global financial services company. Bonnie's doctorate research focused on understanding information seeking and user behaviour in the workplace. Bonnie publishes papers, gives lectures at universities and speaks regularly at international conferences. She is the author of *Social Strategies in Action: driving business transformation* published by Ark Group in 2013.

Dr Mark Childs is a Learning Designer at the Open University. His research is in online collaborative learning, and in learners' experiences of digital identity and online presence. He has co-edited a book on digital identity for Springer (*Reinventing Ourselves*) and co-authored one on the experience of online spaces for Chandos (*Making Sense of Space*). His most recent book, for Routledge (*Online Learning for STEM Subjects*), was published in January 2017. Mark's PhD on learners' experience of presence was awarded in 2010 by the University of Warwick. He is a senior fellow of the Higher Education Academy and a visiting fellow at Edge Hill University. His blog and a summary of his professional work can be found at markchilds.org

Vedrana Vojković Estatiev is an adjunct lecturer in English for academic purposes at the University of Zagreb. She teaches undergraduate and graduate courses to students of communication sciences, using traditional, blended and online delivery, and has co-authored a practice book entitled *English Academic Vocabulary for Social Sciences and Humanities*. She has extensive experience in online course design and moderation, and is particularly interested in how second and foreign language learning may be facilitated in online learning environments. Vedrana holds an MA in English language and literature from the University of Zagreb. Prior to teaching at tertiary level, she was director of studies and part owner of a language school for several years.

Dr Sue Folley is an academic developer based at the University of Huddersfield, with a remit to support the pedagogic development of staff in the use of digital technologies. Her role involves training staff and contributing to the University's strategic developments in this area. She has a postgraduate certificate in education (PGCE) and has previously taught mathematics in the further education sector, but has worked in higher education for the last 18 years. She has a master's degree in multimedia and e-learning and has completed a doctorate in education focusing on tutors' experiences of teaching online. She is a senior fellow of the Higher Education Academy and the University's representative on the Heads of eLearning Forum (Helf). Sue's research interests include digital literacy, learning analytics and curriculum development.

Josie Fraser is a UK-based social and educational technologist, who works across sectors advising on and implementing the innovative and effective use of technology. Her work focuses on digital literacy, digital citizenship and the digital economy. She was awarded honorary life membership of the Association for Learning Technology in 2017. She currently works for the UK government as senior technology adviser on the National Technology Team, based in the Department for Digital, Culture, Media and Sport (DCMS). Josie is chair of Wikimedia UK (https://wikimedia.org.uk/wiki/Main_Page), a charity dedicated to supporting access to knowledge for all, promoting engagement with Wikimedia projects, including Wikipedia. She blogs at Social Tech (http://www.josiefraser.com/) and her Twitter ID is @josiefraser.

Good Things Foundation (https://www.goodthingsfoundation.org/) is a UK charity and digital social change organisation, with a mission to help everyone benefit from digital technology. The Foundation is a key partner of the UK government; since 2010 it has helped over 2.3 million people improve their lives through digital technology. Good Things works with a national network of 5000 community-based organisations, the Online Centres Network, to reach socially excluded people and help them thrive online, and to design and deliver a wide range of funded programmes with UK government departments, the private sector and grant-making bodies. The Foundation is also working across Australia to build a community-based digital inclusion network reaching older Australians, and with the Kenyan National Library Service.

Dean Groom has worked as a lecturer and in senior roles in educational development at Macquarie University since 2008. From 2008 to 2013 he was Head of Educational Development and Design and in 2013–14 he was Head of E-learning in the Faculty of Arts and Social Sciences at University of New South Wales, before commencing a doctorate in 2013 at Macquarie University researching the negotiations of play that takes place between families and digital game media. His work spans early childhood, school-age and tertiary education, continuing a long history of developing innovative learning environments and experiences. In 2014, he received an Australian Postgraduate Awards Commonwealth Government Scholarship for his research into how families and children use digital games as active networks and how this shapes their rituals, routines and belief about media more broadly.

Janet Hetherington is a participatory practitioner specialising in using community arts in a research context. Having established the Arts Programme at Birmingham Children's Hospital, she then worked as a senior lecturer at Staffordshire University, specialising in using community arts as a tool for action research across Europe, and supporting the professional development of artists working in the field. As an independent consultant, she has advised schools, colleges, local authorities and arts organisations on cultural development and creative learning. She currently works in primary education and continues to facilitate and support initiatives to use creativity throughout the curriculum to engage learners and educators.

Dr Charles Inskip is a senior lecturer and the Programme Director on the MA Library and Information Studies at University College London (UCL). His research interests lie around the connections between people, information and technology (of all kinds) and his PhD exploration of the information behaviours of creative music professionals led to an interest in information literacy. He is directly involved in developing and delivering the library studies curriculum and introduced an information literacy module to the UCL MA in library and information studies. He is currently exploring the information work of insurance practitioners with a view to supporting graduate employability and is completing a book on information literacy for Facet Publishing.

Professor Norman Jackson (www.normanjackson.co.uk/) is Emeritus Professor of the University of Surrey and founder of two social educational enterprises: Lifewide Education (www.lifewideeducation. uk/) and Creative Academic (www.creativeacademic.uk/). He is commissioning editor for two digital magazines and facilitator for several Google Plus forums. An important focus of his work over the last 17 years has been higher education's involvement in developing students' creativity, which is documented in four books including *Developing Creativity in Higher Education: an imaginative curriculum* and his recent book *Exploring Learning Ecologies*. He is currently researching creativity in practice and ecologies of learning and practice, including how technology features in creative processes. He tweets as @lifewider1 and @academiccreator.

Rosie Jones is Director of Library Services at the Open University. She has worked in academic libraries since 2001 taking a particular interest in games and learning, information literacy and learning space development. She is particularly involved in the UK academic library Information Literacy community, currently co-chairs the Librarians' Information Literacy Annual Conference (LILAC) and is the Deputy Chair for CILIP Information Literacy Group. Her LinkedIn profile can be found at https://www.linkedin.com/in/rosiejhjones

Gordana Jugo is a head of the Service for Educational Technologies in the Croatian Academic and Research Network (CARNet). She has been involved in numerous projects and activities aiming to implement technology in Croatian schools to enhance teaching and learning, and develop digital skills of teachers, staff and pupils. One of the most important projects in her portfolio is the national E-schools Project; she focuses on developing a model for digitally mature schools in Croatia. Gordana supports innovative uses of technology in teaching, with focus on pedagogy, and shares knowledge and experiences including about open educational resources. She holds a master's in educational technology from the University of British Columbia. One of the projects she has most enjoyed being involved in is the Comenius project AMORES (an Approach to MOtivating learners to Read in European Schools; http://www.amores-project.eu/), which has the motto 'discovering a love for literature through digital collaboration and creativity'.

Clare Killen has 23 years of experience in supporting providers from the higher and further education and skills sectors with various aspects of staff development including in effective use of digital technologies to support educational practices and ambitions. She has led teams delivering national initiatives and provided consultancy services focusing on whole organisational approaches, transformational change, curriculum design and improving professional practice through peer coaching. Clare has authored several guides for Jisc (formerly the Joint Information Systems Committee) on topics such as student–staff partnerships, emerging digital practices and digital capability development.

Adam Micklethwaite is Director of Digital Inclusion at Good Things Foundation. He has built partnerships at national, local and international level that support vulnerable and excluded people to benefit from the digital world. Before joining Good Things, Adam was a senior civil servant in the UK government, where he worked on education and skills policy, the funding of further education, and supporting enterprise. This included developing the first student loans system in UK further education, and launching the UK National Careers Service.

Chris Morrison is the Copyright Support and Software Licensing Manager at the University of Kent, responsible for copyright policy, licensing, training and advice. He was previously the Copyright Assurance Manager at the British Library and before that worked for music collecting society PRS for Music. With Dr Jane Secker he is co-author of the second edition of *Copyright and E-learning: a guide for practitioners* (Facet Publishing), and with Jane co-founded the award-winning copyrightliteracy.org blog. Chris is a member of the Universities UK / Guild HE Copyright Working Group, has a postgraduate diploma in copyright law from King's College London and is currently undertaking a master's research project into the interpretation of copyright exceptions in UK higher education.

Dr Chrissi Nerantzi (@chrissinerantzi) is an experienced academic developer, open practitioner and researcher working in the Centre for Excellence in Learning and Teaching at Manchester Metropolitan University. Her interests are in creative, innovative and open learning and teaching and her work has been recognised nationally and internationally. Chrissi has conceived and initiated a range of open cross-institutional professional development initiatives. Examples include #creativeHE, #LTHEchat and @BYOD4L, which bring practitioners, students and the public together to learn and develop, nationally and internationally, and have inspired others to innovate and engage in creative and open practices. Through her doctoral studies, she explored the collaborative open learning experience using phenomenography. One of her key outputs is the framework for cross-boundary collaborative open learning for cross-institutional academic development she developed. Norman Jackson and Chrissi work closely together in the #creativeHE community and as Creative Academic champions. To find out more about Chrissi, please visit https://chrissinerantzi.wordpress.com/.

Dr Joe Nicholls is a principal consultant in Cardiff University Library Services specialising in digital enablement, and a lecturer in medical education tutoring on distance learning postgraduate programmes. He has a background in psychology, human–computer interaction and learning technology, with research experience in the design and evaluation of interfaces to educational technologies and information systems. He has over 20 years of experience teaching university staff and students on the design, development and effective use of digital media and technologies for learning and teaching. His current interests concern establishing sustainable and scalable approaches to enabling the development of staff and student digital literacies and the design of effective pedagogies for online learning.

Judy O'Connell is a senior lecturer in the School of Information Studies, Faculty of Arts and Education at Charles Sturt University. She has also filled the role of course director for bachelor and masters' programmes in information science, and later was the quality learning and teaching lead in online learning, working with academics in a wide range of science disciplines to support online learning design, innovation, social media and technology for learning and teaching. Prior to joining Charles Sturt University in 2011, Judy was head of information services at a range of large independent schools and education consultant in Web 2.0 developments for 80 primary and secondary schools in the Western Region of Sydney, Australia, where she first began researching virtual worlds, games and online environments in influencing the learning dispositions of young people. Judy has received faculty awards for academic excellence (2014, 2016) for her work. She is pursuing doctoral study in digital scholarship at La Trobe University.

Jo Parker is a senior library manager at the Open University Library, with responsibility for developing digital and information literacy strategy. Her current role is leading institutional digital capabilities development. She is a 'jolly good fellow' – a Winston Churchill Memorial Trust Fellow, a fellow of the Higher Education Academy, and a fellow of the Leadership Foundation, as well as holder of an Open University teaching award. She has co-edited two previous books for Facet Publishing, and was 2017's 'runner up' for the information literacy practitioner award at the Librarians' Information Literacy Annual Conference.

Katharine Reedy is a digital literacy specialist and learning designer. She was active in the field of digital and information literacy for over ten years in different roles within the Open University Library before joining the Open University Learning Design team in 2016. Her focus is on curriculum development, including the award-winning Being Digital collection and the Open University's Digital and Information Literacy Framework. She has a strong interest in learning design and its potential to improve the study experience. Other work includes 'Succeeding in a Digital World', the Open University's free digital literacy course aimed at developing learners' confidence and skills, and writing the digital literacy 'theme' document for the Open University's 2015 Quality Assurance Agency review. Katharine is a senior fellow of the Higher Education Academy and chartered member of the Chartered Institute of Library and Information Professionals (CILIP). Her contribution to digital and information literacy was recognised in 2015 with the award of Information Literacy Practitioner of the Year.

Dr Philip Seargeant is Senior Lecturer in Applied Linguistics at the Open University. He is co-author of *The Idea of English in Japan*, *Exploring World Englishes* and *From Language to Creative Writing* (with Bill Greenwell) and of *Taking Offence on Social Media* (with Caroline Tagg and Amy Aisha Brown), and co-editor of *English in Japan in the Era of Globalization* and *English in the World* (with Joan Swann), *English and Development* (with Elizabeth J. Erling), *The Language of Social Media* (with Caroline Tagg) and *Futures for English Studies* (with Ann Hewings and Lynda Prescott).

Dr Jane Secker is Senior Lecturer in Educational Development at City University London and the former copyright and digital literacy adviser at the London School of Economics, where she provided advice and support for staff and students. She is Chair of the CILIP Information

Literacy Group and the author of several books, including *Copyright and E-learning: a guide for practitioners*. The second edition of this book was published June 2016, co-authored with Chris Morrison. Her research interests include digital and information literacy, copyright education and the role of technologies in supporting learning. She is an honorary fellow of CILIP, a fellow of the Higher Education Academy and co-founder of the Librarians' Information Literacy Annual Conference. She devised A New Curriculum for Information Literacy (ANCIL) with Emma Coonan, which is a framework for supporting learning in higher education, and has written and spoken widely on her research. Jane has been a member of the Universities UK Copyright Working Group since 2006, which negotiates licences for the higher education sector with bodies such as the Copyright Licensing Agency (CLA). Jane and Chris maintain the website UK Copyright Literacy and tweet as @UKCopyrightLit.

Dr Caroline Tagg is Lecturer in Applied Linguistics at the Open University. Her research is in the language of social media. Her previous publications as author are *The Discourse of Text Messaging* (Continuum), and *Exploring Digital Communication: language in action* (Routledge), and as co-author *Taking Offence on Social Media: conviviality and communication on Facebook* (Palgrave, with Philip Seargeant and Amy Aisha Brown); she also co-edited *The Language of Social Media: identity and community on the internet* (2014, Palgrave, with Philip Seargeant).

Dr Geoff Walton is Senior Lecturer in the Department of Languages, Information and Communications at Manchester Metropolitan University. He is currently working on a project on information discernment and psychophysiological wellbeing in response to misinformed stigmatisation funded by the CILIP Information Literacy Group. Geoff previously worked at Northumbria University where he was involved in a British Academy–Leverhulme Trust funded project with Dr Ali Pickard and the late Professor Mark Hepworth. He has also worked on the EU-funded research project AMORES. Geoff's main research interests are information literacy, information behaviour, technology-enhanced learning, data literacy and public libraries. A list of his publications can be found at https://scholar.google.co.uk/citations?user=UwsIXpUAAAAJ&hl=en.

Introduction

Much has been written about the fast-changing world in which we live and the impact that technological change is having on every part of life. Routine services and transactions take place online, whether doing the weekly shop, applying for jobs or accessing the benefits one is entitled to. Students at all stages of education are required to use digital tools and to make sense of online information in order to learn and to be prepared for the workplace. The world of work today may bear little relation to that of tomorrow, so we are educating people not just for current employment, but for jobs that do not yet exist. Alongside all of that, our worldview is likely to be shaped by the interactions we have via social media. This can have positive effects on health, wellbeing and quality of life, overcoming social isolation and loneliness. It also requires the skills and confidence to deal with unwanted behaviour such as cyberbullying, or scams and hoaxes. How can we engage with and make the most of the opportunities that 'digital' offers, while avoiding the negative aspects?

The term 'digital literacy' has been in common usage for some years, with a variety of interpretations of what it means. These range from basic access through to sophisticated 'maker' skills. Many frameworks and models are available, created to support particular constituencies of learners, and often focusing on skills and competencies. More recently, 'digital literacy' has evolved into 'digital capabilities', encompassing the skills that staff and students in further and higher education settings require to teach, learn and thrive in a digital environment.

Our own experience in UK higher education is lengthy and varied. As educators and information professionals at the Open University we have worked extensively to support distance learners by developing resources and frameworks such as the Open University's Digital and Information Literacy Framework and the collection of online bite-size learning materials in Being Digital. More recently, the focus has been on staff digital capabilities, and rolling out a programme of development for frontline teachers. We are also engaged in supporting academic colleagues to design learning that maximises the potential of the digital environment.

Our passion for digital literacy extends beyond our working environments, into other sectors and aspects of our lives. For example, Katharine's work volunteering as a trustee of her local Citizens Advice service has brought into sharp relief the need for vulnerable members of the community to be able to navigate online systems in order to access and benefit from essential services and support. Jo supports her community in local government, and is active in disability campaigning and special needs education. Taken as a whole, this indicates that digital skills – whatever they are and however they are defined – are essential to participation, relevant to all, and have benefits beyond formal education.

'Digital skills' are an aspect of digital literacy, but they are not the whole picture. Critical thinking – about online information, tools and people – underpins digital literacy, giving it a richer dimension than just the ability to use technology. Digital literacy has synergies and overlaps with other 'literacies' too, including media literacy (Ofcom, https://www.ofcom.org.uk/research-and-data/media-literacy-research/media-literacy), 'web' or 'internet' literacy, derived from the teaching of general information and communications technology (ICT) skills; visual literacy (for example, ACRL, 2011, http://www.ala.org/acrl/standards/visualliteracy), data literacy and information literacy. Those aspects of digital literacy relating to inclusion and social mission are highly important and align closely with the aims of the organisation for which we work: the Open University mission puts inclusion, progression and social mobility at its very heart. Open University graduation ceremonies are a celebration not just of academic effort and achievement, but of challenges overcome, boundaries crossed, and the emancipation of individual lives.

It is all of this that has driven us to gather together this collection of chapters, authored by experts in their respective fields. The intention is not only to bring you a snapshot of innovative approaches to digital literacy, but also to provoke discussion, encourage collaboration and inspire you in your own work – whatever your role or context. In short, we aim to open up the whole area of digital literacy in all its kaleidoscopic richness, and provide you with diverse perspectives, content and ideas to inform your thinking and practice. The title of the book, Digital Literacy Unpacked, reflects this aspiration.

The cross-sectoral and global significance of digital literacy has also been crucial to the way we have approached this book. Whilst primarily aimed at librarians and information professionals (in the UK and internationally), it should also appeal to learning developers, educational technologists, institutional leaders, public librarians and library and information science students. If you are new to the library profession, the chapters provide a multi-faceted introduction to digital literacy. If you are a more experienced library and information practitioner, seeking to promote and develop digital / information literacy in your context, you will find a wealth of practical ideas and approaches. If you are a learning designer or educational technologist involved in developing learning materials, there are insights to encourage and inspire you. For those in student or customer-facing roles, you will find many examples highlighting the value you can add to learning and teaching. Institutional leaders also have much to gain from engaging with the material in this book, particularly those chapters that address high-level frameworks and models.

Whatever your interest or background, we hope there is something to draw on in every one of the chapters which our authors have so willingly offered. Digital literacy is relevant to higher education, further education, schools, children, and the workplace – but crucially at its heart it is a citizenship and inclusion issue, necessary for the full participation and achievement of potential of all in society.

The chapters in this book contain a mixture of practical examples, theory and research. They are organised according to four themes, which reflect some of the key considerations we have identified:

- approaching digital literacy
- learning in a digital world
- developing staff digital literacies
- digital citizens and workers.

Within each of the themes, the individual chapters highlight a particular facet of digital literacy and suggest some approaches. We begin with terminology. Digital literacy can mean different things to different people and an important first step, as outlined by Jane Secker, is to come to a shared understanding of what digital literacy means in a particular setting. Jane also emphasises the important role that professional services staff can play when working together to support learning and teaching in higher education settings and recommends a holistic approach involving all the main stakeholders.

This view is reinforced by Joe Nicholls in his discussion of how front-facing staff in professional service units are uniquely positioned to enable staff and students to make a direct connection with the tools and technologies that will be useful to them in their context. Service staff, who understand the context in which educators and students work, can successfully curate and mediate the digital tools and practices that will support and enhance learning and teaching. Communication and conversation are essential to this, in physical and online spaces. This can be supported by a knowledge hub with online examples of how digital practices have been used in context.

Clare Killen summarises a body of work undertaken through Jisc (a UK cross-higher and further education organisation), to enable you to take the most important highlights from this development. She helpfully shares a range of frameworks and models that have been used to communicate digital literacy to stakeholders. Her main point is the fact that collaboration – in its many guises – is fundamental to ensuring success. Peer coaching is a tried and tested approach that enables people to take ownership of their development needs and achieve cultural change at institutional level.

Our second theme, 'Learning in a digital world', kicks off with a collaboratively-authored chapter about children and literacy by Geoff Walton, Mark Childs, Vedrana Vojković Estatiev, Janet Hetherington and Gordana Jugo. Through interactive, collaborative and creative use of ICT, school students from five European countries between the ages of 9–14 were motivated to read for pleasure. This study highlights the importance of participants as partners, where all voices have the opportunity to be heard. It also demonstrates the importance of motivation, with digital literacy a welcome by-product of using technology for a particular task.

The joy of play, and its role in learning, is also evident in Dean Groom and Judy O'Connell's chapter about digital games. Education comes in many forms, and games have a role in this, providing a fun and immersive environment in which real and imaginary worlds blend together and boundaries between formal and informal learning are blurred. Gaming approaches enable children to actively participate in constructing their own experiences, with the opportunity to learn and interact socially. Positive benefits include motivation, problem solving and higher-order meta-cognitive thinking.

Jane Secker's case study on Student Ambassadors for Digital Literacy (SADL) focuses on a co-creation approach between students and faculty to develop digital literacy skills, resulting in benefits for all participants. Like other contributors, this chapter emphasises the importance of partnerships and peer mentoring. Jane also draws attention to the challenges of scalability, evaluating success and embedding successful approaches into institutional strategy. Benefits to students of engaging in the SADL programme extended beyond study, into the workplace.

Finally in this section, Chris Morrison introduces the concept of copyright literacy, and the impact of the online world on traditional print approaches to copyright. This is a complex relationship, but common sense – and, once again, play – have a role in skills development here. Awareness of copyright is a fundamental part of digital literacy, enabling online educational content to be shared openly while respecting the rights of creators.

'Staff need digital capability/literacy in order to teach digital capability/literacy. You can't have one without the other'. These words from Eric Stoller in a presentation at the OU on 11 April 2016 are a good way to frame the chapters you will find in our third section on developing staff digital literacies.

Liz Bennett and Sue Folley from the University of Huddersfield share their 'D4' model for curriculum design. This focuses on what teachers want students to achieve by the end of the course and the skills and practices that will need to be embedded into the curriculum. Using an appreciative inquiry approach as a basis for a short experiential workshop, staff look at what works well in a given context and where their existing strengths lie (rather than thinking about where they lack competencies). This ensures that the focus remains on the teaching and learning purpose, while at the same time motivating staff to develop their digital capabilities.

#CreativeHE is an open and collaborative approach to professional learning developed by Chrissi Nerantzi and Norman Jackson, which provides a space for sharing and discussion of creativity in teaching using digital tools. Culturally diverse and international in nature, #CreativeHE enables a wide range of participants (not all of whom are currently teaching in higher education) to stretch their thinking and practice through scheduled activities, playful experimentation and social interaction. Facilitators aim to build a climate of trust and respect, which empowers participants to express themselves creatively and gain new insights.

Charlie Inskip revisits definitions of digital literacy in the context of the changing role of library and information professionals across different sectors. He highlights the relational and contextual nature of digital literacies and the range of initiatives that have been developed to upskill the workforce. The central role of librarians in supporting and developing digital capabilities is clear. Common themes emerging from these chapters are once again collaboration, partnership and motivation.

Our final section takes a wider view of society, inclusion and the world of work.

Josie Fraser shares the innovative approach taken by the DigiLit Leicester project, which set out to realise the value of technology investment in schools, raise achievement, connect communities and open up opportunities for all. These wide-reaching aspirations were addressed through initiatives to build the skills of teachers and teaching support staff – focusing on priority areas for their context – and encourage the creation and sharing of open educational resources. Copyright literacy was found to be a core underpinning concept for open educational practice and the importance of developing learners' critical thinking skills is highlighted. The 'lessons learned' are widely applicable.

Bonnie Cheuk brings her experienced perspective on what it means to be a digitally capable employee in a fast-changing world. This is about company strategy and change, rather than technology use as such. Achieving company goals involves employees connecting, communicating and collaborating across boundaries (hierarchical and geographical), and requires everyone to take personal responsibility for their own development. Risktaking and collective experimentation are to be encouraged, and a 'human' non-hierarchical style of leadership is needed. Open two-way communication is fundamental to this process of change management.

Caroline Tagg and Philip Seargeant present the concept of fake news, an issue of global concern in recent times, particularly in the context of social media, and the challenges it presents to all of us. They underline the importance of educating people about how information on social media is produced and shared. Developing the skills to sift, evaluate and authenticate information (information literacy) is part of this. They suggest a need to go beyond digital skills, however, to enable people to take a critical approach to information and civic debate more generally.

Finally, Adam Micklethwaite of Good Things Foundation (an organisation which exists to promote digital inclusion) puts forward the crucial role of basic digital skills in combatting social exclusion. Along with other contributors he sees personal relationships as central to enabling digital participation. Building trust helps to overcome the fears of those who are (for whatever reason) offline – and the numbers in the UK and globally are still too high. Identifying a practical application – finding out 'what's in it for me' – gives people a reason to engage. To ensure continued momentum for digital inclusion initiatives, there needs to be support at stakeholder (government and other large organisations) and grassroots level. Ongoing communication and relationship-building is essential.

This book is intended to be used flexibly according to need. You may wish to go straight to the chapters of most relevance to you, or to work your way through it from beginning to end. However you choose to approach it, we hope that you will see the importance of digital literacy in all areas of life and share our excitement at the innovative approaches showcased here. Enjoy reading!

Part I
Approaching digital literacy

1
The trouble with terminology: rehabilitating and rethinking 'digital literacy'

Jane Secker

Introduction

This chapter is based on a paper given at the Society for Research in Higher Education Conference in December 2015, which formed part of a symposium on digital literacy (Bennett et al., 2015). Building on discussions at the symposium and the author's experience occupying several different professional identities (librarian, learning technologist, educational developer, teacher and researcher) this chapter reflects on how terminology around digital and information literacies can cause misunderstandings and divisions between those working in higher education. The focus of this chapter is on student learning in higher education, although it draws on the author's experiences of working with staff as well. This is partly in recognition that in order to support students effectively, it is important for academic and professional services staff to have a nuanced understanding of the terminology in the digital and information literacy fields. Staff also need an awareness of their own knowledge, skills and behaviour when using digital technologies and information in its broadest sense. The chapter provides some practical steps that can be taken to bridge the gaps or overlaps in student support within an institution, it discusses how to overcome the misunderstandings that might arise between professional services and academic staff, and finally suggests ways to build a more holistic approach to supporting student learning in higher education.

The term 'digital literacy' has gained relatively widespread recognition in a short space of time in UK higher education. The chapter will examine why, when there are many other learning literacies, digital literacy seems to have particular resonance and currency. I will also examine the problems that this might cause and why 'digital' is in many ways a distraction for teachers, who really need to focus on developing students' and their own critical abilities to handle information in all its guises effectively. Digital literacy has gained widespread attention: however, this chapter will explore why it is a problematic and ill-defined term. It is also sometimes referred to – interchangeably – as digital capabilities, which is the term used by Jisc to describe the six capabilities that staff in post-16 education need for themselves and their learners (Jisc, 2017). It is also used by the Universities and Colleges Information Systems Association (UCISA), which has undertaken a Digital Capabilities Survey across higher education staff since 2014 (UCISA, 2017). The choice of the word capabilities is perhaps partly in recognition of the problems that have been associated with the use of the term literacy in higher education.

Some academics equate literacy with basic skills, rather than higher-level thinking and cultural and communicative practices, but introducing capabilities into the debate (and also terms such as fluency or competency) may muddy the water further. The misunderstanding and confusion with other 'literacies' but also with terms such as computer literacy or digital skills (which is favoured by the UK government) can lead to a variety of problems. At best, this leads to duplication of effort in some areas of digital literacy support. For example, in UK higher education several learning support services provide students with help around referencing and avoiding plagiarism. However, the misunderstandings may also lead to gaps in provision in significant areas of emerging academic practice, for example, providing advice and support for students in the use of digital note-taking tools or apps or managing their online profile and using social media in a critical and thoughtful manner. Both these important areas of digital literacy support often have no obvious natural professional lead. In some institutions, the library, the learning technology team, careers or the learning development team might all offer different aspects of support, but they may assume that it is another department's responsibility. The misunderstandings and divisions between support services may even lead to turf wars and 'silo' thinking, and reinforce the echo chambers that all professions exist in, to some extent. As I have experience of working at the intersection of several support services, I have seen these challenges being played out in my own and other institutions. I have also noted that without a clear understanding of the language we are using, the misunderstandings will remain, particularly among academic staff, for whom the literacies language may be something of a mystery.

What is digital literacy?

The term 'digital literacy' was first used in a book published in 1997 by Paul Gilster. He defined it as the ability to understand and use information in multiple formats from a wide range of sources when it is presented via computers. The concept of literacy goes beyond simply being able to read; it has always meant the ability to read with meaning, and to understand. It is the fundamental act of cognition (Gilster, 1997, 1).

Importantly for Gilster, digital literacy was not a new term for computer literacy, which focuses on technical abilities to operate a computer and use software effectively. Digital literacy recognised the internet as a medium that needed specific literacies to critique the information that it provides, to separate truth from fiction and understand how hypertext and non-linear reading allows new meanings to be constructed. Put simply Gilster, who was clearly ahead of his time, saw it as literacy in the digital age.

Despite the appearance of this book, the term gained little currency for at least another decade. For a short period of time (from 2002 to 2005) the term e-literacy (the convergence of IT, e-learning and information skills) gained some currency, following the establishment of a conference hosted by universities in Glasgow, and a short-lived journal (Joint, 2005). It has taken almost 20 years for the term to gain mainstream recognition and it continues to be used interchangeably with terms such as digital skills and digital capabilities. The UK government currently uses 'digital skills', and this formed a key part of the Department for Media, Culture and Sports' digital strategy launched in February 2017 (DCMS, 2017). Digital in this sense refers largely to the broadband and network infrastructure; it is about delivering services using digital technology and ensuring the workforce has the skills and capabilities needed to support the economy. However, those critical abilities to analyse the information that is presented in digital format – to separate truth from fiction, which are highly relevant today, when we have all been bombarded with allegations of fake news – seem to be absent from current mainstream policies. Additionally, equating them to skills implies some lower level functional abilities, rather than the critical thinking and ability to be discerning that literacy implies.

The term 'digital literacy' has been used in the higher education sector for a number of years. In 2010 Beetham and Sharpe's model of digital literacy was adopted by Jisc (Figure 1.1). Beetham and Sharpe went on to develop first seven, and then later six, elements of digital literacy (Jisc, 2017).

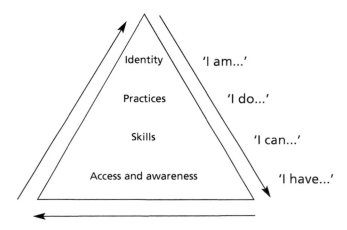

Figure 1.1 *Beetham and Sharpe's model of digital literacies, 2010*
Source: Sharpe, R. and Beetham, H. (2010) p90

Digital literacy was also used by the Higher Education Academy in 2015 and provided a focus for reviews by the institutional Quality Assurance Agency (QAA) carried out after 2015. The term 'digital literacy' is however disputed, reflecting a tension between the perception of technology as either neutral or culturally situated (Hinrichsen and Coombs, 2013). The digital environment opens up possibilities and presents new challenges for staff and learners, so arguably there are a whole host of new literacies that staff and students still need. Underpinning it all is reading, writing and critical thinking: the need for these has not gone away, and they are not things that technology can do for us.

So why exactly might digital literacy be a problematic term? The answer is in part related to the range of other literacies that exist in the educational sphere, which can be regarded as the wider literacies landscape (Figure 1.2 opposite).

Information Literacy Landscape

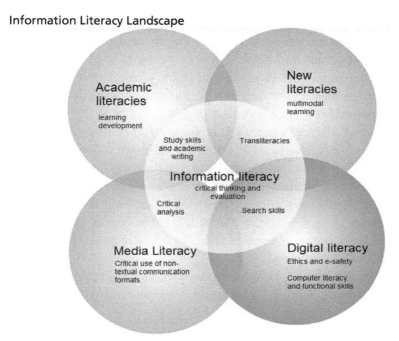

Figure 1.2 *The wider literacies landscape*
Source: Jane Secker

The term information literacy was coined over 40 years ago (Zurkowski, 1974) and academic librarians use it to signify the teaching they do (through formal or informal learning) to develop high-level information handling skills in students. In addition to finding, evaluating and managing information, information literacy involves developing critical thinking skills in students to use information in all its forms. Some of these literacies might be what other professionals in higher education call academic literacies and the term has clear overlaps with terms such as media literacy, digital literacy and the field of new literacies. Terminology is extremely important and is very much tied up with professional identities, particularly in the learning support field. This plethora of literacies with overlapping terms and concepts – which can be used quite differently by learning developers, educational developers, librarians and learning technologists – can also cause confusion for academic staff. And rather than focusing on how best to support students, discussions over which literacy is the container term – which literacy is the most important – has at times hijacked any sensible debate over how to provide practical support within an institution.

There needs to be a way of communicating the value of developing critical abilities in our learners to foster collaboration between higher education professionals and better support students. One suggestion is that given its currency, the term 'digital literacy' might move us closer together, towards a common understanding of the abilities that underpin learning. However, it's not clear that digital literacy is the right term either; the word 'digital' immediately suggests that non-digital information or skills are less valid. It also tends to alienate those professional services staff who are reluctant users of technology, or those who believe it to be a distraction to students. In a recent blog post, Watling (2017) eloquently highlights how language matters, citing Neil Postman's book *Technopoly* from 1992. Describing the belief that pedagogy matters more than technology in higher education, Watling actually came out in favour of the term 'digital pedagogy'.

In this next section, by examining the way digital literacy relates to information literacy, I hope to focus on what really matters: student learning.

How does digital literacy relate to information literacy?

The term 'digital literacy' can be problematic for those who have been teaching and researching what librarians call information literacy, and what learning developers describe as academic literacies. As previously mentioned, the term information literacy was coined in the 1970s by Paul Zurkowski. It was not intended as a library-centric model, but a call to all professions to help people understand the value of information and how to mould it for their needs, which largely went unheeded (Zurkowski, 1974). More recently information literacy has been described as 'knowing when and why you need information, where to find it, and how to evaluate, use and communicate it in an ethical manner' (CILIP, 2013). Librarians increasingly recognise that developing information literacy is a key part of their role, particularly in formal education. Researchers and practitioners have worked to develop frameworks and models of information literacy and to embed it in the curriculum of mainstream education. However, recognition of this term outside the library profession has been slow, and librarians are not commonly considered to be educators, particularly in sectors outside formal education. The author and technologist Seth Godin (2011) argues that the librarian is a 'data hound, a guide, a sherpa and a teacher', not a keeper of books. Librarians have only recently begun developing their role as teachers and many approaches to information literacy still take a functional, skills-based approach.

The use of the word literacy signifies not the teaching of skills or competencies, but practices, attitudes and behaviours that are context specific. While there may be some generic 'literacies' that we all need in order to live, learn and work in society, arguably these are contextual and should be taught in an embedded way in the curriculum to be meaningful. Writing about academic literacies, Lea and Street (1998) advocated moving away from the skills-based, deficit model when supporting students' academic writing practices. This resonates with an increasing recognition of the need to view information literacy as a framework for learning, for example in recent work by the US Association of College and Research Libraries (ACRL) whose researchers used threshold concepts (Meyer and Land, 2003) to reformulate their Information Literacy Framework for Higher Education in 2015 (www.ala.org/acrl/standards/ilframework). Research by Secker and Coonan (2013) on A New Curriculum of Information Literacy (ANCIL) developed a learner-centred model and viewed information literacy as a part of a wider curriculum of critical abilities, attitudes and behaviours that underpin learning. How does digital literacy relate to academic and information literacies? Nowhere in the ten strands of ANCIL is there a technology or 'digital literacy' strand, as this research recognised the term information to encompass digital and print abilities. However, the term information literacy outside the library profession is assumed to be a narrow concept associated with how students find published information, such as books and journals in a library setting. Therefore, much of the teaching that librarians do is not aligned with other literacies and may sit outside or alongside the curriculum.

Despite the apparent currency of the term 'digital literacy' it has largely defied a concrete definition. Hinrichsen and Coombs (2013) argue that defining the term requires taking an ideological position that recognises that technology, like information, is not neutral. They also argue that a functional skills-based approach of IT literacy leads to digital literacy being taught outside the curriculum, rather than taught as part of academic practices and that 'broader literacy practices are not going to emerge spontaneously as a result of technology proliferation' (Hinrichsen and Coombs, 2013, 4). The term 'digital literacy' also risks alienating academic staff who may not perceive themselves to be fully digitally literate, but perhaps the interest in digital literacy presents an opportunity for information and academic literacy experts to reframe their activities. At some institutions, digital and information literacies are presented as interlinked abilities that underpin learning. The 'digital' in digital literacy can be helpful as many teachers recognise that technology and the availability of online resources have changed students' relationship with information. No longer is information scarce, and as there is a wealth of information students need critical abilities to be discerning about what they find online and how they use digital tools to share information for their studies and about themselves.

Whether we call it media and information literacy (UNESCO, 2015), metaliteracy (Jacobson and Mackey, 2013) or digital literacy, terminology matters because it helps academics, librarians, learning developers and learning technologists develop a shared understanding of their aims. However, in many institutions there is still work to be done to map these abilities onto a common framework and to develop an approach for embedding this in the curriculum. By recognising the overlaps and unique aspects of each literacy, those supporting digital, academic and information literacies can work together with academic staff. Moreover, it should then be possible to develop a shared framework that has a measurable impact on student learning, but which avoids prescribing the tools and technologies that students should be able to use. This approach can also challenge the myth of the 'digital native' that persists among many discipline teachers, despite much evidence to the contrary (more on that story later!). Assumptions about how students develop their digital, academic and information literacies need to be challenged if we want to empower students to consider the information they trust, the digital tools and technologies they use, and the ethical issues encountered when using and creating knowledge. The solid foundation in information literacy teaching positions librarians as key players as institutions develop digital literacy programmes, but there is much to learn from critical and academic literacy models and from embedding these beyond the library across an institution.

Academic practice and digital literacy

Working in educational development, teaching academic staff in higher education, has been particularly illuminating in exploring the misunderstandings over terminology. Teacher identity is closely aligned with an individual's discipline and the content or curriculum is the primary focus of many new to teaching. Very few new teachers think about the skills, behaviours and practices they are trying to support and encourage in their students; they focus on the knowledge they are trying to impart. Therefore a common issue over the last 15 years is that staff make readings and resources available in the virtual learning environment (VLE) to ensure students have access to the required knowledge. Conversely, the same staff later regard this as 'spoon feeding' students who do not learn how to use the library and undertake research if (for example) a link is not provided. This is often followed up with a complaint that students are 'lazy' and unwilling to visit the library. Here, technology is to blame; it's the 'fault' of Moodle or Blackboard that students don't read further. What in fact is happening here is an issue related to information or digital literacy and teachers, who often learnt to do research in a pre-digital age, forgetting the process they went through to learn about 'authority'.

The digital native debate
One of the most interesting topics to debate with new teachers is Prensky's much over-used concept of the 'digital native'. What is remarkable is that this research has little or no empirical evidence to support it, and even Prensky has revised his original notion of there being a simple generational divide between the younger, technically fluent, 'digital native' who has grown up with technology and older, less proficient 'digital immigrants'. However, the concept is a useful way of engaging teachers with academic literature in the field of technology and educational development and challenging the assumptions that they might make about young people's skills levels. Many teachers slip easily into the rhetoric that all young people are adept at using technology and have a far greater understanding of how to use technology than their teachers. They confuse technical proficiency with devices such as tablets and smartphones with critical abilities to find, evaluate, analyse and create new knowledge. Prensky cannot be blamed entirely here, for he did modify his digital-native–digital-immigrant hypothesis, but it has retained remarkable resilience as a concept. One of the most enlightening discussions with new academic staff is over the digital native debate. It reveals more about their own insecurities and inadequacies over how to use digital technology than what their students might be doing.

It is important to challenge the view that there is a homogenous generation proficient in using technology, as this belies the huge variety of skills and preferences that exist. The 'residents and visitors' (White and Le Cornu, 2011) typology is viewed by many as a more helpful way of viewing people's interactions in online spaces. This research has been used to develop an activity with learners where they are asked to place their engagement with different online tools on two axes: the personal and institutional, and the resident and visitor. Spaces where one is resident are not just those where you spend a lot of time, but online spaces where people feel comfortable and leave many traces of themselves, whereas spaces you use as a visitor you tend to visit to get the information you need and then leave. The maps that students (and staff) draw can be enlightening, showing there are no simple generational divides and that we all have personal preferences for the online spaces we inhabit. But they have also indicated that many students are resident in social media, rather than the institutional tools we provide for them such as the VLE or their institutional e-mail account. These activities also reveal questions over who best might be teaching digital literacies to students, and often it is clear the expertise does not always lie with academic colleagues.

Practical steps to building a more holistic approach to student learning

This section presents several practical steps that can be taken to bridge the gaps or overlaps in student support within an institution. There are also some suggestions about how to overcome the misunderstandings that might arise between various professional services staff and faculty/academic staff when discussing digital and information literacy. The ideal solution is to build a more holistic approach to supporting student learning in higher education, where academic staff and those across professional services are in alignment. These approaches are presented in sequential order, though your institution may decide to try some of these approaches rather than follow this approach prescriptively. The aim is to help you better equip your students with the abilities they need while in higher education, and beyond in the workplace and their daily lives.

Stage 1 Developing graduate attributes
Create a cross-institutional definition of the critical abilities your

institution aspires to develop in its students. You may call these graduate attributes; they may be your institution's unique selling point and they may already exist, but it's worth undertaking a process to review what these are. What do the students arrive at your institution able to do already and how do you move them to the point where they are fully equipped with these distinct abilities? At this point you do not need to focus on what you call these abilities, but think about what students who graduate from your institution should be able to do. How will they think? How will they approach problems? How will they deal with situations where there is not a reading list or model answer? How does your institution ensure they are lifelong learners?

Stage 2 Creating an institutional framework
If such a thing does not exist already, it might be appropriate to create an institutional framework or model of student literacies or graduate attributes either across your institution or specific to each school or department. You may wish to customise one of the existing models or frameworks that exist or look at another institution that has developed such a framework. The Jisc model of digital capabilities is worth considering. Ensure that all terminology is clearly defined in a way that all staff can understand and relate to, and involve staff from across the institution in developing or customising the framework so it is relevant to the different disciplines.

Stage 3 Undertaking a review or audit
Carry out a review or an audit of the digital literacy provision in the institution. This is an important step to understanding where there might be any gaps in provision or overlaps and duplication. Which departments are responsible for developing students' abilities and moving them towards becoming lifelong learners? Is this embedded in the curriculum? Is it taught alongside the curriculum? Are all students in all departments or schools getting the same opportunities? One approach might be to use an existing framework to map the activity to, but if you have already developed an institutional framework you can use this to audit your current provision.

Stage 4 Identifying overlaps and gaps
Following your review it may not be clear where there is duplication of

effort, or where there might be any gaps in provision. Ensure that expectations are clear about which departments are responsible for leading in specific areas of digital and information literacy support but consider planning joint sessions wherever possible that focus on the tasks students need to undertake in a holistic way, e.g. approaching an assignment from the point of view of the process – doing the research, searching for literature, writing it and citing and referencing.

Stage 5 Sustainability
In order to make it sustainable, embed the framework into the course approval or revalidation process, so that staff have to demonstrate how the courses they teach are supporting student learning. Also ensure that the framework is revised and adapted and a living document, rather than a one-off piece of work that becomes irrelevant. A programme of staff development is also key to ensure that this new approach is supported and sustainable. Staff may need to be up-skilled to provide more effective support to their students, but also so they know where to direct students who need help. It is important to ensure that new staff joining the institution are clear about the graduate attributes and abilities that students leaving the institution need to have. Finally, the culture of the institution needs to help ensure that professional services staff continue to work in partnership with academics on curriculum design.

Conclusion
This chapter highlights how terminology in the two fields of digital and information literacies can lead to challenges in the practicalities of providing learning support services to students and effective staff development. The goal is to ensure that professional services staff and academic staff work collaboratively to provide support for students holistically. The steps outlined in this chapter provide one model for an institutional approach to improving learning support. It is essential to place students' needs at the centre of any approach, rather than develop services that simply mirror the structure of the institution. Working closely with academic departments and discipline specialists is important to ensure that digital and information literacies are embedded into the curriculum, not bolted on as an afterthought. However, staff development also needs to be a key feature of digital and information literacy support, to make it sustainable and to support cultural change across the institution.

References

Bennett, L.; Jefferies, A.; Nicholls, J.; Reedy, K.; Rees, R.; Secker, J.; Whitworth, A. (2015) *A critical focus on digital literacy, Symposium at SRHE Annual Research Conference: Converging Concepts in Global Higher Education Research: Local, national and international perspectives*. Held at Celtic Manor, Newport in South Wales, United Kingdom, 9-11 December 2015.

CILIP (2013) Information Literacy Definition, Chartered Institute of Library and Information Professionals, www.cilip.org.uk/cilip/advocacy-campaigns-awards/advocacy-campaigns/information-literacy/information-literacy.

DCMS (2017) *UK Digital Strategy*, Department of Culture, Media and Sport, https://www.gov.uk/government/publications/uk-digital-strategy.

Gilster, P. (1997) *Digital Literacy*, Wiley.

Godin, S. (2011) The Future of the Library, blog, http://sethgodin.typepad.com/seths_blog/2011/05/the-future-of-the-library.html.

Hinrichsen, J. and Coombs, A. (2013) The Five Resources of Critical Digital Literacy: a framework for curriculum integration, *Research in Learning Technology*, 21, 21334, http://dx.doi.org/10.3402/rlt.v21.21334.

Jacobson, T. E. and Mackey, T. P. (2013) Proposing a Metaliteracy Model to Redefine Information Literacy, *Communications in Information Literacy*, 7 (2), 84–91.

Jisc (2017) Digital Capabilities Framework: an update, https://digitalcapability.jiscinvolve.org/wp/2017/03/09/digital-capabilities-framework-an-update/.

Joint, N (2005) Eliteracy or Information Literacy: which concept should we prefer?, *Library Review*, 54 (9), 505–7.

Lea, M. R. and Street, B. V. (1998) Student Writing in Higher Education: an academic literacies approach, *Studies in Higher Education*, 23 (2), 157–72.

Meyer, J. and Land, R. (2003) *Threshold Concepts and Troublesome Knowledge: linkages to ways of thinking and practicing within the disciplines*, University of Edinburgh.

Postman, N. (1992) *Technopoly: the surrender of culture to technology*, Knopf.

Secker, J. and Coonan, E. (2013) *Rethinking Information Literacy: a practical framework for supporting learning*, Facet Publishing.

Sharpe, R. and Beetham, H. (2010) Understanding students' uses of technology for learning: towards creative appropriation, p90. In R. Sharpe, H. Beetham and S. De Freitas (eds.) *Rethinking learning for a digital age: how learners are shaping their own experiences*. London and New York:

Routledge.

UCISA (2017) Digital Capabilities Survey, Universities and Colleges Information Systems Association, https://www.ucisa.ac.uk/digcap.

UNESCO (2015) Media and Information Literacy, www.unesco.org/new/en/communication-and-information/media-development/media-literacy/mil-as-composite-concept/.

Watling, S. (2017) The Language Matters of Digital Pedagogy and Learning Wheels, blog, https://digitalacademicblog.wordpress.com/2017/07/21/the-language-matters-of-digital-pedagogy-and-learning-wheels/.

White, D. and Le Cornu, A. (2011) Visitors and Residents: a new typology for online engagement, *First Monday*, **16** (9), http://firstmonday.org/article/view/3171/3049.

Zurkowski, P (1974) The Information Service Environment: relationships and priorities, Related Paper 5, National Commission on Libraries and Information Science.

2

Unpacking digital literacy: the potential contribution of central services to enabling the development of staff and student digital literacies

Joe Nicholls

Introduction

Centralised professional services in colleges and universities are uniquely positioned to promote institution-wide development of digital literacies. Front-facing service staff (those who regularly communicate and come into contact with academic staff and students) represent the human interface between available services and the learning, teaching and research practices of students and academics. They can play a pivotal role in raising awareness, informing and helping people to recognise the utility of digital tools and other complementary services (external and internal to the institution). In this regard, digital literacies constitute the knowledge and skills required to be able to use these tools and services effectively to perform useful digital practices. Acting as mediators, service staff are able to promote connections between people who are known to have relevant experience and knowledge, fostering networking and creating the conditions for conversations to take place (Ford, 1999). Through harvesting, managing and disseminating information gathered, service staff can perform a curatorial role, building a knowledge hub to make available what has been identified as useful. The aim is to enable educators and students to make informed decisions about how best to invest their time and effort to recognise and adopt useful digital practices. The challenge for the institution is doing this in a way that scales and is sustainable. Although one-off projects and isolated initiatives have demonstrated that the approaches described here have value in promoting the development of staff and student digital literacies, more needs to be done to ensure there is enduring change.

This chapter presents an interpretation of digital literacies and explores the implications for promoting institution-wide development. The ways in which service staff can enable students and academic staff to make appropriate and effective use of digital technologies are described with reference to examples and key recommendations.

Learning literacies

Digital literacies should be understood as part of a spectrum of related knowledge and skills. The Beetham and Sharpe Learning Literacies Development Framework (Beetham, McGill and LittleJohn, 2009) identifies what should be considered when designing opportunities to promote the development of academic, information, digital, media, social and other literacies. A subsequent modification of the Framework (see Figure 2.1) recognises 'awareness' as an additional contributing factor (Jisc, 2014) and this has provided a useful structure and guide to help clarify the role of service staff and their contribution to the process of developing digital literacies.

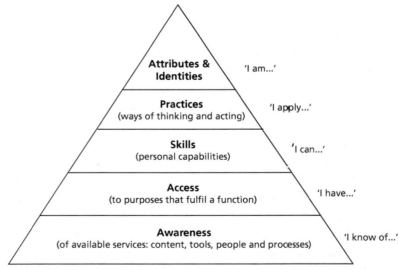

Figure 2.1 *Learning literacies development framework (Jisc, 2013) adapted from Sharpe and Beetham (2010)*

Although the focus here is the development of digital literacies, it is important not to slip into the conceptual trap of thinking of these as separate from other complementary knowledge and skills. A holistic understanding of digital literacies as part of a spectrum of learning literacies is needed, and digital literacies should not be considered in isolation from academic literacies, information literacies, social literacies and media literacies (Goodfellow, 2011). There is much greater educational value in designing learning opportunities to develop a mix of literacies that are appropriate for a given academic challenge and context. Importantly, understanding literacies in this way alerts us to the contribution service staff can make from the different specialisms within centralised services. There is considerable potential benefit in marshalling the complementary expertise of subject librarians, learning technologists, IT trainers, media specialists, student services and careers staff to input to the design of curricula and learning activities to tailor the development of these different kinds of literacies.

Importantly, the concept of digital literacies subsumes and builds on functional IT skills. All too often standalone IT training has focused on instructing how to use the functions and features of an application, such as Microsoft Word or PowerPoint, without creating the opportunity to improve how people write or give presentations in ways that align with their discipline or profession. This disconnection from situated and meaningful practice goes to the heart of the challenge in enabling people to develop appropriate and useful digital literacies. When learning to use technology students should encounter problems and tasks that are typical of their chosen academic domain and subject. If educators manage to achieve this it can profoundly alter the relationship a student has with technology, potentially shifting their attitude and belief about its purpose in relation to their lives and crucially with regard to understanding their own agency in a digital world, in effect their digital identity. A positive digital identity will impact constructively on engagement with all other factors that contribute to the development of digital literacies, and foster the fluency, versatility and adaptability necessary to be able to reappropriate knowledge and skills needed to meet new challenges and new contexts.

With regard to using technology, the practices component of the Learning Literacies Development Framework can be understood as a person's application of digital tools and accompanying thought processes (cognitive practices) in order to perform a challenge. Descriptions and illustrations of such practices provide an excellent starting point for conversations geared towards exploring and devising learning activities to promote the development of digital literacies. This also provides a way to help people recognise requirements and as a prompt to analyse the nature and contribution of the other elements of the framework.

> **An example of digital practice**
>
> Presenting is a familiar and common practice across all subjects and disciplines. All staff and students do it at some time and it provides an excellent means for developing a whole range of literacies, including digital literacies. People construct and deliver presentations in different ways for different purposes (to inform, instruct, motivate, entertain and persuade) and in so doing use a wide range of services and technologies to help them achieve their goal. The aim of describing the practice of presenting is to provide an easily recognised illustration of what is involved (e.g. defining purpose, planning, preparation, design, development, performance) and use this as the basis for linking to simple descriptions and examples of common variations (e.g. academic, PechaKucha, elevator pitch or lightning talk), the digital tools used (e.g. PowerPoint, Keynote, Prezi, Flickr Slideshow or a flip-chart), resources and people with specialist expertise that provide help and support. What is prototypical about the practice – in common to all the variations – is relatively slow to change and can be used to anchor links to

The precise benefit and value of adopting a digital practice is not something that can be determined or guaranteed for someone in advance of them seeking to make it part of the way they do their work. For instance, there are many ways digital technologies can be used to help write an essay, create a presentation or research a topic. What works best must be discovered through a process of critical appraisal of its efficacy in relation to what needs to be achieved. This is why learning to use technology through tackling meaningful challenges is so important educationally. A learner's experience inevitably results in them adapting their performance in response to their idiosyncratic requirements and context specific factors. To promote the development of digital literacies service staff can help educators and students make explicit and share the variety of practices they employ so that others may more easily become aware of what is possible and make judgements as to whether it would be beneficial to adopt them.

Traditionally, a key role of IT service staff has been to raise awareness and ensure access to digital tools and other complementary services, providing access to resources and training opportunities to develop information and technology related skills. However, these are commonly made available as standalone extra-curricula offerings and the challenge has always been how best to contextualise learning. For service staff to be able to do this well requires a shift in perspective and approach. They have to acquire a richer understanding of what educators and students do – their practices. It is the academic context in which these practices take place that is so important in enabling students to tailor and qualify the knowledge and skills they develop. The difficulty is that it cannot be taken for granted that they will be able to articulate and automatically share what they do. The onus is on service staff to increase their knowledge of what is educationally valid, along with gaining an appreciation of the language and terminology used, and developing the prerequisite attitude and confidence that will enable them to have productive conversations about how students learn and staff teach. The ensuing descriptions and illustrations of the practices can then enable others to identify and assess their relevance and value for their own work. It will be what people recognise they have in common, or what they perceive to be useful, that will provide the stimulus for fruitful conversations. This does not require service staff to become experts in the performance of any particular practice, but they need to gain sufficient awareness and understanding to be able to initiate and facilitate connections between people known to have relevant experience and expertise.

It is ultimately the responsibility of the academic educator to ensure learning activities promote the development of academic literacies, such as critical and evaluative thinking. Acknowledging this establishes a clear demarcation with regard to the role, responsibilities and contribution of service staff. The academic subject specialist will always be best placed to think of the kinds of problems and tasks that are characteristic of the discipline and which best promote core thinking abilities and deep learning. The development of essential academic literacies should always be the first concern when formulating pedagogies. Having identified which academic literacies are essential, educators can design and integrate into the curriculum the appropriate digital practices to support these academic literacies.

These digital practices then also foster the development of digital literacies. The challenge becomes to recognise digital practices that are fit for this purpose and then finding the tools and other services that will enable them to be performed. This is where conversations and collaboration between educators and service staff can be most fruitful.

Making conversations happen

It is the conversation that matters. Service staff can act as mediators to help bring those who have relevant expertise and experience together to discuss and share what they know. When the opportunity arises, students and teachers tend to talk quite readily about, and are able to describe in concrete terms, the kinds of things they do during the course of their learning and teaching. The aim is to identify what kinds of digital practices are being performed by whom and create opportunities, through face-to-face and online forums, for conversations about them to happen. These present opportunities for service staff to ask questions about the requirements that relate to the other components of the Learning Literacies Framework, exploring attributes, identities, functional skills, access and awareness. Great things are possible when students, educators and service staff are presented with opportunities to talk to each other. While it is not possible to create communities of practice by design, they can be nurtured through continued contributions to increase their relevance and currency. The important thing is that service staff take responsibility for initiating and fuelling these conversations. The difficulty is that as there are demands on everyone's time, opportunities for face-to-face meetings are rare. Therefore, some mechanism is needed that works to enable more convenient and opportunistic communication and information sharing. This can be achieved through providing an online social space that supports asynchronous ways of communicating (e.g. discussion forums, comment areas, microblogging) and, ideally, synchronous ways of communicating (e.g. instant chat, audio and videoconferencing, presence awareness) as well as file–document sharing and collaborative authoring tools (collectively similar to Google's suite of apps, see http://edu.google.co.uk/). This can be used to maintain continuity between face-to-face meetings and discussions, promote networking, disseminate information and news, as a means for people to ask questions, as well as a place for people to describe what they know and practice. However, do not expect these online social spaces to be active and vibrant all of the time: they will naturally fluctuate in their topicality and popularity. A key role of service staff is to harvest from these discussion spaces anything considered to have enduring relevance and value. This can then be used to build a more stable repository that can be explored to discover and investigate more established forms of digital practice.

Knowledge curation
Service staff perform a valuable role in gathering, summarising and working to consolidate any content from the discussion forums acknowledged to have lasting relevance and value. Describing and modelling practices in ways that showcase their authenticity and situated nature makes it possible to use them as a point of reference and a catalyst for conversations. They function as a framework on which to anchor, and make explicit, links to digital and other services that have been used, along with descriptions and explanations about their utility in helping to perform the practice. Extracting this to create an online repository, a 'knowledge hub', creates a browsable and searchable resource of the digital practices people have found to be effective along with the services they have used in doing so. The purpose of this is to provide a fast-track way to enable discovery of examples of how digital practices and digital tools and services have been successfully integrated into learning activities. Descriptions of the practices, in combination with the application of metadata tags, are what connect the knowledge hub and the conversation spaces. Reciprocal links allow transitions between the validated and relatively stable archive to more discursive and dynamic forums where emergent and niche practices surface. The technology used to build the knowledge hub, such as a wiki (see for example Semantic MediaWiki; www.semantic-mediawiki.org), should allow anyone to flag, comment or amend its content, though service staff should be responsible for managing its content in order to maintain its integrity. As the knowledge hub matures it provides a means to stimulate and promote face-to-face and online discussions about the nature of digital literacies.

Design for learning
Designing learning activities to develop digital literacies requires recognising and formulating pedagogies that engage students in digital practices as the means to learn academic subject knowledge and skills. As has been previously described, educators may find ways to do this independently through their use of the knowledge hub and conversation

spaces to find out what others are doing and to ask for help and advice. This may suffice and be all that is needed to identify appropriate and useful digital practices to integrate into learning activities to develop required digital literacies. However, there are a number of ways service staff can contribute more directly to the design and development of learning activities. Three complementary approaches are outlined: standalone, embedded and integrated. These vary in the extent to which the resulting activity is contextualised for an academic curriculum.

Central services have a history of independently providing standalone resources (digital and hardcopy documents, presentation slides, learning objects) and independent training events (face-to-face and online presentations, tutorials, workshops and webinars) to cater for the varied needs of a broad audience of staff and students. They have therefore often been designed to be as generic possible, e.g. targeting study skills. The rationale for this approach is that it is often considered to be the most efficient use of available resources. However, this is problematic when promoting the development of literacies because it fails to engage learners with the kinds of challenges typical of the subject they are studying. Recognising that the development of digital literacies depends on pedagogies that are effective in contextualising learning, only the academic educator possesses the necessary subject specific knowledge to design activities that are meaningful to students. While service staff may seek the involvement of educators to help tailor what they produce, there are significant logistical challenges in doing so across all subjects and disciplines. Alternatively, resources and activities can be designed and produced in such ways that allow educators to subsequently modify and adapt them to meet subject specific requirements. This does, however, mean that service staff need to become skilled in the production of open and repurposable learning resources. Development tools, such as Xerte (www.xerte.org.uk) greatly simplify the process, presenting a shallow learning curve that enables service staff and academic educators to collaborate in the production of shareable and modifiable e-learning resources (Ball and Tenney, 2008).

Specialist service staff such as subject librarians and learning technologists are often invited to teach topics as a scheduled and embedded component of a planned curriculum. However, all too often, discrete one-off sessions such as these can be untimely with only tenuous links to the curriculum (Stubbings and Franklin, 2006). Since service staff do not have the rich subject knowledge academic educators possess there will always be limits to what they can do to contextualise learning activities appropriately (see case studies 2.1 and 2.2). If conversations between service providers and educators manage to take place, the educator can detail the kinds of problems and tasks that will work well to ensure that the digital practices are appropriate and align with the syllabus and intended learning outcomes. In principle, such opportunities should allow for a richer degree of contextualisation of these embedded learning activities to develop digital literacies.

From an educational point of view, the most desirable approach is for the academic teacher to take full ownership and responsibility for integrating the development of digital literacies into the core curriculum and learning activities. In this case service staff do not themselves do any teaching but contribute their specialist knowledge and perform an advisory and support role. This recognises that the teacher is the person best placed to shape the context in which learning occurs and create the kinds of problems and tasks that will interest and motivate students. Again, using the knowledge hub and social space, service staff would communicate and collaborate closely with the educator.

CASE STUDY 2.1: DIGITAL CURATION TO DEVELOP DIGITAL LITERACIES

A member of library staff collaborated with an academic educator to rethink and redesign learning opportunities for a 2nd year undergraduate cohort in a Welsh language studies module called Language, Policy and Planning. The intention was to enable students to learn digital practices appropriate for studying the academic subject matter. Initially, this was recognised by the students as being of relevance and value to their studies. Previous cohorts had been required to gather, critique and share a wide variety of task-related information. It was recognised by all involved that practices associated with curating digital content would therefore be highly beneficial. In response, opportunities were created to enable the students to search, select, edit, manage, annotate, share and monitor engagement with a broad range of relevant digital multimedia. Because of resource and scheduling constraints the library staff ran sessions themselves instead of scheduled academic lectures – illustrating the embedded approach described above. The problem with this was that the students were concerned about missing out on their academic lectures and questioned the value of learning to practise digital curation if it was not being assessed. The academic educator also eventually voiced concern over the difficulty of getting students enthused and engaged

CASE STUDY 2.2: PRESENTATIONS AND PRESENTING TO DEVELOP DIGITAL LITERACIES

From the inception of a new module on enterprise and entrepreneurism, a member of IT Services collaborated with the academic tutor. The content of the course was intended to enable undergraduate students to explore theory and practices involved in commercialising ideas and products. Student presentations were made central to learning the academic subject matter, allowing for the design of learning activities to develop digital practices as a direct means to engage with the academic subject matter – illustrating the integrated approach described above. These involved planning, preparing, producing and delivering different kinds of presentations, e.g. a business style meeting, an academic report and an elevator pitch. These required students to collaborate in groups and use of a range of digital tools to work with different kinds of digital media to deliver a number of presentations, individually and as part of their group, which were assessed; feedback was provided on content, design and delivery. These were extremely well received by students and academic staff alike. Key to the success of this approach was making the digital practices a seamless part of studying and learning the academic content. For this to work well it is essential that service staff work closely with academic educators from the outset of the

Additional case studies can be found on the Digidol Project website (http://jiscdesignstudio.pbworks.com/w/page/50732611/Digidol%20project).

The different approaches described are not mutually exclusive and can be used successfully in combination to contribute to a curriculum. They vary in the extent to which the academic educator 'owns' and is responsible for the learning activity and in how much they work to contextualise the learning. It requires service staff to develop and apply knowledge and skills that go beyond their conventional role in producing learning resources, to teach themselves and to educate the educators.

Conclusion: the way forward

Although well positioned in the organisation, service staff can only perform these roles if they are given a mandate to do so. With appropriate support, short-term projects have demonstrated that service staff are able to contribute in ways that are valued and effective. However, continued traction and momentum depends on institutional leaders and senior management recognising the need to invest in whole-scale development of staff and student digital literacies. Front-facing service staff have to be empowered to act beyond their traditional role of ensuring the provision of internal services to one that focuses on enabling students and academics to adopt useful digital literacies. This will necessitate them being given the opportunity to develop their own capabilities to become better facilitators, communicators and teachers. Importantly, in so doing, they will be able to better exploit the knowledge and expertise they have of the services they represent and advocate. A variety of professional development options exist that align with recognised career paths and professional accreditation. Postgraduate courses focusing on learning and teaching in higher education have proven to be extremely worthwhile in helping service staff and academic educators develop the necessary understanding and capabilities to work collaboratively to promote effective learning (Newland and Handley, 2016).

The institutional challenge is how to achieve the greatest impact within available resources. A pragmatic way forward is to recognise and focus effort on the practices that most people in the organisation perform most of the time and from which they the gain the greatest benefit. Writing documents, giving presentations, and searching for and managing information are obvious candidates as almost everyone across the institution performs these as a part of learning and teaching. Each practice provides rich opportunities for developing a broad range of learning literacies, including digital literacies. These will present the best candidates for identifying potentially useful digital practices and stimulate the interest needed to get people talking. Focus on exemplars that the educators themselves are willing to evangelise about. Their peers are more likely to be receptive to what they have to say.

In summary, if there is one thing about the enablement role that underpins all else it is concerned with making conversations happen. The onus is on front-facing service staff to create opportunities for face-to-face and online discussions about the development of digital literacies. Although, somewhat ironically, it has to be accepted that it is the voices of academic staff and students that get the ear of senior managers and decision makers and ultimately make the case for enduring change. Service staff must work to empower and support them in doing so through curating the outcomes and outputs of these conversations and marshalling them to promote awareness and catalyse further discussion.

References

Ball, S. and Tenney, J. (2008) Xerte: a user-friendly tool for creating accessible learning objects. In Miesenberger, K. et al. (eds), *[Proceedings of the] International Conference on Computers Helping People with Special Needs*, Springer-Verlag.

Beetham, H., McGill, L. and LittleJohn, A. (2009) *Thriving in the 21st Century: learning literacies for the digital age (LLiDA project)*, https://www.webarchive.org.uk/wayback/archive/20140615060659/www.jisc.ac.uk/media/documents/projects/llidareportjune2009.pdf.

Ford, J D. (1999) Organizational Change as Shifting Conversations, *Journal of Organizational Change Management*, 12 (6), 480–500.

Goodfellow, R. (2011). Literacy, Literacies, and the Digital in Higher Education, *Teaching in Higher Education*, 16 (1), 131–44.

Jisc (2013) *Cardiff University Digidol Project: Institutional Story* http://jiscdesignstudio.pbworks.com/w/page/67472572/institutional-story

Jisc (2014) *Developing Digital Literacies*, https://www.jisc.ac.uk/guides/developing-digital-literacies.

Newland, B. and Handley, F. (2016) Developing the Digital Literacies of Academic Staff: an institutional approach, *Research in Learning Technology*, 24, 31501, http://dx.doi.org/10.3402/rlt.v24.31501.

Sharpe, R. and Beetham, H. (2010) Understanding students' uses of technology for learning: towards creative appropriation, p90. In R. Sharpe, H. Beetham and S. De Freitas (eds.) *Rethinking learning for a digital age: how learners are shaping their own experiences*. London and New York: Routledge.

Stubbings, R. and Franklin, G. (2006) Does Advocacy Help to Embed Information Literacy into the Curriculum?: a case study, *Innovation in Teaching and Learning in Information and Computer Sciences*, 5 (1), 1–11.

3

Collaboration and coaching: powerful strategies for developing digital capabilities

Clare Killen

Introduction

This chapter focuses on holistic strategies for leading and influencing digital capabilities development that make use of structures which already exist within many organisations. It explores how peer coaching strategies and collaborative partnership activities can engage individuals in a co-ordinated and focused way, and generate wider organisational reach and impact.

The examples cited here are drawn from work conducted by Jisc and partners spanning several years. Key projects include the Change Agents' Network (Jisc, 2016a) and Jisc's co-design approach. The Professional Programme for Subject Learning Coaches (Quality Improvement Agency and Learning Skills Improvement Service, 2003–2010), which engaged over 6000 practitioners from the further education and skills sector, is also cited.

After the introductory sections to this chapter, Part 1 explores examples that show different models of partnership and collaboration, Part 2 introduces the concept of organisational digital capability and why this is important, and Part 3 suggests that peer coaching is a means of fulfilling the personal and organisational aspects of partnership and collaboration.

What do we mean when we talk about digital capabilities?

The simplest and yet most encompassing definition of what we understand by the term digital capabilities is 'the capabilities which fit someone for living, learning and working in a digital society' (Jisc, 2014). This neatly encapsulates the three important elements of society, employment and education while accommodating the fluidity of the ever-changing technological environment. Crucially, it also signposts that the route to developing digital capabilities is likely to be a personal journey. There is no magic point at which someone will be easily identifiable as 'digitally capable' – there are too many variables to consider to make this feasible, including how confident each individual feels about their capabilities, their perceptions, self-assessment and evolving practices.

There are several frameworks that unpick digital capabilities further. Some, like the European Commission's Digital Competence Framework (2017) and Go ON UK's Basic Digital Skills Framework (2015) focus on citizenship. Others have been specifically developed for educational audiences and incorporate study and work-related goals. In addition to personal or citizenship goals. These have usually been developed and refined in collaboration with practitioners and sector representatives. Two frameworks designed specifically for higher and further education in the UK and Ireland are the Jisc Digital Capabilities Framework for Individuals and the All Aboard Project.

The Jisc Digital Capabilities Framework for Individuals

The Jisc Digital Capabilities Framework for Individuals explores six elements: information and communications technologies (ICT) proficiency; information, data and media literacies; digital creation, problem solving and innovation; digital communication, collaboration and participation; digital learning and development; and digital identity and wellbeing (Jisc, [2015a]; Figure 3.1 on the next page).

The All Aboard Project

The All Aboard Project (www.allaboardhe.org) takes a different approach to digital capabilities development for staff in higher education in Ireland. Digital confidence is considered within the project's six clustered domains as well as skills levels and infrastructure. Presented as a digital journey accessed from 'Platform 1', resources produced by the All Aboard Project include a metro-style map (Figure 3.2), which provides an overview of the types of technology relevant to staff involved in learning, teaching and assessment; topics presented as 'stations'; and specific themed journeys presented as 'travel cards'.

KILLEN COLLABORATION AND COACHING   31

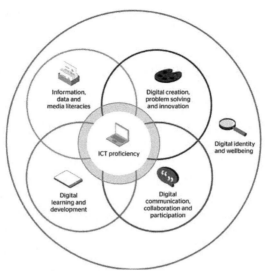

Figure 3.1 *The six elements of the Jisc Digital Capabilities Framework (individual model)*
© Jisc and Helen Beetham, CC BY-NC-ND

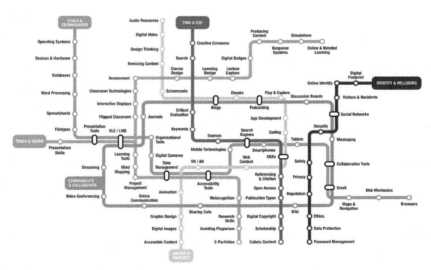

Figure 3.2 *All Aboard's digital skills in higher education metro map*
Source: All Aboard (2017) CC BY-NC 4.0 international licence

Many universities and colleges adapt frameworks such as these or devise their own to explain and make sense of digital capabilities. Indeed, encouraging students and staff from all roles and levels across an organisation to discuss digital capabilities is a powerful way of ensuring engagement and raising awareness of their importance.

Digital capabilities: powerful personal, organisational and economic enablers

It is a digital world, and as well as studying a chosen subject, students are preparing for work and life in a digital society. Digital capabilities are acknowledged as an important enabler for students: 'Gaining cross-disciplinary digital skills is the lifeblood of deeper learning outcomes that lead to fruitful careers' (NMC, 2016).

In addition to providing new and engaging ways to study and affording numerous personal efficiencies (e.g. information finding, online shopping and banking, accessing government services), the ability to use digital technology now features in most forms of employment and there is an expectation that almost all jobs will become digital jobs in the foreseeable future. Matt Hancock MP, Minister of State for Digital, observed: 'One million additional people are expected to be required for digital roles by the middle of the next decade. And it's predicted that within 20 years, 90% of all jobs will require some element of digital skills' (cited in Future Learn, 2017).

The value of digital capability in economic terms for the UK was acknowledged as 'enormous' by the House of Lords Select Committee on Digital Skills (2015), and digital tech industries are a key contributor to the UK economy, 'growing faster in turnover, gross value added and productivity than the rest of the economy' (Tech Nation, 2016).

To all intents and purposes, educational institutions are digital businesses. Colleges and universities need to ensure that their staff and students are adequately trained and supported to take advantage of the benefits and efficiencies offered by today's technologies safely, and to develop the resilience and mindset that will enable their communities to adopt future technologies and to design and develop the next generation of digital innovations.

Yet digital capabilities development is sometimes treated as a separate issue, an 'add-on' or 'nice-to-have' feature rather than an enabler that is recognised as integral to wider strategic objectives. In some cases, the digital capabilities agenda competes for finite resources with other high priority initiatives, rather than being a central consideration.

Objectives such as enhancing the student experience through effective and engaging use of technology, improving student employability opportunities through closer links with employers and providing authentic industry experiences, and widening participation and increasing personal and career opportunities for those facing barriers to learning are just some of the initiatives where developing the digital capability of students and staff will have obvious benefits. Taking a collaborative or partnership approach can elevate engagement and achievement beyond personal or small-scale impact.

Part 1 Collaboration takes many forms and can serve multiple foci

There is a clear symbiotic relationship between collaborative or partnership approaches and the development of digital capabilities: engaging in discussion, exploration and project activity heightens awareness, increases and extends engagement and can offer a deeper, more meaningful and enriched experience for all parties.

Students must be treated as equal in any partnership work – not all contributions are the same but there should be equal respect and value for all partners and support for those adjusting to new working relationships. Establishing a successful partnership initiative requires all players to have a shared understanding of the ethos, culture, nature and purpose of the partnership as well as how it should operate:

> Partnership is fundamentally about a relationship in which all involved – students, academics, professional services staff, senior managers, students' unions and so on – are actively engaged in and stand to gain from the process of learning and working together. Partnership is essentially a process of engagement, not a product. It is a way of doing things, rather than an outcome in itself. Healey, Flint and Harrington, 2014

As the following case studies illustrate, partnership initiatives take many forms and can involve multiple partners – they may focus on one aspect of practice such as content production; peer or cross-partnership support; research, academic practice and research-led change; or improving employability prospects and developing closer links with employers. Some initiatives have multiple foci and some institutions have adopted partnership working as part of a deeper cultural change, applying the principles to all aspects of the student experience.

CASE STUDY 3.1: THE UNIVERSITY OF SOUTHAMPTON: WORKING IN PARTNERSHIP WITH STUDENTS

The University of Southampton places a strong focus on research excellence and reputation with digital scholarship recognised as being of strategic importance. As there is a close working relationship between the library and the digital education team, developments in digital scholarship and digital learning are being addressed in parallel.

The university works with Innovation and Digital Literacies Champions (iChamps; www.diglit.soton.ac.uk/), student digital partners, who lead their own projects and act as advocates and mentor new iChamps, offering workshops to share their skills. In collaboration with the Students' Union, the university is also training course leaders and representatives in how their digital practices can support their roles, using badges and accreditation pathways to recognise and reward their achievements.

CASE STUDY 3.2: FACULTY OF HUMANITIES: THE MISSION EMPLOYABLE PROJECT

In a separate project, students in the Faculty of Humanities at the University of Southampton led the creation of an employability strategy. A team of four interns, supported by a faculty working group, established the brand Mission Employable and launched a VIP alumni scheme and external advisory board to increase employer engagement; collaborated with career destination and faculty staff to develop content for a compulsory undergraduate first year employability module; designed a faculty-wide peer-mentoring scheme; and developed an online tool to encourage students to reflect on their employability-related activities.

Students developed their digital confidence and capabilities throughout the project, using a range of technologies: a blog to support team collaboration and communication, Twitter and Facebook for publicity, LinkedIn to create a professional alumni network, the online application form iSurvey to recruit mentors, an online quiz and the virtual learning

CASE STUDY 3.3: SALFORD CITY COLLEGE: CASCADING SKILLS THROUGH STAFF AND STUDENT CHAMPIONS

Salford City College identified digital learning as one of five strategic priorities in 2015 and is aiming to implement the Further Education Learning

Technology Action Group recommendations by 2018 (FELTAG, 2014). Their digital learning strategy of 2016 sets out how the college will achieve this through seven strands of work: pedagogy, digital learning environments, IT investment and resourcing, digital literacies for staff and learners, collaboration and partnerships, innovation and quality. Skills development is being supported by teams of student and staff digital champions.

Employability and progression are key success factors for the college. As well as developing placement partnerships with employers, the college also aims to help employers understand the value of digital capabilities in their businesses and to help them to make use of the digital expertise the college can provide.

CASE STUDY 3.4: UNIVERSITY COLLEGE LONDON: MODERN VARIATIONS ON A RADICAL TRADITION

UCL's 20-year vision commits the university to 'supporting students to develop their digital capabilities to ensure that they are able to thrive in new working and learning environments'. The 2016–21 education strategy (UCL, 2018) has specific objectives for the digital curriculum and the digital environment for learning. Staff plan to expand their current student ChangeMakers programme (https://www.ucl.ac.uk/changemakers) to increase the number of staff–student innovation projects and site more student change agents within departments.

UCL is also encouraging students to participate in digital learning and scholarship through the Connected Curriculum scheme (https://www.ucl.ac.uk/ teaching-learning/education-initiatives/connected-curriculum), which engages students in research, scholarship and professional practice.

CASE STUDY 3.5: THE UNIVERSITY OF LINCOLN: HOW DIGITAL ARE YOU?

The University of Lincoln has an ambitious digital education plan, which aligns with the university's overall strategic plan and new vision for education. The university places a premium on open pedagogies and student-led production of open content, connecting digital education with the practices of digital research and the public communication of ideas.

The university recognises that staff and students will need support to take advantage of a 'more complex and dynamic digital environment' and are

> also concerned to promote digital safety and wellbeing. The Jisc Digital Capabilities Framework was used to gather a baseline view of digital capabilities across the university and the results are informing priorities for future workshops and development projects.

Partnership in its broadest sense
These case studies highlight examples of collaboration within teams, faculties and sometimes across organisations to enhance digital capability. The growth in student–staff partnership initiatives in recent years has generated collaboration beyond individual institutions through regional cluster networks such as Birmingham Digital Student (https://www.birminghamdigitalstudent.co.uk/). The momentum generated by the Jisc-funded Change Agents' Network (2015–2016) has been sustained by community-led initiatives including an annual national conference hosted by individual universities. Jisc has established a digital capabilities community of practice with a mailing list and national network events.

Not all partnership initiatives have a digital focus – but there will undoubtedly be digital elements within the overall partnership objectives, for example, the UK network for Researching, Advancing and Inspiring Student Engagement (www.raise-network.com) has a digital special interest group.

Part 2 Transformative approaches and the concept of organisational digital capability

Although the development of digital capabilities is unique to each person, with different starting points and different drivers and ambitions that influence individual development pathways, the extent to which the culture, policies and infrastructure of an organisation enable and support digital practices can help or hinder – Jisc calls this concept organisational digital capability (Killen, Beetham and Knight, 2017).

The case study examples in Part 1 offer examples of how colleges and universities are engaging stakeholders but also signpost overarching visions, priorities and strategic plans where digital capability or digital skills are explicitly referenced. The intent is that the digital interventions proposed will be transformative in some way – to the future employability prospects of students, to provide more flexible and engaging learning, to better support learners managing complex lives and to improve organisational performance. It is recognised that students and staff need a supportive culture and environment, as the following two case studies highlight.

CASE STUDY 3.6: LANCASTER UNIVERSITY: DIGITAL FLUENCY FOR EVERYONE

> When we were looking at the Digital Lancaster strategy [we considered] whether people would have the skills to undertake what we were expecting, and above and beyond that, did they have a culture that encouraged them to actually do it?
>
> Rachel Fligelstone, Head of IT Support, Lancaster University

Lancaster University is addressing cultural, infrastructure and skills development needs through Digital Lancaster, the digital version of the overall strategic plan.

Digital Lancaster sets out five goals: digital learning, digital design, digital expansion, digital communities and digital engagement (Digital Lancaster, n.d.) and has identified four key digital capabilities they need to cultivate:

- digital fluency for staff and students
- digital infrastructures
- digital innovation
- digital governance.

With a 'recruit the best' strategy, the human resources function is exploring what this means for a digital organisation.

CASE STUDY 3.7: THE UNIVERSITY OF HERTFORDSHIRE: BUILDING DIGITAL CAPABILITY THROUGH COLLABORATIVE ENGAGEMENT

The University of Hertfordshire established a digital capabilities scoping group sponsored by the chief information officer and endorsed by the deputy vice-chancellor. Group members representing the diverse interests of the main stakeholders across the organisation were tasked to investigate the implementation of the Jisc Digital Capabilities Framework (Jisc, [2015a]) and profiles to assess staff and student skills levels and identify requirements for a programme-based approach to development.

The formation of a digital capability scoping group has been a key

> enabler, engaging senior stakeholders and sponsoring wider participation with their teams. Work is also under way to map where digital capabilities fit into the university's staff development model and broader continuing professional development (CPD) framework. The university has also established a student experience academic research group with a sub group focusing on technology-enhanced learning and exploring whether the academic CPD model can be applied to other role profiles.

Strategic direction and vision on its own is not enough. An approach is needed that combines the macro whole organisation aspects of changes to practice and culture with the micro levels of personal change that motivate and empower individuals. One approach that has had a recognised impact on aspects of educational professional development and transforming culture is peer coaching.

Part 3 Peer coaching: combining vision and strategy with collaborative mechanisms to provide responsive and differentiated support

The challenge for education providers in supporting students and staff is significant and will continue to grow as new technologies and digital practices emerge. A sustained and flexible approach that can accommodate a wide range of starting skills levels and diverse development ambitions is required.

Peer coaching schemes offer personal, customised and responsive support with the advantage of developing tools and techniques that help to develop a resilient mindset capable of coping with ongoing change. Research by Joyce and Showers (1980) led them to conclude that the likelihood of CPD having a positive impact on teacher performance was significantly increased if teachers also received coaching and had opportunities to reflect on their performance in a supportive climate. The findings from this research, combined with the GROW coaching model (Whitmore, 2009), formed the basis for the Professional Training Programme for Subject Learning Coaches, part of the National Teaching and Learning Programme, which engaged over 6000 practitioners from the further education and skills sector (Quality Improvement Agency and Learning Skills Improvement Service, 2003–2010).

Establishing peer coaching as a part of the implementation strategy for organisational change can be powerful at personal and organisational levels. It engages and motivates individuals and reaches more people in a more responsive way, providing more tailored, longer-lasting and cost-effective support. It creates opportunities for students, staff and employers to better understand the needs, problems and challenges others face, and to develop meaningful responses. Additional benefits include the creation of a positive culture and that the resource available expands as more people receive coaching training.

Peer coaching relationships can be between students, between staff or between students and staff. They may be subject-related or more general. Trust and confidentiality are essential in any coaching relationship and adherence to coaching protocols provides a suitably robust framework. Appreciative enquiry is another potential strategy that can be combined with coaching protocols as this approach is also person-centred and encourages self-determined change (Cooperrider, Whitney and Stavros, 2008).

Introducing peer coaching requires careful consideration. It is a powerful model but based on protocols designed to maximise impact while protecting individuals. There are several different models, theories and practices. Regardless of which model you choose it is important to offer training and support as well as to allow time for people to become confident in their coaching practices.

Peer coaching approaches are being used successfully and cost-effectively to support digital capability development, as the following case studies illustrate.

CASE STUDY 3.8: DERBY ADULT LEARNING SERVICE: PEER SUPPORT TUTOR SERVICE LEADS TO EMBEDDED USE OF TECHNOLOGY IN CURRICULUM ACTIVITIES

After changing their approach to the way CPD is delivered, Derby Adult Learning Service staff have noticed a significant improvement in the use of technology to support learning and in tutor confidence in embedding digital interactions within curriculum activities. A small team of six peer support tutors, co-ordinated by the professional development adviser, provide a centrally managed but devolved service that provides cost-effective on-demand support for tutors.

CASE STUDY 3.9: SOUTH EASTERN REGIONAL COLLEGE: A WHOLE COLLEGE APPROACH TO DEVELOPING DIGITAL CAPABILITIES

South East Regional College, Northern Ireland, is committed to enhancing the digital literacy of staff and students to support the Department for the Economy's skills strategy for Northern Ireland and to address anticipated changes to the world of work driven by globalisation, new business models and rapidly changing consumer needs.

The college has a centralised approach to quality enhancement, curriculum design and data management. Every course has a consistent digital presence and technology features strongly in business and learning activities: staff and students use a wide range of apps developed in-house to support day-to-day activities; online staff development is tracked through the college's learning engine and e-registers allow live attendance reporting. The college has achieved a high level of staff digital confidence by investing in CPD at scale, recruiting specialised digital developers and buying out the time of experienced staff to act as mentors.

CASE STUDY 3.10: LEICESTERSHIRE ADULT LEARNING SERVICE: AN INTEGRATED APPROACH TO STAFF DEVELOPMENT USING SUPPORTED EXPERIMENTS AND COACHING TECHNIQUES

Leicestershire Adult Learning Service invites staff to attend three tutor briefings throughout the year including a one-day conference held on a Saturday. The focus is on providing inspirational, high quality and engaging CPD that is directly relevant to teaching practice. The tutor briefings include external speakers and feature collaborative project work with ongoing support from a team of coaches. Heads of service actively support and monitor progress of the projects known as supported experiments. Their virtual learning environment, Moodle, is used to monitor the projects, provide ongoing support and showcase the outcomes.

Conclusion

Many organisations already have programmes and resources to support student and staff digital capability development; open approaches to education have made even more available. Networking infrastructures and champion-type support roles exist in many organisations and some regions also have networks that support partnership and digital capability initiatives. National networks provide a further level of support.

Peer coaching has a role to play in bringing about the sort of cultural change that digital capabilities development requires. If we add it to the mix of collaborative partnerships, networks and resources we have a powerful and sustainable combination that can extend impact beyond that associated with other approaches to CPD – a win, win combination.

References

All Aboard: Digital Skills in Higher Education, (2017) www.allaboardhe.org

Cooperrider, D. L., Whitney, D. and Stavros, J. M. (2008) *Appreciative Inquiry Handbook*, 2nd edn, Crown Custom Publishing.

The Digital Competence Framework 2.0 (2017) European Commission, www.ec.europa.eu/jrc/en/digcomp/digital-competence-framework

Digital Lancaster (n.d.) Five Goals, www.lancaster.ac.uk/iss/info/docs/digital-lancaster-A3.pdf.

FELTAG (2014) *Further Education Learning and Teaching Action Group recommendations report*, Further Education Learning Technology Action Group, http://feltag.org.uk/.

Future Learn (2017) Blended Learning Essentials: developing digital skills, www.futurelearn.com/courses/blended-learning-digital-skills?lr=3.

Go On UK (2015) Basic Digital Skills Framework 2015, www.thetechpartnership.com/basic-digital-skills/basic-digital-skills-framework/basic-digital-skills-framework-2015/

Healey, M., Flint, A. and Harrington, K. (2014) *Engagement Through Partnership: students as partners in learning and teaching in higher education*, Higher Education Academy, https://www.heacademy.ac.uk/system/files/resources/engagement_through_partnership.pdf.

House of Lords Select Committee on Digital Skills (2015) *Make or Break: the UK's digital future*, HL Paper 111, https://www.publications.parliament.uk/pa/ld201415/ldselect/lddigital/111/111.pdf.

Jisc (2014) *Developing Digital Literacies*, https://www.jisc.ac.uk/guides/developing-digital-literacies

Jisc [2015a] Building Digital Capabilities: the six elements defined, www.repository.jisc.ac.uk/6611/1/JFL0066F_DIGIGAP_MOD_IND_FRAME.PDF.

Jisc [2015b] South Eastern Regional College: a whole college approach to developing digital capabilities, http://repository.jisc.ac.uk/6674/1/DigicapSERC.pdf.

Jisc (2016a) Change Agents' Network, https://www.jisc.ac.uk/rd/projects/change-agents-network.

Jisc (2016b) Derby Adult Learning Service: peer support tutor service leads to embedded use of technology in curriculum activities, October, https://repository.jisc.ac.uk/6514/1/Derby_Adult_Learning_Service_case_study.pdf.

Jisc (2016c) Leicestershire Adult Learning Service: an integrated approach to staff development using supported experiments and coaching techniques, October, https://repository.jisc.ac.uk/6516/1/Leicestershire_Adult_Learning_Service_case_study.pdf.

Jisc [2017a] University of Southampton: working in partnership with students, http://repository.jisc.ac.uk/6640/1/DigicapSouthamptonUniversity.pdf.

Jisc [2017b] Salford City College: cascading skills through staff and student champions, http://repository.jisc.ac.uk/6626/1/DigicapSalfordCityCollege.pdf.

Jisc [2017c] University College London: modern variations on a radical tradition, http://repository.jisc.ac.uk/6624/1/DigiCapUniversityCollegeLondon.pdf.

Jisc [2017d] University of Lincoln: how digital are you?, http://repository.jisc.ac.uk/6642/1/DigicapLincolnUniversity.pdf.

Jisc [2017e] Lancaster University: digital fluency for everyone, http://repository.jisc.ac.uk/6639/1/DigicapLancasterUniversity.pdf.

Jisc (2017f) Building Digital Capabilities through Collaborative Engagement: piloting the digital capability discovery tool: the University of Hertfordshire, http://repository.jisc.ac.uk/6683/4/digital-capability-stories-hertfordshire-aug-2017.pdf.

Joyce, B. and Showers, B. (1980) Improving In-service Training: the messages from research, *Educational Leadership*, **53** (6), 12–16.

Killen, Beetham and Knight (2017) Developing Approaches to Organisational Digital Capability, Jisc, https://www.jisc.ac.uk/guides/developing-organisational-approaches-to-digital-capability.

Medland, C., Dudley A., Tribe J., Smith V. and Quince, E. (2015) 'Mission Employable': creating a student-led employability strategy for the Faculty of Humanities, University of Southampton, *Journal of Educational*

Innovation, Partnership and Change, **1,** https://journals.gre.ac.uk/index.php/studentchangeagents/article/view/207/194.

NMC (2016) Digital Literacy: an NMC Horizon Project strategic brief, Volume 3.3, October, New Media Corporation, http://cdn.nmc.org/media/2016-nmc-horizon-strategic-brief-digital-literacy.pdf.

Tech Nation (2016) *Transforming UK Industries*, www.techcityuk.com/wp-content/uploads/2016/02/Tech-Nation-2016_FINAL-ONLINE-1.pdf.

UCL Education Strategy 2016-21 (2018) https://www.ucl.ac.uk/teaching-learning/education-strategy

Whitmore, J (2009) *Coaching for Performance: growing human potential and purpose, the principles and practice of coaching and leadership*, first published 1992, People Skills for Professionals, 4th edn, Nicholas Brealey.

Part II
Learning in a digital world

4

Digital literacy in UK and European schools: enhancing school children's motivation to read for pleasure

Geoff Walton, Mark Childs, Vedrana Vojković Estatiev, Janet Hetherington and Gordana Jugo

Introduction

This chapter explores digital literacy in the context of a project which intended to motivate school students to read for pleasure using information and communications technologies (ICT) and creating digital artefacts (e-artefacts). We define e-artefacts as digital work created in different formats such as text, video, audio, image or animation, or a combination of these. This project, called AMORES (An approach to MOtivating learners to Read in European Schools; www.amores-project.eu), was funded by the EU Comenius multilateral strand of the Lifelong Learning Programme. AMORES ran from 1 December 2013 to 30 November 2015. It aimed to improve students' engagement in reading national and European literature through a methodology based on ICT, interactivity and collaboration. Students from five countries exchanged their e-artefacts on national literature online and at a final event. Preliminary work with teachers enabled them to meet their partner school colleagues to develop an online community to support the implementation of a new digital literacy teaching methodology. The common working language was English and the teaching methodology was subsequently translated into their mother tongues for implementation. The project involved 400 students aged 9–14 from Croatia, Denmark, Poland, Sweden and the UK.

In this chapter we explore the thinking which underpinned the design of the new teaching methodology. An example learning scenario is presented to show how the teaching methodology can be realised. Findings from the pilot implementation are presented. A range of recommendations are discussed including pedagogy, tools and technologies, and social media. The new teaching methodology's potential limitations are also outlined.

Context

Before discussing the project in more detail, it would be useful to begin with a statement of our understanding of what is meant by digital literacy in this context. Digital literacy for our research is defined as 'a combination of all those capabilities which equip an individual for living, learning and working in a digital society' (Jisc, 2011, 2). This includes the critical evaluation of digital content and (in an educational context) its application to learning, for teachers in their pedagogic practice and for students as part of their learning. In addition, we believe that there is a social dimension to digital literacy in that digital literacy includes the ability to use digital media for social participation in any context, whether for leisure, education, work or citizenship.

The project was motivated by a Literacy Trust survey, which noted that more than a fifth (22%) of children and young people rarely or never read in their own time and nearly a fifth (17%) would be embarrassed if their friends saw them reading (Clark, 2012). We wished to address this issue by creating the partnership with schools as outlined above in order to create and test a new teaching methodology. Four of the five partner schools have well-stocked libraries, and all have access to public libraries. Collaboration with local libraries was also very important for the schools, and there were various initiatives, such as bringing in parents and volunteers to read to the students. Sometimes children's authors are also brought into schools through collaboration with local libraries. Most of the schools dedicate time during the week to encourage children to read, and all include reading at home as part of their expectation of the children. This is usually assessed by writing reading reports, and sometimes holding presentations in class. Four of the five schools conduct group work around literature, and use digital technology to create it. These technologies are almost exclusively different types of presentation software, using a series of still images to convey the content. Creating moving images, something we envisaged as a possibility for retelling stories, therefore required additional support. All students were familiar with e-books as a platform and had experience of digital technologies, but the majority did not have experience of learning using online discussion tools. There are varying attitudes generally across the EU to school children using social media. In schools, there is a relatively relaxed attitude to secure social media such as Edmodo, but we found that the UK partner school in particular had a high level of risk aversion to social media tools of any sort being used in the primary setting. Furthermore, safeguarding guidelines necessitated that permission should be sought from parents before any video or photographic images of children are placed online.

Our user needs survey confirmed that many school students lack knowledge of national and European literature. Partner teachers found it hard to interest children in reading literature, but agreed that the use of ICT could help raise the level of students' interest. Staff at four of the five schools in the AMORES project partnership reported that they had difficulty in motivating and engaging students with literature, particularly as the children get older.

Teachers in our survey felt that the competing demands from other media, which require shorter attention spans and more interaction, and the nature of text studies (which may not always appeal to students) meant that many pupils appeared to become switched off from reading. It also became clear that to implement ICT in literacy teaching, teachers need not only expertise in using ICT, but also an innovative methodology that exploits the use of ICT for reading and learning literature.

Models for learning

Creating artefacts is a learning strategy that involves the highest order learning skills, standing at the top of Bloom's revised taxonomy (Anderson and Krathwohl, 2001). The pedagogical theory that best describes learning by creating is that of Papert's idea of constructionism (Lewis, Pea and Rosen, 2010). This not only emphasises the learning that is triggered by the constructivist approach of activity-based learning (or learning by doing), but also the importance of the learning that occurs as a result of discussion leading to shared meanings. These concepts underpin two fundamental elements of the proposed teaching methodology:

- encouraging students to learn by creating
- encouraging students to learn by sharing and discussion.

Our investigation of learning theory also revealed the effectiveness of a learning sequence such as Kolb's learning cycle (Kolb, Rubin and Osland, 1991) in consolidating learning. This involves encouraging students to reflect on their activities and develop them accordingly. The Kolb learning cycle emphasises the value of reflecting on learning and how this can contribute to successful learning. This led to an additional two elements of the methodology:

- encouraging students to maximise their learning by scaffolding activities around creation, observation and reflection
- encouraging students to develop 'meta-cognitive' approaches by reflecting on their learning.

Reflection on learning has the additional benefit of providing much needed data on the effectiveness of the learning activities. As far as social interaction is concerned, this is important because it not only enables annotation, co-creation and feedback on the development of artefacts, but also provides a basis for team and trust-building between participants. However, previous work, for example by Conole et al. (2005), indicates that this trust-building interaction also needs to be scaffolded through the provision of set tasks. What we mean by 'scaffolded' in the educational context is that a structure is used to design learning and teaching activities where the tutor provides guidance to individual learners and also promotes a role for the wider group, or community of practice, in the process (Mayes and de Freitas, 2004; McConnell, 2006). Mayes and de Freitas (2004) note that scaffolding draws on and exploits the Vygotskian notion of the 'zone of proximal development', which is envisaged as a process by which skills, rules and knowledge involved in learning something are internalised by the learner, who in turn creates the cognitive tools to enable self-directed learning. The locus of control passes from the tutor to increasingly competent learners (McConnell, 2006). This structure is recommended in the design of technology-enhanced learning environments (Mayes and de Freitas, 2004; 2007).

In the context of the AMORES methodology, social interaction allows students from participant schools to become better acquainted with national and European literature through collaborating on the creation and discussion of e-artefacts. The methodology has a European dimension, allowing students to discover more about the literatures and cultures of their counterparts from various countries. The recommended instructional strategy is therefore collaborative creation, which is underpinned by the theory of social constructivism. In brief, collaborative learning is described by social constructivism as a means by which meaning is constructed jointly by a community (Conole et al., 2005, 11). Lewis, Pea and Rosen summarise social constructivism as the process by which learners, work together in 'questioning texts and situations, conceptualising problems, designing solutions, building artefacts, redesigning, re-conceptualising and reinterpreting, [where] people generate forms of public knowledge that in turn provide conceptual and relational support for further interaction and learning' (2010, 7).

By bringing these elements together we recommend that teaching methods incorporate the following elements:

- collaborative or individual creating of e-artefacts based on works of literature
- sharing e-artefacts
- discussion of e-artefacts
- reflection on the process of creation of e-artefacts and the whole learning process.

The recommended learning activities should align with the teaching methods, which should include learner-generated content such as creating an e-artefact that can be shared in and between schools and discussed face to face and via videoconferencing. Lewis, Pea and Rosen remark that, 'students engage in deep learning when they research, design and construct an artefact or model as a representation of their knowledge' and that 'constructionism links personal and social influences on learning because the artefact produced is an output of the interaction of personal and social knowledge construction that needs to be meaningful and made public' (2010, 7). It is assumed that enthusiastic early adopters ('technological champions') or those with some experience of technology-enhanced learning (e-learning) are best placed to take the initiative forward (Birch and Burnett, 2009, 121). Therefore, it is recommended that technology-enhanced learning champions who are based in schools are identified, so that they can act as leaders in this process.

A new teaching methodology

This methodology is primarily for teachers to use in teaching national and European literature with the support of interactive ICT tools. The AMORES teaching methodology ('the methodology') draws on the experience of the AMORES project experts and, more importantly, the teachers who conducted the learning activities with students throughout the project. These teachers also participated in the teachers' workshop held at Staffordshire University, Stoke-on-Trent, UK, from 17 to 19 March 2014, during which they shared expertise and started to plan the curriculum during the implementation phase. The methodology is based on participant teachers' experience, the state-of-the-art analysis carried out by the research team, and the user needs analysis developed in the initial stages of the project.

The methodology presented here can be employed by all educators, but primarily those wishing to develop their students' participation in learning about national and European literature through the creation of e-artefacts. This methodology could be used for any subject (the Danish school partner transferred this methodology into history classes) and at any level. It would be interesting to see whether this methodology could be deployed in information literacy classes for example. Using cartoon generators to retell the 'story' of a piece of research may enable students to evaluate a source they are using more deeply or describe an experimental process more succinctly. The teaching methodology and its recommendations offer a set of flexible resources for application across participating schools and other, wider, learning contexts. This methodology provides a framework for teachers to improve reading by enabling students to engage via this methodology, which embodies creativity and collaboration. The methodology responds to the essential need for a mechanism to engage students and has two additional goals:

- to improve the digital literacy of students and teachers by enabling them to create e-artefacts, and to promote sharing and critical reflection on the production of e-artefacts, based on the notion that learning is a social activity (Mayes and de Freitas, 2007)
- to empower teachers to increase their pedagogical competencies by engaging in all these activities.

The development of the new methodology was based on a participatory design (known as participatory research and action), which treated all participants as experts in their own experience and allowed all voices to be heard and consensus achieved in order to make the methodology appropriate and sustainable. Teachers felt empowered and identified the roles and activities which they wished to undertake as part of the AMORES project. The collaborative nature of the venture came through very clearly. It allowed teachers to incorporate their experience into the development of the AMORES teaching methodology. After the draft of the methodology was developed, the educational technology team selected the appropriate ICT tools to support the methodology and correspond to the needs analysis results. The selection of the tools is described in the Technology Selection Report and freely available from http://www.amores-project.eu/results.html. When the technology selection was completed, the learning materials for teachers were designed. The AMORES teaching methodology was tested in a school environment during the school year 2014/15, and the teachers met at a second face-to-face workshop during March 2015. The next section demonstrates how the methodology was implemented.

Example learning scenario
The following is a sample learning scenario employing the AMORES teaching methodology. The teachers who used the methodology with their students during the pilot incorporated most of the steps in this learning scenario, with some slight local variations in the order of steps. Teachers were given these activities as a suggested structure to follow:

- Choose the book(s) – preferably one story only.
- Introduce the books to the students.
- Students read their stories.
- Discuss in class.
- Conduct an analysis of the texts with the students.
- Pose a series of questions about the text to students who then discuss in groups and come up with an agreed set of answers. Example questions are: Who is your favourite character? and Why did you like her?
- Ask students to think about how they might retell this part of the story to students in a partner school.
- Select the tools and activities to use. Keep these varied. Demonstrate

e-tools for possible use to students, for example comic book generators such as Pixton, multimedia poster generators such as Glogster, Video Player, YouTube, Photo Editor, Pixlr.com, interactive timelines such as Toki-Toki and/or a presentation package such as Prezi.
- Students discuss and decide which e-tool to choose, for example a movie film of students acting out an aspect of the story, or a cartoon generator. As movies can be time-consuming to create it is recommended that teachers consider cartoon generators in the first instance as they are quicker to use and complete.
- Design specific activities so that they best combine the type of analysis and the tools chosen.
- Choose the groups for the students to work in.
- Students create their own e-artefact, such as a cartoon strip or a movie.
- Partner schools students share and discuss the e-artefacts via an online social network for example the freely available and secure Edmodo.
- Partner schools' students discuss the process of creating e-artefacts via videoconference.
- Teachers moderate and summarise all discussions.

Findings
The pilot implementation demonstrated that the AMORES teaching methodology, and especially the creation of e-artefacts, is an effective means of encouraging learning for students and staff. The key observations are divided into student and staff perspectives. It was clear from the group work at the teachers' workshop that although the teachers were working in very different contexts, the problems and issues regarding lack of engagement with literature are very similar. This shows that the approach outlined here can be applied across the countries involved – Croatia, Denmark, Poland, Sweden and the UK – and suggests that the methodology may have a wider application across the whole EU.

Student perspective
Students reported that they found the use of digital technologies to be more fun than writing. Examples of the students work can be found at YouTube (2016) and Flickr (2015). It was also noted that less academically able students expressed themselves more easily in other

modes than text. The reframing, or retelling, of a story within an e-artefact (for example a cartoon generator or video) encouraged students to adopt a critical perspective. The extra length of time it took to create an e-artefact required a longer engagement with the text, which led to a deeper analysis of the characters and the narrative.

The collaborative nature involved in the creation of e-artefacts taught students how to engage in effective teamwork and communication. This alternative mode encouraged students with self-efficacy or self-esteem problems to discover new talents and present them to other students. Those activities which were most engaging and participative in nature fostered more productive relationships between students and between students and staff.

While this methodology, centred on the creation of e-artefacts, encouraged digital literacy for younger students, it was less successful with older students. Nevertheless, it showed that the AMORES methodology is extremely helpful for those older students who needed refresher training in technologies they have already been taught in the classroom.

Staff perspectives
The sharing of expertise with peers and the process of implementing the methodology contributed to staff's professional development and classroom practice. It benefitted their professional development by improving their digital literacy and providing more opportunities to collaborate with students and fellow teachers than they had previously enjoyed. It also provided the ability to influence peers, as the methodology became more mainstream and was adopted by other disciplines within each school. Teachers should note that the use of technology makes classroom activities more engaging provided the activities are changed frequently to avoid the novelty wearing off. In light of this, having a range of different tools on hand to use was found to be extremely important. Finally, teachers suggested that it is better to focus on fewer books (or indeed one book) when creating e-artefacts because students then tend to read their chosen book in more depth and can retell it more effectively.

Recommendations
To use the methodology, it is necessary to determine to what extent teachers are familiar with particular categories of online tools. Those who

do not have the expertise required to engage their students in the activities which are to take place partly or wholly in the online environment, or to guide their students in using online tools, are advised to use the AMORES learning materials (AMORES, n.d) for teachers on interactive ICT tools in teaching national and European literature

Teachers may find that the level of support needed for the AMORES methodology is more than for traditional teaching and pupil–teacher ratios may be a constraint on supporting them effectively. Although the technologies are not challenging, the requirement to upload material and keep the technologies running can be a time-consuming. Younger students particularly need more support. It is essential that parents are included in the process by taking part in an introductory workshop. This is helpful in addressing any concerns they may have about the use of the technology and to help them support their children's work.

The activities carried out in the classroom, such as those described in the learning scenario example above, should take into consideration the following recommendations based on findings from students during the pilot methodology.

Recommendations on tools and activities:
- Make activities meaningful to engage and motivate students.
- Structure activities to enable collaboration across institutions.
- Ensure that technologies stretch students but do not overtax resources at schools.
- Students need observation and feedback on their progress throughout the creation process to ensure they are mastering the required skills.
- Provide an opportunity for learners to feed back on each other's work as this is motivating for them, formatively (by enabling annotation and response to each other's work) and summatively (in the form of a final 'show and tell').
- Give adequate provision for learning by creation, as it is a resource-intensive activity, particularly in the time required by learners and teachers.
- Ask students to create a logbook, which can help to order their thoughts and ensure fundamental things do not get forgotten because the process of reading and analysing the book and then creating an artefact can be lengthy.

- Before implementing the activities, review the structure of the activities, for example, how the groups are to be set up, whether the required technology is available, and whether to examine the whole book or just a segment.
- Carefully align tools and activities and think carefully about choosing an appropriate task to encourage students to learn about the book, and pick the right tool to support this task (see learning scenario section above for examples). The timeline tool Tiki-Toki is particularly useful because it can examine and identify the key stages in a narrative.

Facilitating student learning

Recommendations on facilitating student learning:

- The creation of an artefact requires students to adopt a critical perspective on a book in order to retell it, so help students analyse books, which can be a difficult task.
- Give students time to reflect on the creation of e-artefacts. Reflecting together as a class, where students get to see each other's work, can be motivating. Students find video especially engaging, particularly when they appear in them and they are viewed as part of a shared classroom activity.

Recommendations on addressing individual differences between students:

- Be aware of students' individual differences when planning to implement this methodology and observe students to identify whether they need additional support.
- Evaluate their language skills: how good is their English, and how confident are they in their English proficiency (not the same things) in an international collaboration?
- Evaluate their ability to co-operate; some highly competent students are not comfortable with co-operating; some students have limited negotiation skills.
- Evaluate their maturity (or media literacy). When creating artefacts they may include things 'because they're cool' rather than having a relevant academic focus. The methodology aims to address some of the imbalance between academically focused students and those who

are not engaged. Although this provides equality of opportunity for students, those who previously were high-flyers may not be when using a new pedagogy, and could feel alienated by this.
- Be aware that younger students are often not highly digitally literate (like many older students) and may struggle with creating artefacts and collaborating, so need more support.
- Some students may see the creation of artefacts as something to just 'get done' and want to move quickly onto the next thing. Therefore, they do not have the opportunity to explore the narrative and engage with individual perspective, meaning, interpretation and so on. At the other end of the spectrum, others may get so caught up with the process of creation they do not finish. Support both extremes to move somewhere towards the middle.
- Be prepared to assist students who have learning difficulties. These can be verbal, such as stammering, so talking on a video may be difficult, or social, which has a similar effect. One remarkable outcome of the methodology is that some students who were normally withdrawn in class suddenly came to the fore in activities.
- Be aware that some students do not engage with reading because they have created an identity in which they define themselves as someone who does not read. This is more likely among boys than girls. Although the AMORES methodology may not address this self-definition, it has still proven effective in engaging them in analysing the books rather than simply skim reading or, indeed, not reading at all. Be prepared to offer appropriate support but do not expect students to like reading any more than they do at present.
- Be prepared to assist students who have reading difficulties. The AMORES methodology does not address fluency directly, though may motivate some students to try reading more, and is likely to bring these students to the surface.

Digital technologies

In order to select the technologies used for specific learning activities, the following points need to be taken into consideration. According to the theoretical framework on which the draft methodology is based, tools that allow creation and mediation are necessary. Participant (teacher) experience suggests that the technologies chosen need to be ones that allow remixing, annotating and sharing. They should also be engaging for students and flexible enough to allow them to draw on their experiences. Key technologies that are recommended are video creation tools and comic strip generators. These offer a rich media experience, are interesting to students and include the storytelling aspects crucial to creating digital artefacts based on literary works. An important consideration is that schools and students generally have some experience of creating videos, as was evidenced by most of the participant schools. A social network is recommended for asynchronous activities, as a medium for socialisation, while videoconferencing is advised for synchronous ones. Project requirements stipulated the selection of technologies that allow sharing and collaboration at a distance.

Social media
When using online social platforms, there should be sufficient time allocated purely dedicated to online interaction between students. Specific activities requiring interaction need to be integrated into students' learning experiences for them to happen. These pedagogical modes also need to have been modelled for the teachers in workshops so teachers are sufficiently familiar with them as a teaching technique as social platforms take much longer to adapt to than other technologies. Unlike other technologies, social platforms require the development of an online identity, a sense of social space and the development of a range of complex communication strategies, as well as a feeling of being accustomed to the functionality and to become engaged with a community, particularly when this is exclusively online. Teachers need to be aware that students perceive proficient language skills as a necessity for communication on social platforms. Students, especially in an international setting, may understandably be self-conscious about their language skills.

Videoconferencing
Preparation is an essential prerequisite for the process of videoconferencing. Trialling the software and hardware in advance is very helpful in enabling the videoconferences to be effective. This gives students the opportunity to rehearse what they want to say. Sharing artefacts beforehand enables students to prepare fully their responses for discussion. Videoconferencing works best when students on either side of the online conversation are the same age and mismatches in ages of

two years or more can create a stilted and awkward interaction at first. Videoconferencing improves with practice. The second videoconferences are better than the first. Students are more confident presenting material and technical issues that have become apparent in the first round, such as room and equipment set-up problems, can be avoided or minimised.

Potential limitations

For the pilot implementation of the methodology, activities carried out in the classroom demonstrated that the methodology has two general limitations and one specific limitation in the UK context. These should be considered when planning to use the methodology in the classroom. The AMORES methodology encourages in-depth engagement with text and character but not attitudes to reading. Although the creation of digital artefacts improves learning about literature, it has not changed attitudes to reading. It appears that issues associated with reading are too culturally ingrained to be addressed by a learning strategy alone. However, encouraging communication between students who love reading and students who have a negative attitude towards it may enable changes in the attitude of the latter group over the longer term.

Creating e-artefacts can take up much more time than writing traditional essays, and this may limit the degree to which the methodology can be introduced. This can be alleviated by focusing on less time-consuming technologies such as the creation of digital comic strips, which can be created faster than videos.

The UK school system severely constrains autonomy for teachers and hence creativity for students. Whereas most schools in the EU are able to introduce alternative modes within their curriculum, the UK school system has much more accountability built into it, which requires a degree of written work to demonstrate that various targets have been met. Therefore, bringing the AMORES methodology into the UK educational context may only be achieved on a much smaller scale than in other EU countries, although it can still be done.

Conclusion

In implementing this project, it has become evident that school pupils' motivation to engage with their literature can be increased via the use of the AMORES teaching methodology which, in large part, includes creativity in the form of producing e-artefacts to retell a story to an audience of peers, but it does not increase students' love of reading. However, there is a significant caveat to this approach: to maintain students' interest, the ICT used and teaching techniques employed need to change regularly or the novelty wears off fairly quickly. The difference between this project and many others is that the participants were treated as experts in their own experience and therefore the new teaching methodology and the technology selection report were far more effective in meeting the needs of teachers as they implemented this new approach. The final version of the teaching methodology document (D4-2) is freely available on the AMORES project website (www.amoresproject.eu/results.html). This participatory technique demonstrates that treating participants as partners can bring rich rewards in practical outcomes and is strongly recommended as a way of exploring digital literacy, whatever the context.

References

AMORES (n.d) http://www.amores-project.eu/

Anderson, L. and Krathwohl, D. (eds) (2001) *A Taxonomy for Learning, Teaching and Assessing: a revision of Bloom's Taxonomy of educational objectives*, Longman.

Birch, D. and Burnett, B (2009) Bringing Academics on Board: encouraging institution wide diffusion of e-learning environments, *Australasian Journal of Educational Technology*, 25 (1), 117–34, https://ajet.org.au/index.php/AJET/article/view/1184/412.

Clark, C. (2012) *Children's and Young People's Reading Today: findings from the 2011 National Literacy Trust's annual survey*, https://literacytrust.org.uk/documents/144/2012_01_01_free_research_-_children_and_young_peoples_reading_today_sag3x9P.pdf.

Conole, G., Littlejohn, A.; Falconer, I. and Jeffery, A. (2005) *Pedagogical Review of Learning Activities and Use Cases: LADIE project report*, Jisc.

Flickr (2015) AMORES Multimedia, https://www.flickr.com/groups/2767321@N22/pool/.

Jisc (2011) *Developing Digital Literacies, briefing paper*, https://www.webarchive.org.uk/wayback/archive/20140616150918/www.jisc.ac.uk/media/documents/funding/2011/04/Briefingpaper.pdf.

Kolb, D., Rubin, I. and Osland, J. (1991) *Organizational Behavior; an experiential approach*, 5th edn, Prentice-Hall.

Lewis, S., Pea, R. and Rosen, J. (2010) Special Issue: digitize and transfer,

Social Science Information, **49** (3), 1–19.

Mayes, T. and de Freitas, S. (2004) *JISC E-learning Models Desk Study Stage 2: review of e-learning theories, frameworks and models (issue 1)*, www.jisc.ac.uk/uploaded_documents/Stage%202%20Learning%20Models%20(Version%201).pdf.

Mayes, T. and de Freitas, S. (2007) Learning and E-learning: the role of theory. In Beetham, H. and Sharpe, R. (eds), *Rethinking Pedagogy for a Digital Age: designing and delivering e-learning*, Routledge.

McConnell, D. (2006) *E-learning Groups and Communities*, McGraw-Hill Education.

YouTube (2016) AMORES Project, https://www.youtube.com/channel/UCK3IktOiQkWG40cHKfTlbFw/videos.

5

Digital games: providing unique digital literacy challenges in childhood

Dean Groom and Judy O'Connell

Introduction

As they become more accessible and more mobile, digital technologies are increasingly crossing the contexts of home, school, workplace and communities, and offering an expanding range of educational and social affordances (Haddon and Livingstone, 2014). This is a challenge for families and those seeking to better understand, engage and implement digital games in children's education. Technology has become an important feature of family life in many households with children using some form of device with a screen every day (Gutnick et al., 2011; Holloway, Green and Livingstone, 2013; Vandewater et al., 2009. Children use and enjoy technology more and more, in a world of expanding technologies, access and media forms (Buckingham and Willett, 2013; Tyner, 2009; von Feilitzen and Carlsson, 2000). Ongoing improvements to technology have enabled children to access new media and technologies from an early age, and the YouTube clip of a baby manipulating a touch screen is all too familiar. Leathers, Summers and Desollar-Hale (2013) argue that babies who have had ready access to touchscreen technologies since birth learn to point at screens by the age of 10–14 months.

Children do not need to wait until they can operate a keyboard and mouse to begin interacting with digital media. Today, pre-verbal, non-ambulant infants have parents who are comfortable with their children using these child-friendly touch screen devices. Nikken and Schols argue, 'through age 7, children are honing their fine-motor skills, which makes it gradually easier for them to manipulate touchscreens, small keys, gadgets and controllers' and are 'adept at using symbols, playing pretend games, interpreting relevant cues in their social environment, and gain knowledge of story grammar, which is essential for the formation of interpretive schema for processing more demanding media content' (2015, 3423).

This chapter takes a focused look at the emerging opportunities provided by digital games and provides a rationale based on research to encourage individuals and organisations to consider games and gaming as mainstream channels of digital literacy engagement.

Digital childhoods

Digital games are an integral part of children's environments, with findings pointing to continued growth and regular game play across a range of devices, driven by curiosity, challenge and interactivity (Blumberg and Fisch, 2013). Some researchers discuss children's media use as 'screen time' rather than information and communication technologies (ICT) in order to try and encapsulate the ongoing diversity of devices being used, human interaction, preferences and experiences of use as well as the now common interoperability and synchronicity enabled by the internet (Clark, Demont-Heinrich and Webber, 2005). This interest in the notion of 'screen time' (Clancy and Lowrie 2005; Ernest et al., 2014; Randall, 2013; Stager, 2010) increasingly connects the home–school environment, indicating that educators need to consider children's home use of screen time as part of their overall educational development.

Carson and Janssen (2012) investigated the screen time habits of children under the age of 5 in Canada, in order to gain a better understanding of the factors that influence the use of television, video and computer games. They argued that intrapersonal, interpersonal and physical environment factors within the home setting are essential to children's use of 'screens' and that parental cognitive factors at the interpersonal level were of particular importance. This suggests that children's experience of digital media remains diverse but, more significantly, they are actively engaged with media at a very young age. It was found that 37.9% of children (≤ 5 years old) played video games and

93.7% watched television. The authors found increasing parental awareness towards recommendations of 'screen time' improved their self-efficacy to refuse access and better regulate their children's media diet (Carson and Janssen, 2012, 7).

Hakanen (2007, 3) argues that identities are being formed on the social grid and shaped by the dominant medium of the era, which includes digital video games. As players, children are placed into these mediums and their digital identity in part emerges from discourses salient to what media is offered to them and how adults think about what constitutes the self. The image of the child playing as an avatar in a game is a significant expression of the convergence of children's corporeal and hypermediated worlds, also providing an enlarged sense of what media and communications are involved in digital childhoods (Hjorth, Burgess and Richardson, 2012). The real and the imaginary worlds come together to create new forms of engagement, motivation or places for play.

New literacies in and out of the classroom

Digital technologies have become common in children's homes and schools, yet a survey of 2462 teachers about their use of technology at home and in their classrooms suggested that while educators outpace the general adult population in personal technology use, 42% of teachers feel that their students know more than they do about using digital tools (Purcell et al., 2013). Technology use in the home context has been the focus of research (Burnett, 2010; Marsh, 2006; Pahl, 2010; Plowman, Stephen and McPake, 2010) with strong arguments for the need to continue to examine children's literacy and learning practices in these contexts, all the more crucial given the home–school nexus.

A fundamental requirement of learning is to be able to read. But what does 'read' mean in the 21st century? Lamb (2011) argues that reading goes beyond interpreting text to also include graphics, sound, motion and other kinds of symbols in addition to or instead of text. To become fully literate, students must become proficient in the new literacies of 21st century technologies (International Reading Association, 2009). Literacy educators have a responsibility to integrate these new literacies into the curriculum. This interpretation (for example) is supported by the *Australian Curriculum: English*, which states that students 'listen to, read, view, speak, write, create and reflect on increasingly complex and sophisticated spoken, written and multimodal texts across a growing range of contexts with accuracy, fluency and purpose' (ACARA, 2014, par. 1).

These new literacies are multimodal, comprising multiple modes – visual, sound and text – and are more participatory (Wilber, 2010). In other words, literacy as metaliteracy action (Ipri, 2010) – where information being accessed and read takes many forms online and is produced and communicated through multiple modalities (Mackey and Jacobson, 2011) – happens whenever children and young people read and interpret their world, as many young people comfortably use a wide variety of the literacies associated with new technologies to construct and distribute knowledge (Coiro et al., 2014; Lenhart et al., 2007).

Essentially the field of new literacies focuses on how language and literacies are shaped by the ongoing development of new tools and technologies. Learning in online environments involves skills and processes that are common to print literacy but also important skills that are unique, such as using search engines, reading websites, selecting appropriate hyperlinks, and comparing information (Asselin and Doiron, 2008). Understanding how the use of technology is distributed in multiple settings includes understanding how, when and why access to information and novel kinds of technologically mediated learning environments – such as online special interest groups, tutorials or games – can support learning for children on their own terms (Barron, 2006, 194).

Digital games

A digital video game as a concept is an 'electronic' game that involves human interaction with a user interface to generate visual feedback on a device. The forms grow increasingly diverse and some of the most commonly used games by children or for educational purposes with children includes alternate reality games, massively multiplayer online games, multiplayer online battle arenas and social, casual and mobile games.

The alternate reality game genre is much more than simply being a pre-coded application, and can be flexible enough to allow teachers to create a narrative or plot, and to use some free web-based tools to create a playful and immersive environment which is not real, but which engages with the real world in a way that draws players into the fantasy narrative. Popular alternate reality games include Ingress (2013; www.ingress.com) and Pokémon Go (2016; www.pokemongo.com). Alternate reality games can also be games driven by storyline and typically supported through some type of online game portal that manages the game, such as a website. They often remain active online for some time, such as World Without Oil (2007; http://worldwithoutoil.org). Examples of massively multiplayer online games are World of Warcraft (2004; http://us.battle.net/wow/en) and World of Tanks (2010; http://worldoftanks.com). Multiplayer online battle arenas include League of Legends (2009; http://oce.leagueoflegends.com) and Robocraft (2016; http://robocraftgame.com). Popular casual and mobile games include Angry Birds (2009; https://www.angrybirds.com), Minecraft (2011; https://minecraft.net) and Highlights Monster Day for pre-schoolers (2016; www.highlights.com/store/apps/highlights-monster-day).

These digital games demonstrate the developments taking place in the history of this genre. The rapid expansion of game types, platforms, experiences, media-convergence, human interfaces and growth of game popularity in our society increasingly requires parents and educators to address the challenges, opportunities and potential of digital games.

Player participation and engagement
Players do not just engage in ready-made gameplay but also actively take part in the construction of these experiences: they bring their desires, anticipations and previous experiences with them, and interpret and reflect the experience in that light (Ermi and Mäyrä, 2003). Digital games allow 'the full experiential flow' by linking perceptions, cognitions and emotions with first-person actions (Grodal, 2003). Digital games provide a fertile environment for learning (Gee, 2005). Role-playing games allow child players to take an ontological position that may be unavailable in their lived existence. This allows a player to make sense of the play experience and construct an interpretation of the game that draws on personal and social contexts of their life or builds beyond current situational, social or cultural contexts. Additionally, games are a force in the (re)construction of contemporary childhood (Papazian, 2010); this provides models of good learning practices which can be used to develop practical competencies and social practices in early childhood (Manessis, 2011). Because children test out an idea by acting on parts of it, the boundaries between the real world and the game world can become blurred.

Where games differ from other media is that they require the participation of players and, unlike older media, the actions of players themselves play a key role in reshaping them as a multimodal experience of enjoyable playful interaction. Digital games provide an active process of meta-cognitive engagement and decision making within creative action. They can provide authentic learning situations, promote social interactions, increase motivation, encourage higher-order thinking, and foster 21st century skills (Qian and Clark, 2016) as well as promote collaboration, problem solving and communication (Johnson, Adams and Haywood, 2011).

Craft (2003, 42) identifies that this action of creativity involves passing of control to the learner; placing a value on learners' ownership and control to encourage thinking and debate as well as co-participation in learning. Reilly argues that children are learning through new media as a 'set of social skills and cultural competencies, are not tied to traditional curriculum standards and practices, but instead are best developed through creative and engaging projects' (2011, 473). These new literacies merge the creative modes fostered through a variety of media tools, to encourage socially constructed meanings and forms of self-expression. There are strong links with discourses surrounding digital childhoods (Buckingham, 2013) and implications for education (Steinkuehler, Squire and Barab, 2012). Essentially, this process of creative 'dialogue' reveals how metaliteracy transactions are being transformed in digital games.

Gaming literacies

During gameplay, gaming literacies (elements of game play and complex understanding of computer systems) as a metaliteracy are used to accomplish difficult but motivating tasks in order to develop new knowledge by navigating a complex, changing virtual environment (Apperley and Walsh, 2012). Learning can become an immersive participatory experience (Barab and Dede, 2007) where the knowledge learned in the game and the knowledge learned at school scaffolds disciplinary content (Barzilai and Blau, 2014). Games can also convey meaningful messages that young people value, and through active game creation can motivate and improve the capacity to learn (Altura and Curwood, 2015). Games give educators the opportunity to introduce layers for conceptual learning and new taxonomies for pedagogical design, and herein educators are understanding the complex learning that gaming can involve (Steinkuehler, Squire and Barab, 2012, 271).

Felicia (2011) argues that playing video games stimulates affective, cognitive and communicational processes, thus facilitating the emergence of knowledge. These strategies can be viewed through a pedagogical classification of games; they can develop psychomotor, intellectual, identity and relational skills, which support a range of academic, problem solving and sense-making situations. In essence, games provide spaces for accelerated and simultaneous information processing, competence and skill development (St-Pierre, 2011), however understanding how information behaviour affects game design and gaming interactions is also critically important.

Boundaries of engagement

When playing digital games, players must make choices about game mode and challenge levels (Sit, Lam and McKenzie, 2010), retrieve information to solve problems or make sense of situations, in a variety of ways that may well be different from their other experiences (Adams, 2009). Knowledge construction in games is also an extension of game design, which ideally supports the learner's needs within the information-seeking context while also generating successful immersive experiences for problem solving (Liu, Cheng and Huang, 2011). It is also suggested that in games it is helpful to create a flow experience (Thin, Hansen and McEachen, 2011), in which students are motivated to apply trial-and-error, learn-by-example and analytical reasoning strategies. Inal and Cagiltay (2007) also found that challenge and complexity elements of games had more effect on flow experience in an interactive social game environment than clear feedback only.

A game does not exist without players (Bourgonjon, 2014, 4) and the learning that takes place is an intersection of the experience designed by the game designer and the intentions of players (Steinkuehler, Squire and Barab, 2012, 247). Zimmerman outlines these intersections as gaming literacy through systems, play and design (2008, 24). Harviainen, Gough and Sköld (2012) introduced the concept of games as information systems, in the sense of systems that inform. The authors explain that in order to progress through digital games, players must recognise and process information from the user interface, cues and clues embedded in the game environment, and through interacting with non-player characters. They also explain that as reasons for seeking game-related information touch on cognitive issues, the conceptual connection between information seeking and information behaviour is significant to the construction of games as information systems.

There is also evidence of games as being an important constituent of media education, literacy and information fluency learning (Beavis, Dezuanni and O'Mara, 2017; Buckingham, 2007; Buckingham and Burn, 2007; Buckingham and Willett, 2013). All games are systematic and use an array of information and techniques to communicate with players (Squire, 2006). Video games often provide players with just-in-time information through a range of audio, visual and haptic clues triggered by choices and interaction with the game world. Steinkuehler and Williams (2006) say that the way information is revealed to players is part of the socialisation needed for them to behave in certain ways. The information from the environment is then processed by players, who then select appropriate behaviours. Players in multiplayer games are part of the information giving process. For example, watching the mistakes of another player is a way of processing information to improve a player's performance without verbal communication between those players. Information giving is common in games (asking others how they did something, what they need, how to find and so on). Players are involved in an ongoing social relationship with an audience, drawing on language and communication to reproduce information. In this way, the hardwired, 'designed in' informational boundaries are supplemented with additional knowledge inside and outside the game.

Digital player identity is another complex topic related to literacy through body, gender, age, race and ethnicity to demonstrate affiliation and relationships as players adopt certain storylines and discourses in online gaming (Thomas, 2007, 9). Martin (2012) argues that player self-identity is an important component of online play where participants' skill and level in the game as well as their play style and information practices influence their success at school.

It is important, therefore, not to see digital video games as a homogenous whole, but rather as a complex and changing set of technologies which by their very nature include literacy requirements and experiences. Through gameplay and narratives found in today's digital video games children are clearly being immersed in transmedia navigation, which is contributing to the ongoing development of theories about the literacies of game play in formal and informal settings (Barnett, 1976; Kafai, 2006; Kangas, 2010; Yee, 2006). Previous boundaries between informal and formal learning are blurring and so are the required literacies that reflect contemporary life (Hagood, 2009).

Games and gaming action involve a dynamic, active process of knowledge construction in which learners constantly strive to make sense of new information. This information behaviour is influenced not just by information seeking that a participant may engage in, but also by the game mechanics that have been established in the game itself.

Examples in action

Quest Atlantis (now maintained as part of the Atlantis Remixed Project at http://atlantisremixed.org) was created by Indiana University and allows students to complete educational tasks in 3D multi-user environments. In this digital game students can move around freely and complete quests based on educational goals and chat to collaborate with other students about work and tasks. The most beneficial part of Quest Atlantis is its inclusion of curriculum-appropriate tasks that students are required to complete directly connecting curriculum and learning goals in the game (Turkay et al., 2015, 3). Quest Atlantis encourages students to take risks and use their failures as exploration of topics (Gee, 2005, 35). Students develop better motivation, confidence, knowledge and understanding, creative thinking and negotiating skills (DEECD, 2011, 14). Other key learning outcomes included enhanced motivation, confidence, reading and comprehension skills (DEECD, 2011, 21–7). Students had also begun to develop their creative writing skills, by creating their own characters and quests for other students to complete (DEECD, 2011, 14). It was also found that Quest Atlantis allowed students to develop or extend knowledge at their own rate without feeling overwhelmed (DEECD, 2011, 18).

Scratch (https://scratch.mit.edu/) is a game created on the Scratch platform using blocks of code in a drag and drop interface, to manipulate sprites on the screen. Scratch promotes mathematical and computational skills as well as creativity, reasoning and collaborative working. The internet is populated with Scratch resources and professional learning opportunities, including Code Club Australia, which is establishing a network of events for students aged 9–11. There is a wealth of literature on the application of Scratch for learning (Breen, 2016).

Minecraft (https://minecraft.net/) is not simply a digital game that allows children and youth to build and create virtual worlds, but also an educational tool used as a vehicle for teaching critical content. Through the ability to take control and be active learners, motivation is enhanced in areas as diverse as science, maths, history, engineering, architecture and computer coding (Ellison and Evans, 2016).

Transmedia storytelling (https://www.coursera.org/learn/transmedia-storytelling) provides a digital game experience and learning tool that has the power to motivate, persuade, entertain as well as educate. Inanimate Alice creates an experience that immerses the reader in the complexity and emotional journey of a story through the impact of sound and vision of the multilayered story, with new storylines emerging to enrich the tale, making Alice a unique digital reading experience built on the mesh of game, puzzle, sight and sounds to embellish a story (Fleming, 2013).

Unity (https://unity3d.com/) is a complex digital programming game tool with advanced graphic capabilities. Free learning resources can be accessed via the Unity website and there is a wide variety of assets and a community of developers across the web. An understanding of general programming language such as C# or UnityScript is required to make best use of the features. However, this does not prevent youngsters from becoming capable and enthusiastic game builders. In a short video 12-year-old Cooper explains that Scratch can be too easy and describes what motivates him to play Unity (YouTube, 2017). Learning what 'real' game engines are and becoming involved in the game-building opportunities of coding provides such youngsters with unique meta-cognitive and metaliteracy learning opportunities.

On a novel twist on digital games, Breakout EDU (https://www.breakoutedu.com/) is similar to the popular 'escape room' game, but has a marked difference as this game is about opening a locked box. It is a timed challenge that involves solving puzzles, discovering clues, finding hidden items and red herrings, and ultimately figuring out how to unlock a series of locks to open the box. The sessions have an underlying theme or story that underpins each Breakout, focusing on collaboration and problem solving. Breakout EDU is often used to introduce new concepts, reinforce learning, bring closure to a lesson, and reinforce skills and concepts learned, all in a fun way (Goerner, 2016). While this is a 'physical' game, Breakout EDU Digital (https://www.breakoutedu.com/digital/) encourages teachers to play alongside students to model a growth mindset playing the game completely online. This has been used successfully to create many game challenges. Among the many available a game on the French Revolution, Escape the Guillotine! (https://sites.

google.com/site/escapeguillotine/), involving solving various clues about events around the revolution, has been used successfully in Years 11 and 12 curriculum studies in Australia. The riddles and puzzles resulted in social interaction between group members creating multiple stories, confirming the finding that students learn more when they are left to engage with a game in a group competition (Admiraal et al., 2011).

Museums are developing serious games to engage students in history content with successful results. The project Playhist (http://www.experimedia.eu/2014/02/25/playhist/) in Carnegie Mellon University uses 3D technology to immerse students into the environment of Tholos (virtual theatre) in the Foundation of the Hellenic World of Athens, requiring players to engage in some mini games. Progress in the game through 'learning by playing' provides a better understanding of an historical subject (Perez-Valle, Aguirrezabal and Sillaurren, 2014).

The portability of devices for gameplay is also demonstrated by Game 1910 for learning history, which allows a player to live through the 1910 revolution that led to the establishment of the republic of Portugal (Cruz, Carvalho and Araújo, 2017). This game was designed after research into students' game preferences to understand rules, obstacles and choices, and players need to learn through failures to be successful (Gee, 2007).

According to Squire and Steinkuehler (2005), when Santa Monica Public Library, CA, hosted gaming nights for teens to come and play games, there were many positive benefits. Not only did the gaming nights reorient young people towards the library and allow librarians insight into youth culture, but half of the students who attend game nights and played games such as Age of Empires (https://www.ageofempires.com/), Civilization (https://www.civilization.com/) or Rome: Total War (https://www.totalwar.com/) ended up borrowing a book based on an interest generated through gameplay. Such games require serious thought and stimulate an interest in multiple topics including history, politics, economics and geography. For many, they raise curiosity, spark passions and inspire lifelong interests, and should be included and promoted in public library collections for these reasons (Squire and Steinkuehler, 2005, 41). Brown and Kasper (2013, 756) argue that games can be fused with library agendas and posed three questions to investigate how games affect reading, learning achievement, information literacy and library use:

- What do participants in a library's video game program learn?

- How do library gaming programs assess participants?
- What steps can programs take to improve their assessment?

Next steps

When we think about game-playing, where fun and immersion drive meta-cognitive, reflective experiences playing games such as World of Warcraft, Destiny, Halo, Guild Wars, Lord of the Rings and so on, many players are almost entirely focused on the gap between their current position and the 'next level' and the term 'levelling up' is a common phrase applied to gaming success. The game level, or rather information processes at that game level, are entirely designed to give feedback to players such that no external 'judge' is required. Arguably, educational games are more likely to be considered for implementation if the intended learning outcome has recognisable curriculum facing materials. Where teachers and designers are required to deliver the object of study as concepts, definitions, formulae, facts and problems, the intention may seem less obvious and so lead to questions about implementation.

According to Burgun (2012) planning to incorporate digital games in community or education contexts should involve asking what kinds of actions will be possible in the game and what types of interactions could take place. Burgun suggests we begin by asking, 'Will interactivity help me do what I want to do? . . . Will a game system, with its goals, its competition and its player interaction be helpful?' If the answer is no, then a game might not be the right medium (2012, 21).

Some educational games are simple in design, focused on content with low levels of literacy demand, which emphasise drill and practice or memorisation. Research has shown that other games can promote meaningful learning by providing players with adaptive challenges, curiosity, self-expression, immersion, collaboration, competition, variable rewards and low stakes failure (Qian and Clark, 2016). Such games can provide situated learning, promote social interactions, increase motivation and engagement, and provide opportunities to develop valued 21st century skills (e.g. collaboration, creativity, communication and critical thinking).

Games in general, and educational games in particular, pose unique requirements on the perception and processing of information by gamers–learners. Any education or community organisation is able to introduce games and gaming in the context of the services to children and youth, and provide intrinsic integration of learning content for knowledge and skills exploration and acquisition. Schools and libraries share in the unique opportunity to foster literacy and knowledge construction through digital games. Games fit the mission of libraries to promote literacy and informal learning as they encourage reading and information literacy, and are great for students with diverse learning styles, by people of all ages, families and other intergenerational groups (Gilton, 2016, 37).

Digital literacy and/or metaliteracy transactions are the enabling factors connecting literacy, systems, play and design. Ultimately, where knowledge has been successfully integrated, the game mechanics can also serve as platforms for trying out and experimenting with ideas that have been acquired outside of the game:

> Imagine learning about avionics and how wing designs affect speed and manoeuvrability, or reading historical descriptions of the British longbow and how it changed the way battles were fought, and imagine having a tool to try out and experiment with those concepts, seeing how they play out and how changes made by the player effects the outcome.
>
> Mozelius et al., 2017, 352

Conclusion

The growth of digital video games is likely to continue and therefore remain a fixture in educational discourses. Likewise, digital games have also captured the attention of institutions that wish to harness the engagement and motivational qualities of games for a variety of non-gaming purposes from consumer loyalty to advocacy and education (McGonigal, 2011).

Children have been shown to play video games as part of their leisure and learning time in numerous studies. Arguably, this has helped to drive teacher interest in using games (Kenny and McDaniel, 2011). Young people are increasingly engaging in practices that remix traditional and newer literacies (Gainer and Lapp, 2010), creating an imperative to understand the knowledge construction process in games as information systems, driven by new and emerging literacies as metaliteracy transactions, digital identity and knowledge construction. Game play can consist of single or multi-aged player groupings, and can support developmentally determined expectations beyond the normal curriculum learning and teaching imperatives. In such contexts, the importance of new and emerging literacies become a priority consideration. To succeed in today's interconnected and complex world, workers need to be able to think systemically, creatively and critically. Equipping students with these 21st century competencies requires new thinking not only about what should be taught in school but also about how to develop valid assessments to measure and support these competencies (Shute and Ventura, 2013). Digital games provide a unique environment for engaging with conceptions and constructions within digital childhood experiences – and understanding the participatory new literacies involved provides a rich field for ongoing and expanding research in digital childhoods.

References

ACARA (2014) *Australian Curriculum: English: aims*, Australian Curriculum and Reporting Authority, https://www.australiancurriculum.edu.au/f-10-curriculum/english/aims/.

Adams, S. S. (2009) What Games Have to Offer: information behavior and meaning-making in virtual play spaces, *Library Trends*, **57** (4), 676–93.

Admiraal, W., Huizenga, J., Akkerman, S. and Dam, G. T. (2011) The Concept of Flow in Collaborative Game-based Learning, *Computers in Human Behavior*, **27** (3), 1185–94.

Altura, G. J. and Curwood, J. S. (2015) Hitting Restart, *Journal of Adolescent & Adult Literacy*, **59** (1), 25–7.

Apperley, T. and Walsh, C. (2012) What Digital Games and Literacy Have in Common: a heuristic for understanding pupils' gaming literacy, *Literacy*, **46** (3), 115–22, http://doi.org/10.1111/j.1741-4369.2012.00668.x.

Asselin, M. and Doiron, R. (2008) Towards a Transformative Pedagogy of School Libraries 2.0, *School Libraries Worldwide*, **24** (2), 1–18.

Barab, S. and Dede, C. (2007) Games and Immersive Participatory Simulations for Science Education: an emerging type of curricula, *Journal of Science Education and Technology*, **16** (1), 1–3.

Barnett, L. A. (1976) Current Thinking About Children's Play: learning to play or playing to learn?, *Quest*, **26** (1), 5–16.

Barron, B. (2006) Interest and Self-Sustained Learning as Catalysts of Development: a learning ecology perspective, *Human Development*, **49** (4), 193–224.

Barzilai, S. and Blau, I. (2014) Scaffolding Game-based Learning: impact on learning achievements, perceived learning, and game experiences, *Computers & Education*, **70**, 65–79.

Beavis, C., Dezuanni, M. L. and O'Mara, J. (2017) *Serious Play: literacy, learning, and digital games*, Routledge.

Blumberg, F. C. and Fisch, S. M. (2013) *Digital Games: a context for cognitive development*, Wiley.

Bourgonjon, J. (2014) The meaning and relevance of video game literacy. CLCWeb: *Comparative Literature and Culture* 16.5 (2014):https://doi.org/10.7771/1481-4374.2510

Breen, D. (2016) *Designing Digital Games: create games with Scratch!*, John Wiley & Sons.

Brown, R. T. and Kasper, T. (2013) The Fusion of Literacy and Games: a case study in assessing the goals of a library video game program, *Library Trends*, 61 (4), 755–78, http://search.proquest.com/docview/1443260853?accountid=10344.

Buckingham, D. (2007) Digital Media Literacies: rethinking media education in the age of the internet, *Research in Comparative and International Education*, 2 (1), 43–55.

Buckingham, D. and Burn, A. (2007) Game Literacy in Theory and Practice, *Journal of Educational Multimedia and Hypermedia*, 16 (3), 323–49.

Buckingham, D. (2013) *Beyond technology: Children's learning in the age of digital culture*. John Wiley & Sons

Buckingham, D. and Willett, R. (2013) *Digital Generations: children, young people, and the new media*, Routledge.

Burgun, K. (2012) *Game Design Theory*, CRC Press.

Burnett, C. (2010) Technology and Literacy in Early Childhood Educational Settings: a review of research, *Journal of Early Childhood Literacy*, 10 (3), 247–70.

Carson, V. and Janssen, I. (2012) Associations Between Factors Within the Home Setting and Screen Time Among Children aged 0–5 years: a cross-sectional study, *BMC Public Health*, 12 (1), 539.

Clancy, S. and Lowrie, T. (2005) Multiliteracies: new pathways into digital worlds, *International Journal of Learning*, 12 (7), 141–5.

Clark, L. S., Demont-Heinrich, C. and Webber, S. (2005) Parents, ICTs, and Children's Prospects for Success: interviews along the digital 'Access Rainbow', *Critical Studies in Media Communication*, 22 (5), 409–26.

Coiro, J., Knobel, M., Lankshear, C. and Leu, D. J. (eds) (2014) *Handbook of Research on New Literacies*, Routledge.

Craft, A. (2003) The Limits to Creativity in Education: dilemmas for the educator, *British Journal of Educational Studies*, 51 (2), 113–27, http://web.nsboro.k12.ma.us/algonquin/faculty/socialstudiesteachers/

smith/documents/thelimitsofcreativityineducationarticle.pdf.

Cruz, S., Carvalho, A. A. A. and Araújo, I. (2017) A Game for Learning History on Mobile Devices, *Education and Information Technologies*, **22** (2), 515–31, https://doi.org/10.1007/s10639-016-9491-z.

DEECD (2011) *Innovating with Technology: game-based learning research trials: findings to inform school practice*, Department of Education and Early Childhood Development, Victoria, Australia.

Ellison, T. L. and Evans, J. N. (2016) Minecraft, Teachers, Parents, and Learning: what they need to know and understand, *School Community Journal*, **26** (2), 25.

Ermi, L. and Mäyrä, F. (2003) Power and Control of Games: children as the actors of game cultures. In Copier M. and Raessens, J. (eds) *[Proceedings of] Level Up: digital games research conference*, University of Utrecht and Digital Games Research Association.

Ernest, J. M., Causey, C., Newton, A. B., Sharkins, K., Summerlin, J. and Albaiz, N. (2014) Extending the Global Dialogue About Media, Technology, Screen Time, and Young Children, *Childhood Education*, **90** (3), 182.

Felicia, P. (2011) *Handbook of Research on Improving Learning and Motivation Through Educational Games: multidisciplinary approaches*, IGI Global.

Fleming, L. (2013) Expanding Learning Opportunities with Transmedia Practices: inanimate Alice as an exemplar, *Journal of Media Literacy Education*, **5** (2), 3.

Gainer, J. S. and Lapp, D. (2010) Remixing Old and New Literacies = Motivated Students, *The English Journal*, **100** (1), 58–64.

Gee, J. P., (2005) Learning by Design: good video games as learning machines, *E-Learning and Digital Media*, **2** (1), 5–16.

Gee, J. P. (2007) *Good Video Games + Good Learning: collected essays on video games, learning and literacy*, Peter Lang.

Gilton, D. L. (2016) *Creating and Promoting Lifelong Learning in Public Libraries*, Rowman & Littlefield.

Goerner, P. (2016) Breakout EDU Brings 'Escape Room' Strategy to the Classroom, *SLJ Review*, www.slj.com/2016/09/reviews/tech/breakout-edu-brings-escape-room-strategy-to-the-classroom-slj-review/.

Grodal, T. (2003) Stories for Eye, Ear, and Muscles: video games, media, and embodied experiences. In Wolf, M. J. P. and Perron, B. (eds), *The Video Game Theory Reader*, Routledge.

Gutnick, A. L., Robb, M., Takeuchi, L., Kotler, J., Bernstein, L. and Levine, M.

(2011) Always Connected: the new digital media habits of young children, Joan Ganz Cooney Center at Sesame Workshop.

Haddon, L. and Livingstone, S. (2014) EU Kids Online Network.

Hagood, M. C. (2009) *New Literacies Practices: designing literacy learning*, Peter Lang.

Hakanen, E. (2007) *Branding the Teleself: media effects discourses and the changing self*, Lexington Books.

Harviainen, J. T., Gough, R. D. and Sköld, O. (2012) Information Phenomena in Game-related Social Media. In Widén, G. and Holmberg, K. (eds) *Social Information Research 5*, Emerald Group Publishing.

Hjorth, L., Burgess, L. and Richardson, I. (eds) (2012) *Studying Mobile Media: cultural technologies, mobile communication, and the iPhone*, Routledge.

Holloway, D., Green, L. and Livingstone, S. (2013) *Zero to Eight: young children and their internet use*, EU Kids Online, London School of Economics.

Inal, Y. and Cagiltay, K. (2007) Flow Experiences of Children in an Interactive Social Game Environment, *British Journal of Educational Technology*, **38** (3), 455–64.

International Reading Association (2009) *New Literacies and 21st-century Technologies: a position statement of the International Reading Association*.

Ipri, T. (2010) Introducing Transliteracy, *College & Research Libraries News*, **71** (10), 532–67.

Johnson, L., Adams, S. and Haywood, K. (2011) *The NMC Horizon Report*, https://www.nmc.org/pdf/2011-Horizon-Report-K12.pdf.

Kafai, Y. B. (2006) Playing and Making Games for Learning: instructionist and constructionist perspectives for game studies, *Games and Culture*, **1** (1), 36–40.

Kangas, M. (2010) Creative and Playful Learning: learning through game co-creation and games in a playful learning environment, *Thinking Skills and Creativity*, **5** (1), 1–15.

Kenny, R. F. and McDaniel, R. (2011) The Role Teachers' Expectations and Value Assessments of Video Games Play in their Adopting and Integrating Them into their classrooms, *British Journal of Educational Technology*, **42** (2), 197–213.

Lamb, A. (2011) Reading Redefined for a Transmedia Universe, *Learning & Leading with Technology*, **39** (3), 12–17.

Leathers, H., Summers, P. W. and Desollar-Hale, A. (2013) *Toddlers on*

Technology: a parents' guide, AuthorHouse.

Lenhart, A., Madden, M., Macgill, A. and Smith, A. (2007) *Teens and Social Media*, Pew Internet & American Life Project, www.pewinternet.org/files/old-media/Files/Reports/2007/PIP_Teens_Social_Media_Final.pdf.pdf.

Liu, C. C., Cheng, Y. B. and Huang, C. W. (2011) The Effect of Simulation Games on the Learning of Computational Problem Solving, *Computers & Education*, **57** (3), 1907–18.

Mackey, T. P. and Jacobson, T. E. (2011) Reframing Information Literacy as a metaliteracy, *College & Research Libraries*, **72** (1), 62–78.

Manessis, D. (2011) Early Childhood Post-educated Teachers' Views and Intentions about Using Digital Games in the Classroom. In *[Proceedings of the] European Conference on Games Based Learning*, Academic Conferences International Limited.

Marsh, J. (2006) Emergent Media Literacy: digital animation in early childhood, *Language and Education*, **20** (6), 493–506.

Martin, C. (2012) Video Games, Identity, and the Constellation of Information, *Bulletin of Science, Technology & Society*, **32** (5), 384–92.

McGonigal, J. (2011) *Reality Is Broken: why games make us better and how they can change the world*, Penguin Press.

Mozelius, P., Fagerström, A., & Söderquist, M. (2017) Motivating factors and tangential learning for knowledge acquisition in educational games. *Electronic Journal of e-Learning*, *15*(4), 343-354.

Nikken, P. and Schols, M. (2015) How and Why Parents Guide the Media Use of Young Children, *Journal of Child and Family Studies*, **24** (11), 3423–35.

Pahl, K. (2010) Changing Literacies: schools, communities and homes. In Lavia, J. and Moore, M. (eds), *Cross-Cultural Perspectives on Policy and Practice: decolonizing community contexts*, Routledge.

Papazian, G. (2010) A Possible Childhood: video games, narrative, and the child player, *Children's Literature Association Quarterly*, **35** (4), 450–58.

Perez-Valle, A., Aguirrezabal, P. and Sillaurren, S. (2014) Playhist: play and learn history, learning with a historical game vs an interactive film. In Ioannides, M., Magnenat-Thalmann, N., Fink, E., Žarnić, R., Yen, A.-Y. and Quak, E. (eds), *Digital Heritage: progress in cultural heritage: documentation, preservation, and protection: [Proceedings of the] 5th International Conference*, EuroMed 2014, Limassol, Cyprus, 3–8 November, Springer International Publishing, https://doi.org/10.1007/978-3-319-13695-0_54.

Plowman, L., Stephen, C. and McPake, J. (2010) Supporting Young Children's Learning with Technology at Home and in Preschool, *Research Papers in Education*, **25** (1), 93–113.

Purcell, K., Heaps, A., Buchanan, J. and Friedrich, L. (2013) *How Teachers Are Using Technology at Home and in Their Classrooms*, Pew Research Center's Internet & American Life Project, www.lateledipenelope.it/public/513cbd4d55a81.pdf.

Qian, M. and Clark, K. R. (2016) Game-based Learning and 21st Century Skills: a review of recent research, *Computers in Human Behavior*, **63**, 50–8, http://dx.doi.org/10.1016/j.chb.2016.05.023.

Randall, M. (2013) Combining Screen Time and Face Time in a Hybrid Class, *Teaching Music*, **20** (4), 60.

Reilly, E. (2011) Art as Experience, Rather Than Appreciation, *Journal of Children and Media*, **5** (4), 471–4.

Shute, V. and Ventura, M. (2013) *Stealth Assessment: measuring and supporting learning in video games*, MIT Press.

Sit, C., Lam, J., McKenzie, T. L. (2010) Children's Use of Electronic Games: choices of game mode and challenge levels, *International Journal of Pediatrics*, http://europepmc.org/articles/PMC2905688.

Squire, K. (2006) From Content to Context: videogames as designed experience, *Educational Researcher*, **35** (8), 19–29.

Squire, K. and Steinkuehler, C. (2005) Meet the Gamers, *Library Journal*, **130** (7), 38–41.

St-Pierre, R. (2011) Learning with Video Games. In Felicia, P. (ed.), *Handbook of Research on Improving Learning and Motivation Through Educational Games: multidisciplinary approaches*, Waterford Institute of Technology.

Stager, G. (2010) Should There Be Limits on Students' Screen Time? No, *Learning & Leading with Technology*, **38** (2), 6–7.

Steinkuehler, C. A. and Williams, D. (2006) Where Everybody Knows Your (Screen) Name: online games as 'third places', *Journal of Computer Mediated Communication*, **11** (4), 885–909.

Steinkuehler, C., Squire, K. and Barab, S. A. (2012) *Games, Learning, and Society: learning and meaning in the digital age*, Cambridge University Press.

Thin, A., Hansen, L. and McEachen, D. (2011) Flow Experience and Mood States Whilst Playing Body-movement Controlled Video Games, *Games and Culture*, http://journals.sagepub.com/doi/abs/10.1177/1555412011402677.

Thomas, A. (2007) *Youth Online: identity and literacy in the digital age*, Peter Lang.

Turkay, S., Hoffman, D., Kinzer, C. K., Chantes, P. and Vicari, C. (2015) Toward Understanding the Potential of Games for Learning: learning theory, game design characteristics, and situating video games in classrooms, *Computers in the Schools*, **31** (1–2), 2–22.

Tyner, K. (ed.) (2009) *Media Literacy: new agendas in communication*, Routledge.

Vandewater, E. A. and Lee, S. J. (2009) Measuring Children's Media Use in the Digital Age: issues and challenges, *American Behavioral Scientist*, **52** (8), 1152–76.

von Feilitzen, C. and Carlsson, U. (2000) *Children in the New Media Landscape*, UNESCO, Nordicom.

Wilber, D. J. (2010) Special Themed Issue: beyond 'new' literacies, *Digital Culture & Education*, **2** (1), 1–6, www.digitalcultureandeducation.com/cms/wp-content/uploads/2010/05/dce_editorial_wilber_2010.pdf.

Yee, N. (2006) The Labor of Fun: how video games blur the boundaries of work and play, *Games and Culture*, **1** (1), 68–71.

YouTube (2017) Game Makers – Connected Learners, https://youtu.be/lAdmppn0mwA.

Zimmerman, E. (2008) Gaming literacy: Game design as a model for literacy in the twenty-first century. In *The video game theory reader 2* (pp. 45-54). Routledge.

6

Students in the SADL: lessons from LSE's digital literacy programme

Jane Secker

Introduction

Student Ambassadors for Digital Literacy (SADL) was a student digital literacies programme that ran at London School of Economics and Political Science (LSE) from 2013 to 2016. This chapter provides an overview of the lessons learned during its three years. It draws on the evaluation work conducted at the end of each academic year to understand the impact of SADL and reflects on the approach taken and challenges faced. It also highlights several important issues that student partnership projects and digital literacy progammes need to address if they are to be successful. Although the programme ultimately did not continue and recruited relatively small numbers of students, the impact on the students who took part was considerable. The benefits to students who became senior ambassadors and worked alongside staff was particularly significant. SADL also influenced a number of other universities to set up similar digital literacy ambassador schemes and was highlighted by Jisc as an example of good practice in developing staff–student partnerships and in supporting student digital literacies (Jisc, 2016).

The programme was modified after the first two years and enhancements were made following feedback from the student participants and staff teaching on the programme. Devising the content of the course and engaging with students was one of the least challenging aspects of SADL. Student feedback on the format and content of workshops was highly positive and suggested they developed a range of skills through participating in the programme. However, one of the biggest challenges was justifying the resources required to sustain and make the programme scalable. This chapter highlights two important issues for others to address when working in this field:

- establish, scope and acquire the resources needed to ensure a programme is scalable beyond a small-scale pilot
- build evaluation into the programme and have jointly agreed measures of success with all project stakeholders.

These issues are explored in the chapter in the section 'Challenges' and should be of particular interest to those developing digital literacy programmes in further and higher education.

The institutional context

LSE is specialist, research-led university focusing on the social sciences, based in central London, with approximately 9000 full-time equivalent students. It has an international reputation for research with a relatively small undergraduate population (approximately 4500 students). Students study across the social sciences in quantitative subjects such as economics, mathematics and statistics, and qualitative subjects such as social policy, international history and anthropology. Students attend LSE from around the world, and it has a high percentage of international students and an excellent rating for graduate employment. The SADL programme was partly launched because an earlier study at LSE (Bell, Moon and Secker, 2012) suggested that undergraduate students had relatively few opportunities to develop their digital and information literacies, either as part of their course of study or as an extracurricular activity. There was a concern that many undergraduates did not attend workshops offered by the Library and Teaching and Learning Centre. The research also highlighted how academic staff made assumptions that students were already 'tech savvy'. However, as students attended LSE from all around the world, it was difficult to make assumptions about what tools and technologies they might be familiar with. While they were all high achieving students, experience showed that their digital and information literacy skills varied enormously.

Aims of the programme
The SADL project started in 2013 as a pilot in two academic departments following a successful bid for a small external grant from Jisc and the Higher Education Academy under their 'Changing the Learning Landscapes' fund. The bid was jointly led by Learning Technology and Innovation and the LSE Library, and also secured support from the Students' Union and the Teaching and Learning Centre, whose representatives joined the project steering group. An important aspect of the project from the start was the idea that staff would work in partnership with students to better understand their needs in this field and to explore the feasibility of providing digital and information literacy support though a peer-mentoring network. The SADL programme was also an attempt to plug the 'digital skills crisis' identified in a House of Lords report (House of Lords Select Committee on Digital Skills, 2015).

SADL aimed to develop students' digital literacies, but also provided an opportunity to understand more about what their needs might be. So throughout the three years of the programme, research was undertaken with the cohort to measure their abilities at the outset of the programme and to track how they might have improved by the end of the year. Students completed a pre-course survey on their research practices adapted from a survey devised by Purdy (2013) before they embarked on the programme. Many of the same questions were then included in the post-course evaluation survey to enable the team to collect data on how students' abilities might have improved. The programme was therefore partly a research project, aimed at better understanding students' needs in this field, while also attempting to work with them to improve the support available.

Funding and set-up
A relatively small external grant was sufficient to establish the project in its first year and was largely used to fund the student workshops. Staff time was provided by the participating departments; however, the funding allowed the team to provide catering and Amazon vouchers for students, which were offered as an incentive in the first year for all students who attended workshops. In subsequent years ongoing funding was secured from the Library and Learning Technology and Innovation departments at the same rate. Meanwhile we decided that Amazon vouchers would only be offered to students as rewards for additional

activities, beyond simply attending the workshops. In years 2 and 3 the budget was primarily used to employ senior ambassadors. These were students who completed the programme the year before; they were employed on an hourly rate to support workshops and help plan sessions.

Recruitment and operation of the programme

As a pilot programme in year 1, SADL was promoted to all undergraduate students in the Department of Social Policy and Department of Statistics at LSE at the start of the first term, during the induction week. It was advertised through social media, a poster campaign, departmental e-mails and a 'shout out' in introductory sessions from the Students' Union education officer. A job description and person specification was devised and students were encouraged to apply competitively. The Students' Union help to recruit and advertise the SADL programme was important, but personal contacts in the departments in years 1 and 2, such as the department administrator and the undergraduate programme leader, were also key.

In the first year 20 students came forward to join the programme and this allowed the team to try out ideas with a relatively small cohort of ten students from each department. Shortlisting was not required and all students were invited to a welcome event early in the first term. In year 2 SADL was extended to two further departments, the Department of Law and the Department of International Relations. Recruitment in these two years was relatively straightforward as we could target invitations at first-year students in the departments. Students in their second year were also able to join the programme, but we did not promote it to third-year students who we thought would be too busy to commit. In the third year of the programme, 2015/16, we decided to allow first and second year students from any undergraduate department at LSE to join, and recruitment proved to be far harder, as it was more difficult to target the publicity, partly because it proved impossible to send someone to promote SADL to every departmental induction, as had happened in the first two years. Recruitment therefore focused on a stall outside the Library during the induction week. The programme in its final year recruited 50 students in total, a relatively small number of students given it was advertised across all departments.

Senior ambassadors

In order to try to make the programme sustainable and relevant to students' needs, we decided to run it as a staff–student partnership project, so students were teaching alongside staff in years 2 and 3 of the programme and had an input into the design of the workshops. These students were known as senior ambassadors and the idea came about at the end of Year 1 when several students indicated they were keen to stay involved in the programme. In Year 2 four senior ambassadors supported the programme, and in Year 3 this was increased to nine senior ambassadors. They undertook a number of important roles in addition to teaching alongside staff: they supervised students working on group projects, they wrote blog posts and they generally helped to promote SADL. This even led to two students attending a staff–student partnership conference, organised by Jisc and giving presentations about the work they had been doing.

The workshops

Several features remained constant throughout the three years of the programme, including the four workshops that provided most of the digital and information literacy content. In Year 2 a welcome event was introduced, and students were expected to take part in a group project, which they presented at the end of the programme in a final celebration event. The student projects came from a suggestion by a graduate of the programme in year 1, who felt this might help the group bond and allow them to put their new digital and information literacy skills into action. Blogging was another consistent feature of the programme, and the SADL blog had numerous posts written by students to share their experiences and what they were learning more widely. The first workshop introduced students to writing blog posts and in later years students were rewarded with Amazon vouchers for their contributions to the blog.

Workshops aimed to develop students' capabilities around four main areas: finding and evaluating information, using digital tools for academic practices, managing and sharing information, and reflecting on their digital identity. They were taught in a highly interactive way and also worked on a group project to consider the role of technology in learning at LSE. The team was keen to develop the peer support aspects of developing digital literacy to enable the skills to be cascaded to students outside the programme; however, there was also an important community learning aspect to being part of this programme, which the team was keen to maintain. Providing students (and staff) with enough guidance and support, but also helping to empower them as change agents, was an important balance to achieve within such a programme.

Workshops were spread across the academic year with two held in the first term and two workshops in the second term. Each workshop was repeated at least twice to cater for students' timetables and to keep the group size relatively small. The content of the workshops covered a range of digital and information literacies and evolved over the course of the three years, but it was the style of the workshop that was particularly different from traditional library skills training. From the outset we had decided to run participatory, interactive style workshops, which would be unlike the traditional information skills sessions offered by the Library. The team wanted students to share their practices and knowledge by working in small groups, and undertaking activities to engage them in the topic. We devised lesson plans so different teachers could run the sessions and students would get a consistent approach to the content.

We decided at the outset that computer classrooms were not suitable for the workshops, as in these learning spaces students tended to work alone and spend their time behind a computer screen. Therefore we adopted the 'bring your own device' approach and made laptops and iPads available for loan in the session if students did not bring a device. In year 1 teaching took place in a variety of classrooms around LSE, but in years 2 and 3 the team could use a dedicated library teaching room, where the room layout could be controlled. Being within the Library encouraged a greater link with library staff. To keep the workshops friendly and informal we provided drinks and refreshments, and the room was arranged in cabaret style for group discussions. There were four workshops, whose content is described below.

Workshop 1 Finding and evaluating information
The first workshop was a chance for the ambassadors to meet each other and the SADL team, and discuss the kinds of skills students need to excel in their studies. Students and staff discussed how to find and evaluate information for their studies and social lives. These were the main activities in this session:

- First there was a welcome and an ice breaker activity.

- In group work students discussed the digital and information literacy skills they found useful to have on their courses, and considered the differences in skill sets required by their peers in their department and in other departments.
- Students considered search engines, comparing and evaluating methods for finding resources on Google, Google Scholar and the LSE Library search engine and the different sources found by each tool.
- Students considered how to evaluate the quality of the information they find online, and how to spot spoof websites. They also reviewed the value of different types of information sources.
- The SADL group project was introduced where students were to be supervised by a senior ambassador to explore one of three topics: improving learning spaces at LSE, improving feedback and assessment, and the role of peer learning.
- Finally students were introduced to the idea of blogging and given editing access to the SADL blog.

Workshop 2 Academic practices: reading and research
This workshop covered how to use reading lists and strategies on how to use readings effectively. It also explored how to use tools to facilitate note-taking and getting organised. These were some of the activities:

- Students worked in groups to discuss how they approached an assignment and to draw out the stages in the process. This could include everything they did, from distraction avoidance techniques to actual research methods. They presented and compared their maps.
- Students analysed reading strategies, looking at what, how and how much to read, and how to read beyond reading lists.
- Students looked at tools to plan their time, get organised and take notes better.

Workshop 3 Managing and sharing information
In this workshop students explored how they stored, shared and used information they found for their studies. They discussed different approaches to their 'information behaviour' and looked at some tools that can help, depending on their way of working. The group shared their favourite tools and discussed ideas with each other. Finally students

discussed issues related to academic integrity with the message that sharing is important, but students must be mindful of plagiarism. Activities included:

- a review of student ambassadors' role and sharing activities
- an information behaviour activity and current techniques for managing, storing and citing information
- a review of tools that can help in this process
- a discussion about what plagiarism is, with a quiz to find out how much students knew about plagiarism, citing and referencing.

Workshop 4 Managing your digital identity and the digital future
In this final workshop students explored how to manage their digital identity and digital footprint through social media. They reviewed different aspects of their identity including their use of social networking, production of online media, issues related to online security and their online image. As this was the final workshop, we also reviewed some of the concepts covered throughout the programme. We invited students to capture feedback on their experiences over the course of the programme through recording short video clips. The session also provided some guidance on creating videos, which was useful for the research project students were working on. These are some of the activities undertaken in the workshop:

- Google another student and review the type of personal information available online about people.
- Students were asked to consider how to improve their digital identity and give advice to other students.
- Students learned how to interview other people to collect information from them and how to use cameras and voice recorders for the SADL group project.

The SADL teaching team
The teaching team was drawn from LSE Library and Learning Technology and Innovation. In the first year the Students' Union education officer helped to deliver several of the workshops and there was a contribution from the Teaching and Learning Centre. In years 2 and 3 the teaching was mainly undertaken by academic support librarians and learning

technologists. It was important to brief the teaching team on the content and approach to the workshops, because of the new content that was included and the style of the workshop. Lesson plans were produced and a standard set of PowerPoint slides was developed for each workshop, though staff were encouraged to be responsive to the needs of their group. They were also encouraged to view themselves as much as learners as the students and to encourage students to contribute their ideas. In years 2 and 3 the teaching team included the senior ambassadors. They helped to plan the content of the workshop in years 2 and 3 and gave invaluable feedback on what worked well and less well in sessions.

SADL as a student–staff partnership

The interactive nature of the workshops, where staff teach some aspect of digital literacy, but are keen for students to share their ideas and experiences, lay at the heart of the SADL model. Student ambassadors were encouraged to discuss their approaches to using technology in their daily life and they learnt lessons that could be applied to academic study and the workplace. Senior ambassadors helped to shape the content of the workshops and to lead of some activities in them, to bridge the gap between staff and students. The impact of the programme was measured through an evaluation survey, which considered how students' digital skills had developed over their time on the programme. The team also carried out interviews with students at the end of each year. This research suggested that leadership, collaboration and team-working skills were gained through the programme. The interviews revealed that the opportunity to gain skills valued by employers was a key motivation for students who joined the programme. The students were also rewarded with a statement on their personal development record, although most acknowledged this was less important to them than the other motivators. Amazon vouchers were considered useful but many students did not say these had motivated them to join the programme. The opportunity to develop their own digital literacy skills came across as the main motivating factor in each year.

SADL built a deeper level of engagement with students than would be possible during one-off workshops. It also provided a supportive community where students could share their current digital practices, learn about new tools and technologies, and develop a range of skills including digital literacies. Students from across LSE departments had an opportunity to reflect on disciplinary differences in digital and information literacy and to discuss their ideas with staff. Technology was used in all the four workshops but group work, discussions and creative teaching techniques were important to learning in a fun and collaborative way.

Impact and benefits
The impact of SADL was measured in several ways, and after each year an extensive evaluation study was undertaken (Lau, Secker and Bell, 2015; Secker and Karnad, 2014; Wang, Secker and Gomes, 2016). Evidence that was collected included:

- data on students' research practices pre- and post-SADL using a survey and interviews
- evaluation data collected via interviews with students on the value of the workshops and the programme as a whole, including one interview with a student following her graduation, one year after leaving LSE
- statistical data to analyse hits on the SADL website and the number of blog posts written by students
- metrics gathered from outputs of the teaching team through presentations at national and international conferences
- interviews with staff to assess the benefits of being involved in a collaborative project and their experience of teaching different types of interactive sessions with staff from other teams.

The SADL programme was unlike other teaching undertaken at LSE and attempted to change the dynamics of the relationship between staff and students. One of the key features was that staff and students learnt together, and the evaluation of the staff experience suggested they had a better, deeper understanding of the students' needs. It was also challenging because LSE students tended to be uncomfortable with being asked to share their practices with others and it took many of them some time to develop their confidence and trust in staff. Our experience suggested that student ambassadors and champions would be valuable in any university or school. Furthermore, if those students can be supported to act as peer mentors then the model becomes sustainable and scalable. However, there was a challenge to build student confidence, to empower students to act as 'change agents' without a relatively high degree of structure and support from staff on the programme.

Student research practices

SADL's reach and impact on the students who took part in the programme was significant, in particular for those who acted as senior ambassadors. The students developed digital skills but in the final year evaluation it was clear that they also valued the non-technical skills they gained in the programme, such as leadership, presentation skills and team working. The data collected over the three years into students' research practices showed small changes in student behaviour: they made greater use of the library search engine and Google Scholar, felt better organised when undertaking research and had a greater awareness of their digital footprint. Perhaps unsurprisingly, students remained unsure of their ability to evaluate information critically and often relied on their reading lists. Undertaking a pre and post-course survey was a particularly valuable way to try and measure students' improvements, if only in their perception of their ability.

Challenges

One of the drawbacks with SADL was its resource-intensive nature and the fact it did not reach large groups of students. The relatively small class size worked well given the interactive nature of the workshops and helped to build trust and the sense that the cohort was a learning community. The personal contact with students over an academic year arguably enabled staff to learn about how to support all students at LSE better. In the third year the team decided to cap the programme at 50 students to foster a sense of community and to allow workshops to be run for no more than 20 students at a time. As a result, each workshop had to be run at least twice, often three times, and with two staff and two senior ambassadors teaching each workshop.

Perhaps one of the biggest challenges to SADL proved to be securing an ongoing commitment towards funding and resources, including a commitment to staff time being invested in maintaining the programme in this format. Staff development also required an additional time commitment to ensure that all the teaching staff understood the aims of each workshop and were confident with the new approaches and content that was used. Consequently it proved difficult to get all the teaching staff to attend pre-workshop briefings or evaluation sessions, because of time pressures. Therefore the lesson plans and resources that were developed by the team sometimes had to be used by staff who were less clear about their intended learning outcomes, or less comfortable teaching in a more interactive way, than the core team members were.

Another key challenge proved to be providing students with guidance and support to develop as peer mentors, so that they could cascade their learning to others. We had intended to allow the student ambassadors to develop their confidence and skills to become workshop leaders. Measuring the success of this, and whether the cascade effect of SADL had been achieved was more challenging than originally envisaged, owing to the support students required. Had the programme continued, greater effort would have been invested in training for students in how to act as peer mentors. Related to this was a tension between student autonomy and agency and the level of support they needed. So while the intention was for students to lead a group project and hold drop-in surgeries, sometimes staff found the students were unsure how to do this effectively. While the senior ambassadors were invaluable in helping to plan and facilitate the workshops, it became clear that they needed greater training and support to lead them. Our experiences showed the training we gave was not adequate to develop their confidence as teachers until relatively late on in the term.

In any programme that requires significant resources, demonstrating impact and having agreed measures of success between the project team and the stakeholders is vital. Our programme evaluated the impact on staff and students each year; in the end it became clear that senior managers had not agreed the measures of success and wanted the programme to deliver support to greater numbers of students than had been possible. This was disappointing for the project team but highlighted how important ongoing dialogue with senior management is. It also highlights the challenges of reaching large numbers of students while building an in-depth understanding of students' needs. Many students stated in the evaluation that the reason they liked SADL was because it was small and personal, and they got high levels of support. This often contrasted to how they were taught in their undergraduate programmes at LSE.

Key points and lessons learned

Over the course of three years at LSE the SADL team learnt a lot about what motivates students to get involved in digital literacy programmes, what rewards they might want, and how challenging building a network of peer support can be. Our experience suggested that students are motivated by recognition and rewards such as Amazon vouchers, but that digital literacy skills are valued by students in their personal, professional and academic lives. Student feedback in the final year of SADL suggested that more advanced digital skills could be included, such as advanced use of Excel and coding skills. Our experiences also suggested that developing digital and information literacy skills for students will benefit them beyond higher education in 'the real world'. Graduates from the programme who kept in touch with the team told us this was their experience after entering the workplace. One senior ambassador blogged about her experiences on the programme, shortly before completing her course, but after being offered a job. She had remained part of the programme throughout her three years at LSE, and said: 'Being a student ambassador helps you build the confidence and leadership skills required to become employable, but to me, it also meant differentiating myself from other candidates because of the set of skills that I gradually picked up from the SADL programme' (Delior, 2016).

Technology is an integral part of students' lives and understanding how to use it effectively while at university is something many students value. The benefit of the wider skills, such as communication, teamwork, being a peer mentor and a leader were some of the most valuable experiences students gained from this programme.

Conclusion: looking to the future

In autumn 2016 LSE created a new learning space within the Library known as LSE Life, as a focus for academic, personal and professional development activities. A wide range of new workshops were developed by the Library so staff resources were significantly stretched. It was decided to suspend SADL for the academic year 2016/17 while LSE Life was established and the resource implications could be better understood. However, a number of new workshops that were developed as part of SADL continue to run as part of other learning support activities. The value of a peer-mentoring study skills scheme was recognised and the provision of a dedicated space in the library will make it far easier to take forward in the future. LSE remains committed to enhancing student digital literacies and a variety of options are currently being discussed. There were many lessons learnt from the three years of SADL and the notable successes and challenges outlined in this chapter should help those working in a similar field at other institutions.

More information
For more information about SADL visit the SADL blog, which contains historic information about the programme: https://blogs.lse.ac.uk/lsesadl/.

References
Bell, M. and Moon, D. and Secker, J. (2012) *Undergraduate Support at LSE: the ANCIL report*, London School of Economics and Political Science, http://eprints.lse.ac.uk/48058/.

Delior, D. (2016) *How SADL Got Me Hired*, blog, http://blogs.lse.ac.uk/lsesadl/2016/03/07/how-sadl-got-me-hired/.

House of Lords Select Committee on Digital Skills (2015) *Make or Break: the UK's digital future*, HL Paper 111, https://www.publications.parliament.uk/pa/ld201415/ldselect/lddigital/111/111.pdf.

Jisc (2016) Jisc Change Agents Network Case Study: student ambassadors for digital literacy at LSE, London School of Economics and Political Science, https://can.jiscinvolve.org/wp/files/2016/09/CAN-LSE.pdf.

Lau, D., Secker, J. and Bell, M. (2015) *Student Ambassadors for Digital Literacy (SADL): evaluation & impact report*, Learning Technology and Innovation, London School of Economics and Political Science, http://eprints.lse.ac.uk/63357/.

Purdy, J. P. (2013) Scholarliness as Other: how students explain their research writing behaviors. In McClure, R. and Purdy, J. P. (eds), *The New Digital Scholar: exploring and enriching the research and writing practices of nextgen students*, Information Today.

Secker, J. and Karnad, A. (2014) *SADL Project Evaluation Report*, Learning Technology and Innovation, London School of Economics and Political Science, http://eprints.lse.ac.uk/59478/.

Wang, Y., Secker, J. and Gomes, S. (2016) *Student Ambassadors for Digital Literacy (SADL): evaluation & impact report 2015/16*, Learning Technology and Innovation, London School of Economics and Political Science, http://eprints.lse.ac.uk/67579/.

7
Copyright and digital literacy: rules, risk and creativity

Chris Morrison

Introduction and definitions

Copyright is now an inescapable aspect of learning and research when using digital technologies, and therefore awareness of it is a fundamental part of digital literacy. Rather than being a separate concept that can be considered in isolation, copyright implications arise whenever anyone creates, interacts with or shares content with others. It is therefore woven through all the key aspects of digital literacies and capabilities, with particular relevance for the ethics of sharing.

Copyright has traditionally been seen primarily as a compliance issue for educational and cultural institutions such as libraries, universities, colleges and museums – protecting an institution from claims of infringement by 'locking down' processes and procedures. Copyright literacy however seeks to situate the subject in a critical and empowering context. It draws on developments in the field of information literacy, which have been shaped in recent years by theories of critical pedagogy (see for example Elmbourg, 2006; McNichol, 2016; Smith, 2013; see also chapter 1 in this volume). Jane Secker and I recently defined copyright literacy as: 'Acquiring and demonstrating the appropriate knowledge, skills and behaviours to enable the ethical creation and use of copyright material' (Secker and Morrison, 2016, 121).

The term was first used in Bulgaria 2012 by Tania Todorova who carried out a survey of librarians' levels of knowledge and understanding of copyright, calling this 'copyright literacy' (Todorova, 2014). The survey was subsequently carried out in 14 countries (Todorova, 2017), highlighting a need for greater awareness of copyright issues among the library profession. Following the multinational survey, copyright literacy has been recognised as an important area for library and information science education and continuing professional development, though an awareness of and an ability to discuss and communicate copyright issues within educational and cultural institutions extends beyond the library profession. We are all now creators and consumers of artistic, scientific and cultural expression, so copyright and licensing affect the daily lives of everyone in education and research. It governs how we can access and use content in all forms, and it is important for it to be part of the professional skillsets of other learning support staff as well as teachers and indeed students.

However, copyright literacy is not developed simply by teaching librarians, educators or the wider public more about the arcane workings of the copyright system. It requires a critical approach to the subject, recognising that uncertainty and risk are inherent components of working creatively with copyright material. This involves examining the history and philosophy of copyright; demarcating the boundaries of what it covers and protects; understanding the practicalities and power dynamics of licensing systems (including open licensing); helping people interrogate the mechanics, ethics and cultures around 'sharing'; and finally looking at the consequences and remedies if a dispute does arise. See Figure 7.1 on the next page for a diagrammatic representation of these five elements of critical copyright literacy first presented at the IFLA Conference in 2017 (Secker et al., 2017).

Although this chapter does not intend to expand on this model of critical copyright literacy, it is worth starting briefly with the history and philosophy of copyright in order to set some context.

The history of copyright and its relationship with digital technology

Before the widespread use of digital technologies, copyright had little relevance to the day-to-day lives of most people. The first copyright legislation was enacted just over 300 years ago to regulate the publishing industry by providing exclusive rights to authors for reproductions and translations of their literary works. The means of production for literary

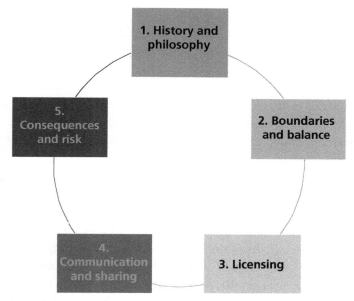

Figure 7.1 *The five elements of critical copyright literacy*
Source: Chris Morrison

works – the printing press – was expensive and therefore it was physically impossible for most people to infringe copyright.

Over the following three centuries copyright law has been expanded to cover most types of creative work. From its roots as a way of protecting the written word (hence the 'right' in 'copy') it brought artistic, musical and dramatic works under its umbrella. Then in the 20th century it was also applied to sound recordings, films and computer programs, thus providing protection for 'entrepreneurial' works, the owner of which was normally a commercial 'producer' rather than the more romantic notion of 'author'.

Another important aspect of copyright law is that, following international agreement in the Berne Convention of 1886, copyright protection arises automatically as soon as a work is created. Again, the consequence of this for most ordinary people before the digital age was limited. Yes, private letters, amateur paintings and family photographs were all protected by copyright, but without the means to reproduce and distribute copyright works there was a clear distinction between organisations whose business was investing in and communicating creative content, and everyone else. Effectively only commercial organisations needed to concern themselves with copyright law.

The internet has of course changed this dynamic fundamentally and the web is now awash with copyright opinion, mythology and huge volumes of unauthorised content. Copyright has become the site of an ideological battle between those who believe that online activity needs to adhere to the long-standing tradition (not to say moral duty) of not copying others' work without their permission, and others who believe that copyright law should adapt or even disappear given the potential of the internet to connect and empower humanity through delivery of free access to information (Doctorow, 2010).

Between the two extremes of the copyright enthusiasts – those who follow legislative developments and case law closely in order to notch up the points scored against the other side – are the vast majority: those who realise that there needs to be some kind of system of rewards and penalties to avoid a complete free-for-all, but also note the enormous social and cultural benefit of consuming, sharing and re-using content without having to engage with complex legalities. It is certainly not a clear case of doing the 'right' or the 'wrong' thing. Studies into unauthorised file sharing demonstrate that there are a range of reasons why people engage in this activity, a major one being the lack of clarity over the way the law applies to private uses of copyright material and how it is enforced (Watson, Zizzo and Flemming, 2014).

It is also within this group of 'ordinary people' that the majority of those who are teaching or learning will sit: people who have limited time to think about copyright but nonetheless realise that there may be some aspect of it and their use of digital technologies which has an impact on their educational goals. Recent studies found that most UK students felt they didn't understand enough about copyright and other types of intellectual property for their studies or future careers (IPAN, 2016; NUS, 2013). Studies in other countries have also shown a lack of copyright awareness among academics (Di Valentino, 2015). This is an issue not just in 'creative' subjects such as art and design, which have always required an understanding of originality and transformation of existing ideas into new forms. Students in all subjects are increasingly asked to write blog posts, make videos or create visually appealing presentations and posters for their assignments. The temptation simply to repurpose content found on the web without providing sufficient acknowledgement or giving sufficient thought to the wider implications is powerful.

But the question remains, how do institutions communicate and model the appropriate knowledge, skills and behaviours relating to copyright that students are asking for, when it is such a complex and contested space? Before setting out the approach that I've been following with Jane Secker as part of UK Copyright Literacy (www.copyrightliteracy.org), it is important to consider the 'limitations and exceptions' of the copyright system as these are intrinsically linked to the activities of education and research.

Fair use, fair dealing, education and risk

An essential aspect of all copyright systems is that there should be some limitation on the exclusive rights provided to authors and producers. If it was possible for these copyright owners to successfully sue anyone who reproduced or communicated any part of their works without permission, it would significantly limit any kind of quotation, parody, homage or illustrative teaching use. This would clearly have a negative impact on freedom of expression and cultural participation. Therefore, in addition to having a time limited duration (usually 70 years following the death of the author, or date of creation, depending on the type of work) copyright law also includes a series of 'exceptions', which allow people to make reasonable use of others' work without having to ask permission.

One of the most well-known systems of exceptions is 'fair use', which is a doctrine within US law, providing a flexible test to determine whether a specific use of copyright material without permission is lawful. Fair use itself emerged from the British concept of 'fair dealing', which still applies in UK law as well as other Commonwealth jurisdictions such as Canada and Australia. Although fair use and fair dealing seek to achieve the same thing, the UK system of fair dealing can only be applied to specific uses as expressed in the legislation (e.g. fair dealing for the purpose of illustration for instruction).

However, regardless of the jurisdiction under which a person is operating (something that can be extremely unclear in an online environment), anyone wanting to make use of a copyright exception will have to make individual judgements as to whether any given activity is lawful and/or ethical. Making and relying on such judgements will rarely involve a clear cut 'right' or 'wrong' answer and will necessarily involve an element of risk. For example, is it 'OK' to take an image from the internet and use it as the stimulus for an online psychology experiment if it is not possible to get permission? The answer to this question will depend on a number of factors including the nature of the image (is it by a well-known artist? will only that image work for the experiment?), the nature of the use (will it be available to a closed group of participants, or openly accessible to all?) and the economic impact on the rights holder (does it tarnish their reputation or undermine their ability to make money?). Ultimately it is a question of whether the benefits outweigh the risks once all the options are considered. Although risk is an unavoidable element of everyday life, the problem with copyright-related risk is that for those without necessary levels of copyright literacy to appreciate the nuances there is the strong potential to either over-estimate or under-estimate the level of risk involved.

Risk, rules and compliance

From the perspective of an educational institution, the desire to minimise risk is understandable. A school, college or university is a high-profile organisation with a reputation for safeguarding trust and modelling best practice. No educational establishment would want its name associated with lawlessness or a cavalier attitude towards creators' rights, particularly given its role of instilling responsibility in their students. However, viewing copyright as simply a 'compliance' issue potentially undermines the ability to communicate copyright's importance as a key component of digital literacy. Rather than seeing copyright as a set of 'rules' which must be adhered to, lest the perpetrator face arbitrary punishment, seeing copyright as an essential component of digital literacy challenges teachers and students to consider how best to approach it in relation to their own discipline and cultural context. This is on the basis that each discipline is likely to have its own (sometimes unwritten) rules about what is and isn't acceptable behaviour when using the work of others and how creators are credited.

Communication to the public and open practice

One of the main concepts that entered the lexicon of UK copyright law around the turn of the millennium was that of 'communication to the public'. Before these changes copyright law didn't explicitly pertain to activities on the internet, but after the implementation of the EU Information Society Directive in 2001, rights holders were provided with another exclusive right covering online communication. Communication to the public remains one of the most vexed issues of European (and therefore for the time being UK) copyright law – with much complex case law defining what communication is, what a public is, what type of public they might be (new or not), and whether those communicating further had knowledge of the intention of the copyright owner regarding their original communication.

But this idea of restricting communication to the public doesn't sit well in many educational contexts if we work on the basis that education is about communicating ideas freely for the public good. This sharing for the benefit of public good is the ideology behind the Creative Commons movement (https://creativecommons.org/) – the free licensing toolset developed by Laurence Lessig and others in 2002. Creative Commons licences allow creators to freely license their work for use by others, particularly online, and as of 2016 there were over 1.2 billion Creative Commons-licensed works in existence.

Creative Commons has now become a fundamental component of education and scholarship with the rise of open access publishing and the open educational resource movement. It is based not on antipathy towards copyright, but rather uses legal and digital tools to allow authors to indicate that they want others to reproduce or remix their content, while still using the copyright system to set the boundaries of acceptable behaviour. There are numerous case studies of the success of Creative Commons licences from businesses and individual authors, to governments and perhaps the internet's greatest collaborative achievement – Wikipedia.

The limits of open licensed content
However, despite the potential of open licensing not everything can be open within the confines of a market-based economy. Most mainstream publishing, broadcast and other media business models are based on legally enforced scarcity. Some creators want greater control over the way their content is shared, consumed and used, and it is difficult to conceive how sophisticated industrial art forms such as motion pictures could be financed without the legal protection afforded by copyright, and the ability of the rights holder to prohibit copying and performance of the work in question. In addition, those who create content for the purposes of public good such as teachers, scholars and curators need to have the economic security to release the fruits of their efforts into the public

sphere with no further monetary payment. To this extent it could be said that the extent to which someone is able to participate in 'open practice' is in direct relation to their level of privilege (Bali, 2016).

Regardless of whether the current situation is a transitional one or a reflection of the inescapable economics of creation, clearly for the foreseeable future not all content will be made available under open licence terms. Given that this is the case, how can we ensure that people's access to culture, science and education is not limited? This is where copyright exceptions show themselves to be a fundamentally important part of a functioning information society. And arguably the most important thing about either relying on exceptions or using copyright material under licence is that it is essential to attribute the creator and cite the source properly. This is the common denominator that unifies the different ideological positions on copyright – respect should be paid and recognition should always be given to the act of creation and the institutions that support and preserve creativity.

Playful approaches to copyright education

Having determined that there are a range of different copyright concepts that the digitally literate person needs to understand, what is the best way to get these across? Particularly when copyright remains at its heart quite a dry and difficult subject for some, and an extremely emotive one for others.

One approach that I have been following is to use playful methods to engage learners in critical and practical consideration of copyright. In creating resources with my research partner Jane Secker, such as Copyright the Card Game (2017) and a new board game exploring scholarly communications choices called the Publishing Trap (2017) we have drawn on the success of games-based learning as a method for teaching information literacy (Walsh, 2015). The value of using games to teach 'difficult' subjects is that they provide participants with a 'safe space' and an opportunity to fail (Whitton and Moseley, 2012).

Copyright the Card Game allows players to grasp physically the abstract concepts associated with copyright as they are printed on colour-coded cards with clear associated icons. The aesthetic impact of the resource itself is an important part of the learning, deliberately designed to contrast with text-heavy, presentation-led copyright training sessions. This was in part influenced by the resource Copyright User (www.copyrightuser.org/), which is informative and visually appealing, as well as the Creative Commons icons. The card game was initially created following the reform of UK copyright law in 2014 to introduce librarians and other education professionals to the updated exceptions. The team-based approach to the game encourages conversation among peers and provides ample opportunity for interaction with the subject specialist leading the game. Although no detailed evaluation has been undertaken to measure the impact on librarians' knowledge, Walters (2017) recently completed a study reviewing the potential of games-based learning to address copyright literacy needs, citing Copyright the Card Game as a key resource and a potential model for building an interactive online game.

Play testing of the Publishing Trap has already revealed that the use of fictional game characters and satirical humour allows people to deal with contentious subjects, by taking them out of the potentially emotive real-world context. For example, research students find it easier to think clearly about the choices that Brian the Microbiologist (a hipster with a large beard who likes to spend time on his allotment) has to make, rather than considering directly their own research and the impact it has on their lives.

Copyright the Card Game has proven to be very popular with librarians (Morrison and Secker, 2015) and versions for other jurisdictions are in development (it is licensed under a Creative Commons, Attribution-NonCommercial-ShareAlike licence). Similarly, the Publishing Trap is currently generating a lot of interest in the UK and internationally. It would be interesting to see further research into whether games-based learning truly does provide the deep learning required to develop an understanding of copyright in practice.

Conclusion

There is no denying it: copyright can be a difficult subject for many people to grasp. This is possibly because they find it difficult to make sense of the abstract concepts underpinning it, or the implications of applying them to any given situation, or because they are looking for certainties where none exist. In addition to this, the line between something being acceptable and not is often painfully thin and seemingly arbitrary. In many cases it is the difference between crediting someone properly, or forgetting to do so. However, simply applying credit to any use and believing it to be some kind of get-out-of-jail-free card is clearly not an appropriate response to the law or the risks that it poses.

Despite these challenges there are many examples of good practice. Applying the seemingly dry and alien concepts of copyright law to an educational and research environment *can* be done effectively by using creative and engaging methods from information literacy and games-based learning. My own experience as co-founder of the UK Copyright Literacy research team has uncovered huge potential for exploring these difficult concepts in ways that allow them to be critically examined as well as practically managed.

Ultimately, the underlying values behind copyright literacy involve applying common sense and demonstrating common courtesy in a digital environment. To be digitally literate involves being copyright literate – being assertive yet respectful. It involves accepting that creativity is not a one-way process that pushes content from commercial producer to private consumer, but also appreciating that those who do invest greatly in creativity should be rewarded for their efforts on socially acceptable terms. Despite the temptation to want to communicate a set of neat rules to teachers and students about what is 'right' and 'wrong', we must constantly strive to bridge the gap between culture, art, science and the law to provide creative copyright education in the service of universal copyright literacy. After all, in the words of Philip Pullman (2005), 'true education is where delight falls in love with responsibility'.

References

Bali, M. (2016) On Attribution vs Privilege of CC0, https://blog.mahabali.me/whyopen/on-attribution-vs-privilege-of-cc0/.

Di Valentino, L. (2015) Awareness and Perception of Copyright Among Teaching Faculty at Canadian Universities, *Partnership: The Canadian Journal of Library and Information Practice and Research*, **10** (2), http://dx.doi.org/10.21083/partnership.v10i2.3556.

Doctorow, C. (2010) What Do We Want Copyright To Do?, *Guardian*, https://www.theguardian.com/technology/2010/nov/23/copyright-digital-rights-cory-doctorow.

Elmbourg, J. (2006) Critical Information Literacy: implications for instructional practice, *Journal of Academic Librarianship*, **32** (2), 192–9.

IPAN (2016) *University IP Policy: perception and practice, how students and staff understand intellectual property policy at their HEI*, Intellectual

Property Awareness Network, http://ipaware.org/wp-content/uploads/ 2016/10/IPAN_NUS_University_IP_Policy_16aug16.pdf.
McNichol, S. (2016) *Critical Literacy for Information Professionals*, Facet Publishing.
Morrison, C. and Secker J. (2015) Copyright Literacy in the UK: a survey of librarians and other cultural heritage sector professionals, *Library and Information Research*, 39 (121), www.lirgjournal.org.uk/lir/ojs/index.php/lir/article/view/675.
NUS (2013) *Student Attitudes Towards Intellectual Property*, National Union of Students, www.nus.org.uk/PageFiles/12238/IP%20report.pdf.
Pullman, P. (2005) Common Sense Has Much to Learn from Moonshine, *Guardian*, 22 January.
Secker, J. and Morrison, C. (2016) *Copyright and E-learning: a guide for practitioners*, Chapter 6, Copyright Education and Training Available Online, Facet Publishing.
Secker, J., Morrison C., Nilsson, I.-L., Landøy, A., Todorova, T., Kurbanoğlu, S., Repanovici, A. and Coello, M. (2017) Copyright Literacy and the Role of Librarians as Educators and Advocates: an international symposium, IFLA off-site meeting, Models of Copyright Education in Information Literacy Programs, 23 August, Wroclaw, https://www.slideshare.net/seckerj/copyright-literacy-and-the-role-of-librarians-as-educators-and-advocates-an-international-symposium.
Smith, L. (2013) Towards a Model of Critical Information Literacy Instruction for the Development of Political Agency, *Journal of Information Literacy*, 7 (2), 15–32.
Todorova, T., Trencheva, T., Kurbanoğlu, S., Doğan G., Horvat, A. and Boustany, J. (2014) A Multinational Study on Copyright Literacy Competencies of LIS Professionals, presentation given at 2nd European Conference on Information Literacy held in Dubrovnik, October, http://ecil2014.ilconf.org/wp-content/uploads/2014/11/Todorova.pdf.
Todorova, T. et al. (2017) Information Professionals and Copyright Literacy: a multinational study, *Library Management*, 38 (6/7).
Walsh, A (2015), Playful Information Literacy: play and information literacy in higher education, *Nordic Journal of Information Literacy in Higher Education*, 7 (1), 80–94, https://noril.uib.no/index.php/noril/article/view/223.
Walters, G. (2017) Collection: an analysis of academic, library and learning technology staff attitude to copyright literacy being taught through online

game based learning; what are enablers and barriers?, https://www.foliospaces.org/view/view.php?id=85845.

Watson, S. J., Zizzo, D. J. and Flemming, P. (2014) *Determinants and Welfare Implications of Unlawful File Sharing: a scoping review*, CREATe Working Paper, Research Councils UK Centre for Copyright and New Business Models in the Creative Economy, www.create.ac.uk/publications/determinants-and-welfare-implications-of-unlawful-file-sharing-a-scoping-review/.

Whitton, N. and Mosely, A. (2012), *Using Games to Enhance Learning and Teaching: a beginner's guide*, Taylor and Francis.

Part III
Developing staff digital literacies

8

D4 curriculum design workshops: a model for developing digital literacy in practice

Liz Bennett and Sue Folley

Introduction
Finding effective strategies to engage academic staff in developing their digital literacies is a challenge familiar to the higher education sector. The Association for Learning Technology (ALT) examined uptake of digital practices in the UK further and higher education sectors and found teacher time to be a significant part of this challenge (Laurillard and Deepwell, 2014). Similarly, the Universities and Colleges Information Systems Association (UCISA) identified that staff development is the most commonly cited issue for institutions when considering development of digital capability (overtaking technical infrastructure and legal and policy issues) (Walker et al., 2016, 3). Many academic staff might be described as 'hard to reach' to participate in training and other staff development courses (Newland and Byles, 2014, 322). In the Rogers' (2003) model for the diffusion of an innovation in organisations, this group has been termed the late adopters, and members are characterised as being cautious about their use of technology, more sceptical about the benefits of technology than the early adopters, and unlikely to adopt a particular technology until it is used by the majority (Kahn and Pred, 2001). Despite a plethora of staff development activities, online learning opportunities and other academic development initiatives, finding ways to encourage and motivate lecturers to make better use of technology remains a difficult challenge to address.

We have found that there are dangers in focusing on the lack of digital competency of academic staff as this problematises the skills and practices of the academic staff and is experienced as blaming them for being deficient. In response they often act defensively, attacking the need for these skills, or seeking to locate the teaching of digital skills in other parts of the students' experience (their study at school, the support from the library). We wanted to approach the issue in a different way, to use the curriculum as a way to motivate and engage academics.

This chapter describes the approach that we designed and have been running for the last few years at the University of Huddersfield, a D4 (Discover, Dream, Design, Deliver) Curriculum Development Model. The model is based on working within course teams to examine digital literacy from the perspective of students' skills and practices and how they are developed within the taught curriculum. The chapter outlines the nature of digital literacies in the higher education context then introduces the D4 Curriculum Development Model, then discusses why it has been a successful approach.

Digital skills and practices in the higher education curriculum

Introducing digital literacies into the curriculum is challenging because they are not merely skills but practices. Beetham and Sharpe's (2011) model for students' digital literacies provides a useful way to visualise the difference between a skill and a practice: the hierarchical model shows that practices build on skills (Figure 8.1 opposite) (see chapters 1 and 2). Skills are the technical aspects of a tool, whereas a practice expresses how the tool is used to achieve a particular purpose. For instance, the use of a blogging tool within a fashion marketing course involves knowing how to create, upload and tag a blog post, but it is also about understanding who reads fashion blogs, the appropriate tone and language for a blog, and how fashion blogs might be used alongside other media to support a marketing campaign. In other words, it's not just about technical skills and know-how, but also about context and understanding of an audience. Thus knowing 'how to blog' is only a small part of the knowledge that is needed for using blogs within the fashion marketing.

This example from fashion marketing illustrates the nature of the challenge of embedding digital literacy in the higher education curriculum. It raises questions such as who is responsible for the

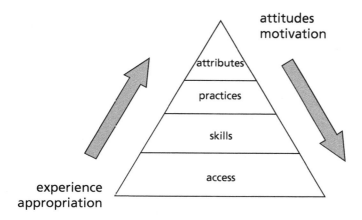

Figure 8.1 *A hierarchical model to depict learners developing effective strategies for learning with technology*
Source: Beetham and Sharpe (2011)

development of digital literacy skills? Is it the learning technologist who knows about use of different blogging tools; or the librarian who has an understanding of the copyright issues, and knows how to find and judge the information sources; or the academic who knows about the way that the fashion industry works? And who is responsible for planning these skills and practices? And how do all these groups work together to design a curriculum that develops them? Our D4 Curriculum Design Model addresses the embedded and distributed nature of digital literacies by focusing on these skills as part of the academic curriculum and by working in course teams, with librarians and learning technologists participating, so that the response is co-ordinated.

The D4 Curriculum Design Model

The D4 Curriculum Design Model takes the form of a facilitated experiential workshop, for course teams to work through the design of a learning activity and to do so with support and guidance from expert facilitators with knowledge of how digital practices can be incorporated into teaching and learning. The workshop, which lasts 2.5 hours, supports course teams to work as a group through a series of tasks (explained below). It provides a platform for discussion, collaboration and action planning, and to create a shared vision of their course. It is a holistic approach, which enables the course team to step back from the detail of the contents of each module. Instead they can focus on what they want their students to achieve by the end of their degree course, including practical knowledge and skills, and graduate attributes such as confidence, team working, leadership and agility.

The model is based on the Appreciative Inquiry approach to change management (Kadi-Hanifi et al., 2014). This methodology focuses on framing the topic in a positive way, looking at what *does* work well in a given context, and where the strengths of the staff and course lie. This methodology contrasts with a problem-based or deficit-model approach, which takes a negative stance by examining what is going wrong or what does not work well, and then trying to come up with solutions to fix these issues. This traditional approach to change management can lead to people feeling defensive in trying to establish causes of what is not working well. This can in turn result in a negative downward spiral and people feeling dissatisfied or, worse still, blamed for their less-than-perfect situation. In contrast, the Appreciative Inquiry approach helps to motivate staff through seeing change as a positive development, which acknowledges their course for its strengths, and creates a vision for the future, which they can work together to deliver. The staff then become more engaged in adopting strategies that include digital technologies.

The Appreciative Inquiry methodology involves four stages: discover, dream, design and deliver (Figure 8.2), and these form the basis of the

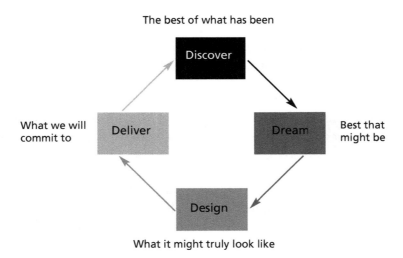

Figure 8.2 *The Appreciative Inquiry Model, the basis for D4 curriculum design workshops*

workshop, with a practical task designed for each stage. The four stages also provided the name for the workshops, branded as the D4 curriculum design workshops (Bennett and Folley, 2016).

For the first task, the discover stage, the participants reflect on their own experiences in small groups. They discuss positive learning that they have experienced, telling their personal stories, and making notes of the elements of what contributed to those experiences. These elements are then shared with the whole group.

The second task, the dream stage, is about imagining what *can be*: so the small groups recognise the attributes, skills and knowledge that they would expect from a first-class student graduating from their course. Again the small groups share these with the whole group.

In the design stage task, the participants first map their current modules onto the list of graduate attributes (from the previous task). They identify where these graduate attributes are currently developed in their curriculum. They work together to design a learning activity which will address one or more of the gaps they noticed in their mapping exercise. For this task we used the Jisc ViewPoint cards; the front of each card contains a single word based on a student activity (e.g. debate, explore, create). These Jisc ViewPoint cards are available under creative copyright licence (Figure 8.3 on the next page) (Jisc, 2012; 2014). Once the learning design has been agreed, the participants turn over the cards and decide on the finer details of each stage of their learning activity. The back of the cards contain a list of potential digital tools and technologies that could be used to achieve that task.

The final task, the deliver stage, is to action plan, so the group develop a set of actions to take the team's ideas and discussions forward. The action planning sheet that is used during the deliver stage is found on the website ipark.hud.ac.uk/content/training-development.

The intention of the workshop is not to design a whole new curriculum in half a day (which clearly takes much longer), but rather to give the participants a starting point for their curriculum development process and the tools and confidence to continue this development. The workshop provides participants with a space to get together and share ways of thinking about their curriculum, and gives the teams a shared vision of what they want their curriculum to deliver for their students. It provides them with the impetus for change through this experiential approach alongside some practical action planning.

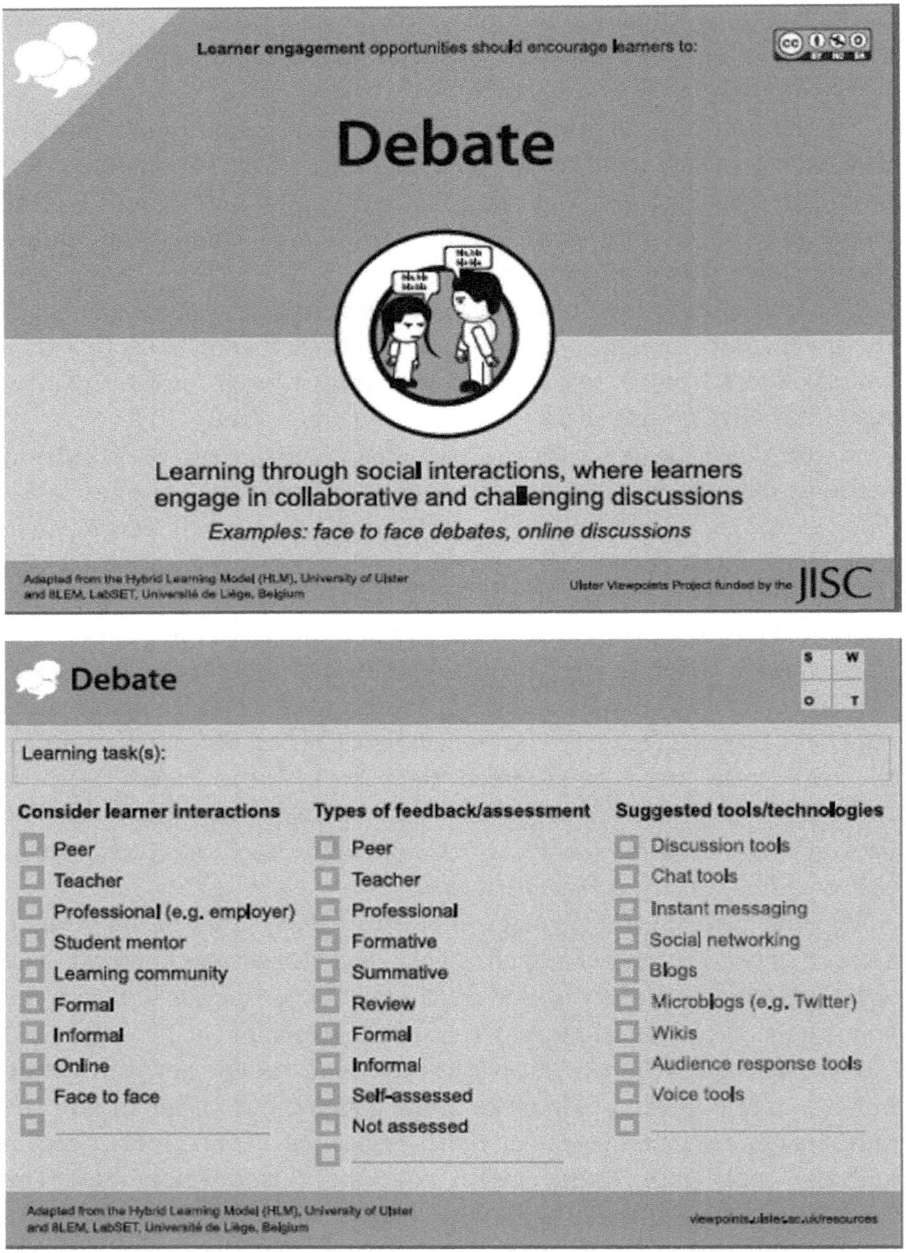

116 PART III DEVELOPING STAFF DIGITAL LITERACIES

Figure 8.3 *Example of the Debate Jisc ViewPoint card used in the design stage*
Source: Jisc, 2012; 2014

An important role of the facilitators is to set expectations at the outset, so that this workshop is seen as the first part of a process of curriculum development. In the deliver stage we remind the teams that they now have a shared vision and a set of the tools to take forward, but that they need to use their action plan to turn their ideas into a practical set of tasks, which will bring their ideas to fruition. Another key role of facilitators is to seed the discussion with ideas for how technology might be used effectively and to provide examples of how technologies work in practice.

The workshops can be particularly successful in developing a coherent and embedded approach to developing students' digital literacies if participants in the workshop include not just academic staff but also the wider team, such as learning technologists, librarians and academic support tutors.

D4 curriculum design workshops – discussion

Using this Appreciative Inquiry Model has resulted in very positive uptake of digital practices by course teams from across the institution. In this section of the chapter we analyse why these D4 curriculum design workshops have been so well received and have had a positive impact on practice. By focusing on the course team we engage the staff who might be classified as 'late adopters' (Rogers, 2003).

Rather than focus on the staff development needs of individuals, the D4 curriculum development workshops address digital literacies through the lens of the curriculum, and as embedded practices within the curriculum. Because of this focus, we find that academic staff are more motivated to explore the potential of different technological approaches if they can see that the tools might add value to their students' learning. This echoes the findings from a study of the early adopters of technology, which found that lecturers were mainly motivated in their adoption of technology by the desire to achieve their pedagogic goals (Bennett 2014, 11). Salmon and Wright (2014, 57) found that working to achieve practical outcomes that support students' learning is a way to engage academic staff. Brown (2013) found that participatory collaborative approaches to embedding technology into the curriculum were far more successful than either top-down approaches from management, or bottom-up approaches from technology enthusiasts.

The discipline-based focus of the D4 curriculum development

approach has additional value because it plays to academic staff strengths: their confidence in their subject knowledge. We know that introducing technology into one's teaching can be unsettling and challenging for even the most technically confident (Bennett, 2014). We also know that discipline fields dominate academic identities (Barnett, Parry and Coate, 2001, 2). Thus the D4 curriculum development approach, which focuses on the curriculum rather than tools or skills, engages academics in creative and exciting approaches to delivering their pedagogical aims and by doing so it helps them to feel safe and in control of the change. As Powell and Varga-Atkins (2013, 12) note, the discipline context impacts significantly on how staff conceive of and value digital skills.

The Appreciative Inquiry approach has a positive way of framing change, which is a critical feature of the success of the D4 curriculum design workshops. We have worked with a range of teams including reluctant participants who defend their existing approach, for instance by arguing that their course has a professional requirement. However, the Appreciative Inquiry approach has enabled us to unfreeze these stuck behaviours (Lewin, 1943) through its positive framing of the change. The team members have been able to engage in principled dialogue about the values that underpin their curriculum (dream stage) and to see how technology and digital literacy fit into this picture as a graduate attribute or in order to achieve a particular pedagogical goal, for instance to enable staff to support students' greater analytical and critical skills. Similarly, Newland and Handley (2016) found that course level approach to digital literacies was improved adoption from staff.

The design stage ensures that the pedagogy leads the technology or, put differently, that the technology flows from the teaching and learning purpose. This helps even those academics who are most critical of technology to engage actively and enthusiastically in evaluating new approaches because they are focused on their pedagogical goals and how technology might support them. Keeping the pedagogical goals to the fore through the design stage helps academics to feel confident because they are the people who understand the curriculum and their students' needs; our role as facilitators is to make suggestions for how technology might be used.

The D4 curriculum design workshop provides a strategic response to development of digital literacies in that it challenges the nature of digital literacies as individually owned. This approach helps to ensure that digital literacies are systematically planned across the range of modules rather than siloed into areas of innovation supported by enthusiastic early adopters (Russell et al., 2014, 1).

Taking a more theoretical view, the D4 curriculum development workshops offer a potentially powerful way to bring about change in the higher education curriculum. Barnett, Parry and Coate note that in higher education pedagogy is not well understood and practised and is often seen as filling space, e.g. forms, minds, timetables rather than designing space. They say: 'Designing a curriculum and bringing it off cannot be a purely technical matter but poses large questions of ultimate educational aims: in short, what is it to educate in the contemporary world?' (2001, 2). The D4 curriculum development workshops offer a space to address these significant high-level questions about the nature of education and its fitness for purpose in the 21st century, and to challenge colleagues to look beyond their immediate concerns and beyond seeing curriculum as an act of reproduction.

Our approach is not unique. Similar work in the field of educational change has identified the value of curriculum approaches working in teams: see for example Salmon and Wright's (2014) Carpe Diem Workshop Model and Healey et al.'s (2013) discipline-based Change Academy Model. However, our D4 curriculum development workshop offers a more time-efficient model; D4 lasts just 2.5 hours compared with Carpe Diem's two days and Change Academy's four day residential. In addition, the Appreciative Inquiry approach has some advantages, as we have argued above, for framing change in a positive way that enables even reluctant participants to engage with the workshop and be won over by it.

Developments of the D4 model

We have developed the model to focus on other contemporary issues for UK higher educational institutions including employability, retention and attainment. Each of these topics has become the focus for a different workshop, which follows the Appreciative Inquiry four-stage process. The workshops have been wellreceived as they too provide a constructive, co-ordinated approach to tackling a topic that colleagues frequently struggle with addressing. We have found that the team approach and the positive framing of the topic has again helped to unblock and move forward the complex and challenging issues of employability, retention and attainment. The materials for all the workshops are available under

Creative Commons licence (see http://ipark.hud.ac.uk/content/training-development).

Conclusion

Developing digital literacy practices within higher education is an area that is challenging, yet by working through the D4 curriculum design workshop we have found that we can harness academic colleagues' commitment to their students' learning leading to developing revised approaches to digital skills and practices becoming embedded into the curriculum. We have found that using the D4 curriculum design workshop is an efficient and effective approach, and that Appreciative Inquiry methodology provides a positive and supportive framework for course teams to work together on improving their course designs. Their holistic nature allows the focus to be on developing graduate attributes and practices rather than on content knowledge. The workshops have the potential to be used in a variety of ways, for instance by curriculum course teams, or by librarians, staff developers or academic developers with a remit for developing digital literacies.

References

Barnett, R., Parry, G. and Coate, K. (2001) Conceptualizing Curriculum Change, *Teaching in Higher Education*, **6** (4), 435–49.

Beetham, H. and Sharpe, R. (2011) Digital Literacies Workshop, paper presented at the Jisc Learning Literacies Workshop, Jisc, http://jiscdesignstudio.pbworks.com/w/page/40474566/JISC%20Digital%20Literacy%20Workshop%20materials.

Bennett, L. (2014) Learning from the Early Adopters: developing the digital practitioner, *Research in Learning Technology*, **22**.

Bennett, L. and Folley, S. (2016) D4 Curriculum Design Workshops, http://ipark.hud.ac.uk/content/training-development.

Brown, S. (2013) Large-scale Innovation and Change in UK Higher Education, *Research in Learning Technology*, **21**, http://dx.doi.org/10.3402/rlt.v21i0.22316.

Healey, M., Bradford, M., Roberts, C. and Knight, Y. (2013) Collaborative Discipline-based Curriculum Change: applying Change Academy processes at department level, *International Journal for Academic Development*, **18** (1), 31–44.

Jisc (2012) Enhancement of the Curriculum Design and Delivery Lifecycle

Through Technology, https://www.jisc.ac.uk/rd/projects/curriculum-design.
Jisc (2014) Viewpoints Workshop Toolkit, http://jiscdesignstudio.pbworks.com/w/page/29473453/Viewpoints%20Workshop%20Toolkit.
Kadi-Hanifi, K., Dagman, O., Peters, J., Snell, E., Tutton, C. and Wright, T. (2014) Engaging Students and Staff with Educational Development Through Appreciative Inquiry, *Innovations in Education and Teaching International*, **51** (6), 584–94.
Kahn, J. and Pred, R. (2001) Evaluation of a Faculty Development Model for Technology Use in Higher Education for Late Adopters, *Computers in the Schools*, **18** (4), 127–53.
Laurillard, D. and Deepwell, M. (2014) *ALT Survey of the Effective Use of Learning Technology in Education*, Association for Learning Technology.
Lewin, K. (1943) Defining the Field at a Given Time, *Psychological Review*, **50** (3), 292–310.
Newland, B., & Byles, L. (2014). Changing academic teaching with Web 2.0 technologies. Innovations in Education and Teaching International, **51** (3), 315-325. doi:10.1080/14703297.2013.796727
Newland, B. and Handley, F. (2016) Developing the Digital Literacies of Academic Staff: an institutional approach, *Research in Learning Technology*, **24**, 1–12.
Powell, S. S. and Varga-Atkins, T. (2013) *Digital Literacies: a study of perspectives and practices of academic staff*, version 1, written for the SEDA [Staff and Educational Development Association] Small Grants Scheme, University of Liverpool.
Rogers, E. M. (2003) *Diffusion of Innovations*, 5th edn, Free Press.
Russell, C., Malfroy, J., Gosper, M. and McKenzie, J. (2014) Using Research to Inform Learning Technology Practice and Policy: a qualitative analysis of student perspectives, *Australasian Journal of Educational Technology*, **30** (1).
Salmon, G. and Wright, P. (2014) Transforming Future Teaching through 'Carpe Diem' Learning Design, *Education Sciences*, **4** (1), 52–63.
Walker, R., Voce, J., Swift, E., Ahmed, J., Jenkins, M. and Vincent, P. (2016) *Survey of Technology Enhanced Learning for Higher Education in the UK*, Universities and Colleges Information Systems Association, www.ucisa.ac.uk/tel.

9
#creativeHE: an animated Google Plus platform for challenging practitioners to think differently

Chrissi Nerantzi and Norman Jackson

Open, collaborative social learning
Bringing together individuals from diverse backgrounds, who would perhaps normally not learn together, has been enabled through freely available internet-connected social media and learning and teaching approaches that are open, collaborative and explorative or inquiry based. The #creativeHE initiative can be characterised as a 'little' open educational practice based on Weller's (2011) idea of 'little' open educational resource, as it is a practitioner-driven undertaking that is flexible and an informal collaboration among practitioners in different higher education institutions and other organisations.

Crawford's (2009) and Beetham's (2015) work suggests that academics reach outside their institutions to engage in professional networks to enhance their teaching as it gives them a sense of belonging and development opportunities that are tailored to their needs and aspirations. This happens especially after they have completed their teaching qualification internally. While Conole (2013) recognises that the boundaries between formal and informal learning have started to blur, the call for more open and connected higher education and cross-institutional collaboration is advocated by the British Council (2015), HEFCE (2011) and the European Commission (2013), for example, and creates new opportunities for making this happen further. Academic development can play an essential role in modelling such approaches and provide academic staff opportunities to experience these as learners first, which research shows is an effective strategy to change perceptions and practices (Beetham, 2015; Smyth, 2009). Nerantzi's (2011) phenomenographic study is such an example. She explored an informal cross-institutional collaboration in an academic development context and brought together postgraduate certificate participants from different higher education institutions in the UK to learn about assessment and feedback using problem-based learning in facilitated groups. This led to Nerantzi's PhD study (Nerantzi, 2017) through which she explored the collaborative open learner experience and developed a cross-boundary collaborative open learning framework for cross-institutional academic development, which is one of the key outputs.

Pedagogical thinking and practices

The #creativeHE Google Plus community platform provides a virtual space within which people can interact, share and comment on ideas, experiences, practices and resources. For it to have educational value it must attract people who are willing to participate in social learning processes and be animated by people who are able to create frameworks for discussion, experimentation and learning (the course or discussion leaders).

Figure 9.1 shows Stodd's (2014) model for understanding the type of open, online, social learning enterprise that #creativeHE represents. He says that scaffolded social learning is built around two types of components: formal elements ('boxes') and informal social elements ('bubbles'). At the boundary between each, there is a gateway. In this

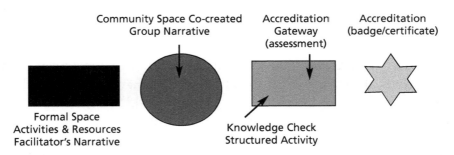

Figure 9.1 *Model of scaffolded social learning in an online learning environment*
Source: Stodd (2014)

way formal and informal ways of learning can be brought together. The bubbles are co-creative, community spaces, places where we can share our experiences or resources, feed in questions and responses to opinions, or in the case of #creativeHE, the artefactual products of creative thinking and action. The boxes are formally defined learning, for example, classroom (or other prescribed activities) or the use of defined resources. The overall arrangement is defined by an overarching narrative with a defined outcome in terms of skills (knowledge) and capability. The overarching narrative for #creativeHE events (courses and discursive events) is developed by the lead facilitator(s) of each event. But it is adapted and contextualised by all the participants as they make their contributions and comment on the contributions made by others.

In the courses such as the #creative course in January 2017 the framework for the overarching narrative is formed around the daily themes, challenges and activities (Willis and Jackson, 2017). It is formed around fundamental questions like 'what does creativity mean?' and 'how can we encourage students to use their creativity?' The emerging narrative is created by all the participants as they share their responses to the challenges by engaging in activities or open discussion around the things that interest them. The learning process for #creativeHE involves individuals participating in open-ended activities that encourage exploration, play, experimentation, making artefacts (the rectangular boxes) and sharing artefacts, commentaries and reflections in community spaces. One of the consequences of this approach is that participants are often surprised by what emerges.

Underlying the #creativeHE founder's thinking is the idea that the social learning enterprise encourages and facilitates experimentation and play. #creativeHE is all about creating a learning environment and culture (an ecosystem) that encourages participants to immerse themselves with others in such experiences. In this way the self-contained but open ecosystem enables individuals to connect and develop their own ecologies for learning, developing and creating and making.

Playground pedagogy
Nerantzi (2015, 44) developed the playground model based on #creativeHE. It provides a scaffold and space that aims to support playful experimentation that progressively leads to autonomy, just like play on a children's playground. Full immersion in experiences, risk taking and

making mistakes are essential features of this. Such experiences stretch our minds, help us to make novel connections and consider new and creative ideas in our own practice. The playground model consists of:

- community spaces connecting people
- open spaces creating expansive minds
- story spaces connecting hearts
- making spaces connecting hands
- thinking spaces connecting minds.

From the perspective of people leading courses and discussions, pedagogic engagement is not through an instructional mode, rather, the behaviours of those leading a course or discursive event are consistent with a predominantly facilitative mode and, perhaps at times, in a disruptive mode through comments that cause individuals to think again (Jackson, 2017). An essential element of the pedagogic approach being used is for lead facilitator(s) to get out of the way. Jackson (2017) used the terms 'instigator' or 'activist' to denote an approach to facilitation that essentially sets things off then gets out of the way, which is the broad pattern of interaction in #creativeHE challenge-based learning processes.

One of the most important aspects of the #creativeHE learning environment is a climate or culture within which an individual's creativity can flourish. The importance of building a climate or culture of trust and respect as a dimension of pedagogy for encouraging learning in any social group should not be underestimated. We can appreciate what this might mean from the study by Amabile and Kramer (2012) of the socio-cultural work environment. These authors identify four factors that nourish a culture in which people feel supported, and positively influences their motivation, productivity and creativity: respect, encouragement, emotional support (e.g. empathy) and affiliation.

Illustration of #creativeHE

It must be appreciated that the #creativeHE learning environment is not specifically aiming to develop competency in using digital technologies. Rather it is using digital technologies as tools to help participants express themselves creatively and consider creative approaches in their practice. The main emphasis is on exploring concepts and practices relating to creativity. The development of familiarity and competency in the use of digital technologies is typically a by-product of activity rather than the goal of the activity.

Each day begins with a post from the leader(s) inviting participants to engage with a challenge, which involves them in some form of activity through which creative thoughts could flourish and ideas can be turned into a tangible artefact that is shared and discussed within the Google Plus community:

- Day 1 Monday: creativity in higher education
- Day 2 Tuesday: play and games
- Day 3 Wednesday: using story
- Day 4 Thursday: learning through making
- Day 5 Friday: celebrating creativity: reflection and action planning.

Note that the final day encourages participants to reflect on what they have learnt and to share how they intend to use what they have learnt in their future educational practices. The January 2017 iteration of the #creativeHE course has been curated, collated and published in *Creative Academic Magazine* (Willis and Jackson, 2017).

All the challenges have the potential to utilise digital technologies, some of which are suggested by the course leader(s), others selected by the participants themselves. To illustrate this, the challenge for Day 3 is shown in Figure 9.2.

Day 3: (Wednesday 18 January) THIRD CHALLENGE – Tell a story Tell your story!
Find one of the five chapters of the following book that speaks to you and create a picture book that captures the key ideas and messages of that chapter – but in a story format.
Consider using Storybird at https://storybird.com/ – or use another tool if you prefer.
Interested in Comic Books or Graphic Novels? Why not tell your visual story that way? (Check out this blog from Nick Sousanis on using comic book formats – which he liked so well, he delivered his PhD as one: http:// spinweaveandcut.com/ – especially the section on comics: http://spinweaveandcut.com/comics/.)
When you have created your story, share it here in the community & comment on stories contributed by others.
As always, reflect on this experience at the end of the day: what were the key take aways for you today? What aspects of story are you thinking about using with your own students?
The book is the following: Piaget, J. (1972) To understand is to invent. The future of education, New York: Grossman Publishers, available at http://unesdoc.unesco.org/images/0000/000061/006133eo.pdf Further suggested reading: CELT Storytelling resources www.celt.mmu.ac.uk/teaching/storytelling.php

---

Figure 9.2 *Day 3 challenge for the #creativeHE course in January 2017*
   Source: Chrissi Nerantzi and Norman Jackson

In this example, participants are encouraged to read a short book, find something in the book that is particularly meaningful, and create a picture book that captures essential ideas in a story format. A number of possible formats and digital tools are suggested but participants can choose others if they want to – choice is an important intrinsic motivator. Participants create their own story and effectively produce a digital artefact that is shared via the Google Plus platform, and in this case Storybird.com. Many of the participants are using these technologies for the first time and must develop a basic level of competency simply to fulfil the task. The stories produced by using these technologies and the responses of participants who read each other's stories have been curated (Willis and Jackson, 2017).

The digital artefacts can be appreciated at two levels – the first recognises the competent use of the technology, the second appreciates the meaning that has been made. It is the making of meaning and the use of a digital tool to enable this that creates the insights and motivations for participants to see how they might adopt and adapt the idea to their own teaching and learning contexts.

Evaluating the impact of #creativeHE

#creativeHE currently has over 450 subscribers but only about 10% engage in the courses and discursive events held throughout each year. Mostly, people dip in and out but there is usually a 'hard core' of people in each conversation who commit and create in way that is quite humbling to witness. Also #creativeHE is an open platform and many of the people who subscribe and participate are not practising teachers. This diversity is considered to be a strength.

In order to gain insights into the perceived value of #creativeHE for participants' teaching practice a qualitative survey was conducted. All registered participants in the Google Plus community who had participated in #creativeHE between January 2015 and December 2016 were invited, via a post on the Google Plus community to respond to a short online survey. The responses were entered into an Excel spreadsheet and analysed thematically.

Changes to thinking and practice

Nine of the fifteen anonymous respondents reported they had changed aspects of their thinking and practice. Five reported that they had not changed their practice and one was still hoping to if the right opportunity presented itself. Examples of changes in practice included the use of storytelling, running creativity sessions, and using the digital tools that had been encountered on the course. 'I have gained new knowledge regarding online learning environments and tools and am currently using many of these tools on my everyday life and work.' Some respondents reported changes in perspectives that would undoubtedly influence the way they behaved:

> I find myself more open to taking risks connecting with people.

> There's something about creativity that was drilled into me as a kid that I misunderstood as being 'special' and separated from others and now I feel the importance lies in not being 'safe' behind barriers.

> This group and its ideas on the creative ecology have changed my thinking and practice.

> My thinking about creativity has changed. My conception of creativity has changed.

Valuing #creativeHE design characteristics
These are some of the pedagogical characteristics that participants valued and which helped them change their thinking and practice:

- the opportunity to interact, discuss and share practices with and be inspired by other participants
- the novelty of the Google Plus community learning environment
- having to use the digital technologies in order to accomplish the tasks
- exposure to theoretical frames that were new to the participant
- being encouraged to write and reflect.

These are some of the comments participants made about the course:

> The creative technology itself – communicating professionally via Google+ was new to me!

Reading inspiring ideas stimulated my thinking.

I think it was a combination of the course being a prompt to think about what is possible and seeing others' creativity was motivating.

I enjoyed the resource materials that encouraged reflection and exchange of views. In order to use these, I had to be competent with the technological tools.

New theoretical frameworks, many contributions, supportive papers

Sharing examples of creative practice, valuing uncertainty, playfuness and purposeful risk.

Involvement in the blogging and writing activities offered through #creativeHE, particularly the week-long structured blogging

Suggestions for improvements

These are some of the suggestions participants made for improving the course experience in using the digital technologies:

More practice of the suggested tools or methods in order to feel more familiar with them and comfortable using them.

Some sort of lab or practice workshops In addition to the five-day intensive focus topics? For instance, if someone has a thinking tool to test or a new idea to talk out that might even be a tangent to the topic, would there be volunteers to do a Skype or Hangout and test the ideas in a safe space for maybe a ten- to twenty-minute separate session?

Generally the exchange of perspectives aids learning and everything new is welcome from my side. I would like greater freedom so that anybody could share a topic around learning and teaching.

The Google Plus community includes the facility to create group spaces, which have been used on the longer #creativeHE courses, but one way they might be used is to hold Google Hangouts for real time conversation and demonstrations of the tools, which some participants could find useful. Some thought it was desirable for there to be greater flexibility regarding discussion topics, with more input from the participants.

Three participants in the January 2017 #creativeHE course were invited to provide reflective essays on their involvement in the course and how it had affected their thinking and practice. These reflective essays are published in *Creative Academic Magazine*, CAM7B (2017). Extracts have been included in Appendix 1.

Conclusion: lessons learnt

The findings of this evaluation confirm that #creativeHE courses and discussions have been valuable for participants, including facilitators, to reflect on their practice and consider alternative, more creative approaches to learning and teaching, including the use of a range of digital technologies. For facilitators (at least ourselves) the learning has been about how to facilitate learning and creative achievement using the Google Plus platform and associated technologies.

The supportive approach used within #creativeHE provided opportunities for participants (including facilitators) to feel part of a community, develop a sense of belonging, reflect on their practice and consider informed changes to practice. For some participants this translated into being brave and experimenting with new approaches, a step some of the participants were prepared to take. According to Gunn (2011) the modelling of innovative practices and inviting participants to immerse themselves into actively experiencing these and take risks also appears to influence participation. Gunn (2011) also reported on the impact active experimentation plays in considering and adopting technology-supported learning and teaching interventions.

Encouraging a critical mass of engagement is essential to creating a good experience for participants. This requires quite a lot of effort before an online event to encourage people to get involved and to create assets to stimulate thinking and discussion. It also involves active participation of facilitators to show people who are new to the process how they might get involved.

The longer #creativeHE iterations included synchronous opportunities for interaction, in the form of regular Google Hangouts in the groups as well as some webinars. This worked best when the group developed a project to which all members of the group could contribute. Some participants expressed a wish to integrate such activities in the shorter, weekly #creativeHE iterations, as the findings suggest. Although, given the time needed to develop trust and discover interests within the group this might be difficult to achieve. Research about synchronous online communication, especially in the form of video technologies, has shown the value of creating opportunities for more natural communication that come near face-to-face interaction (Holmes and Gardner, 2006; Meloni, 2010). The findings of this evaluation study seem to confirm this as it would enable participants to get to know each other, notwithstanding the energies and efforts required to co-ordinate and facilitate such encounters: effort which is rarely factored into such projects.

While the Google Plus community provides a platform where discussions can be archived, its functionality to support curation and follow discussion threads has not worked well. Because of this we developed an approach to curation using *Creative Academic Magazine*. This publication creates new learning objects and allows the products of conversation to be made available to the wider community. It also creates affordance for reflection and synthesis, as well as new opportunities for participants to publish their ideas and share their practices. The effects of this way of distributing the knowledge developed has not been evaluated.

Finally, #creativeHE provides opportunities for people to develop their skills in facilitating online open discussions. A good example of this is provided in the most recent conversation on the role of the body in creative processes and practices in which Lisa Clughen, who has done much work in this area, was coached and supported to take on a lead role in the facilitation process.

Acknowledgements

We would like to thank all our co-facilitators who embraced the concept of #creativeHE and have worked with us to bring diverse individuals together and create novel and stimulating learning experiences for academic staff, students and the public, which is enriching us and our practices.

References

Amabile, T. M. and Kramer, S. J. (2012) *The Progress Principle: using small wins to ignite joy, engagement, and creativity at work*, Harvard Business Review Press.

Beetham, H. (2015) *Developing Digital Know-how: building digital talent: key issues in framing the digital capabilities of staff in UK HE and FE*, Jisc, https://digitalcapability.jiscinvolve.org/wp/files/2015/08/5.-Report.pdf.

British Council (2015) *Connecting Universities: future models of higher education, analysing innovative models for Afghanistan, Bangladesh, India, Nepal, Pakistan and Sri Lanka, an economist intelligence unit report produced for the British Council*, www.britishcouncil.org/sites/britishcouncil.uk2/files/new_university_models_jan2015_print.pdf.

Conole, G. (2013) *Designing for Learning in an Open World*, Springer.

Crawford, K. (2009) *Continuing Professional Development in Higher Education: voices from below*, University of Lincoln, Doctor of Education thesis, http://eprints.lincoln.ac.uk/2146/.

European Commission (2013) *High Level Group on the Modernisation of Higher Education: report to the European Commission on improving the quality of teaching and learning in Europe's higher education institutions*, http://ec.europa.eu/education/higher-education/doc/modernisation_en.pdf.

Gunn, C. (2011) Innovation and Change. In Stefani, L. (ed.), *Evaluating the Effectiveness of Academic Development: principles and practice*, Routledge.

HEFCE (2011) *Collaborate to Compete: seizing the opportunity of online learning for UK higher education*, http://www.hefce.ac.uk/pubs/year/2011/201101/.

Holmes B. and Gardner, J. (2006) *E-learning Concepts and Practice*, Sage.

Jackson, N. J. (2017) Pedagogical Perspectives on the #CreativeHE 'Course': an open ecology for personal and social learning, creativity and the making of meaning, *Creative Academic Magazine*, 7B, www.creativeacademic.uk/magazine.html.

Kozbial, S. (2017) My Short Journey Through the Enchanted Waters of Creativity: why 'a smooth sea never made a skilled mariner' aka an easy course will never encourage you to use your creativity, *Creative Academic Magazine*, 7B, www.creativeacademic.uk/magazine.html.

Meloni, J. (2010) Tools for Synchronous and Asynchronous Classroom Discussion, Chronicle of Higher Education blog, http://chronicle.com/blogs/profhacker/tools-for-synchronousasynchronous-classroom-discussion/22902.

Nerantzi, C. (2011) Freeing Education Within and Beyond Academic Development. In Greener, S. and Rospigliosi, A. (eds), *Proceedings of the 10th European Conference on E-learning*, Brighton Business School,

University of Brighton, Academic Conferences International.

Nerantzi, C. (2015) The Playground Model for Creative Professional Development: exploring play in higher education, *Creative Academic Magazine*, **2A**, 40–50, www.creativeacademic.uk/.

Nerantzi, C. (2017) *Towards a Framework for Cross-boundary Collaborative Open Learning Framework for Cross-Institutional Academic Development*, PhD thesis, Edinburgh Napier University.

Smyth, K. (2009) Transformative Online Education for Educators: cascading progressive practice in teaching, learning and technology. In Remenyi, D. (ed.), *Proceedings from the 8th European Conference on E-learning*, University of Bari, Italy, Academic Conferences International.

Stodd, J. (2014) Scaffolded Social Learning, Julian Stodd's Learning Blog, 5 November, https://julianstodd.wordpress.com/2014/11/05/scaffolded-social-learning/.

Weller, M. (2011) *The Digital Scholar: how technology is transforming scholarly practice*, Bloomsbury Academic.

Willis, J. and Jackson N. J. (eds.) (2017) Curating the #CreativeHE Course, *Creative Academic Magazine*, January, www.creativeacademic.uk/uploads/1/3/5/4/13542890/cam_6.pdf.

Appendix 1

We include the final day's reflection and action plan post of one of the participants in the most recent #creativeHE course to show the sort of impact on thinking and future intentions that the course can have when a participant engages in a deep and committed manner:

> Day 5: Wow – what a frustrating week . . . each day I wanted to create something that I had never done before; moreover, I also wanted it to be fun and meaningful. I am not entirely certain if I had succeeded, but I gave it a try. All comments from the moderators and my course mates were great, hopefully a few more will come as I write this, and I've tried my best (despite a terrible teaching load this week, 18 hours) to reply and comment on other posts. The first day was probably the most frustrating in terms of changing my thinking slightly, I often work with clear guidelines and objectives but here I was given a lot of freedom. My box ended up being quite . . . good – if I may say so myself – after an hour of planning and deliberating, I decided to use Photoshop and stick several labels that represented various ideas. I enjoyed this so much that after posting my box

online, I created another one – a better representation with more logical construct. This showed me that re-thinking something that works is often the way to 'greatness' – just like in teaching.

The second day gave me headache, again originality was my aim and I tried to create something from scratch. My task might be slightly complex to implement, as shrewdly observed by one of my course mates, especially with lower-lever learners (English as a second language), but the concept of 'possibility thinking' was at the heart of designing this. When planning this activity I felt frustrated and excited, on the one hand I wasn't sure if I was going in the right direction, but on the other hand – I felt exuberant when thinking about various possibilities and how students could react to such a game using Lego. The next opportunity I have, I shall definitely try this one out. I need to be more adventurous when it comes to new tasks and new ideas.

The third day was just excellent. I am a huge fan of supporting/encouraging reading practice, and learning through stories is simple, encouraging, powerful and creative! After reading all chapters from Piaget's *To Understand Is To Invent*. The future of education, I decided to focus on the one that speaks out to me the most – Chapter 5. Despite making notes and then transferring these and adding pictures, using Storybird, I wasn't entirely happy with the outcome. Then I decided, that's right, to be more creative and write a poem – to convey my understanding of Chapter 5. Through simple rhymes, I wanted to illustrate that our lives are often controlled and structured in a way that we dislike – that power can be misused and mixed with ill intentions. When rhyming stops, the message changes – we have a right to our believes but we need to be tolerant . . . I cannot express how much I enjoyed this activity. Without a doubt, this one is my favourite so far!

The fourth day was quite difficult, so I decided to seek help and I ask my student if the description of my ideal learning space, which I had created, was to their liking. Some agreed, some added extra items, new ideas . . . but one student surprised me saying that supportive teachers who believe in their students are more important than any equipment . . . I welcome any comments.

Looking at a draft action plan, there are several aspects of my teaching that I am planning to change after these four days – at the same time, I think that with time there will be more to add to this list – as my reflection needs more time and focus (and research too):

- I will try being more creative – (wow, how insightful) I really liked the idea of students being responsible for their own learning through stories – I want to create a small project where students find their favourite story (in their first language) and then they create a picture story in English – this way they can share a cultural aspect of their country and use English as a medium of communication.
- All discussions that we have had this week also made me think about the use of technology (blogs, Google Classroom, Edmodo) to support learning through the concept of ongoing conversation/sharing content. I used to think that my students wouldn't be interested, but I will give it a try and I think it is a great way of practising English – here students could take ownership of their digital spaces too – they could suggest good ways of learning, useful websites – all these little things that we encourage them to do but never fully support . . . or can't check.
- When completing Day 2, I've also realised the need of teachers' participation – I will definitely try being more actively involved in doing various tasks with students. After Day 2, I started researching more about this concept, and I have found a few publications that support the above. In my context, this can be particularly useful when, for instance, creating a paragraph essay – I usually help students, offer useful language and suggest improvements – in the future, I will also write one in class, so the students see the process, corrections, cross outs, imperfections that then can be improved. This should build their motivation and help understanding the process of writing . . . and this is just the beginning.

Sebastian Kozbial, 2017

And finally this extract from Kozbial's reflective essay connects nicely the ways in which the use of technology, challenge and activity-based learning and reflection are nurtured in the #creativeHE experience in such a way as to effect change:

> Facing new tasks with a constant pressure of time, using unfamiliar platforms to display my work (Google+, Twitter – yes I know – and

WordPress), putting my work under scrutiny or working on tasks that were outside my comfort zone, such as my induction task, could be given as examples of times when my anxiety was taking over. On the other hand, learning new things and realising I can be more organised than ever before, learning new skills and technology, receiving constructive criticism and designing creative tasks, were definitely examples of overwhelmingly positive moments during this course – something I would love for my students to experience.

Sebastian Kozbial, 2017

10

Developing library staff digital literacies

Charles Inskip

Introduction

As the 21st century progresses it has become increasingly apparent that the library and information profession's role needs to adapt continually to the dynamic context caused by the impact of digitisation. The development of the profession over the last century has reacted to regular changes in circumstances and ways of thinking, so this is nothing new (Abbott, 1988). While there are some obvious important stakeholders to be considered – the individual, the employer, the professional association and the library school – there are others that have a key role to play in contributing to and supporting the development of librarians. In this chapter, we will look at a variety of these stakeholders, and explore how they are supporting librarian development, focusing on digital literacies.

We will look at some of the literature around the changing roles of librarians and consider the recent professional context. We will then examine some of the fundamental drivers in library staff development, including the recent impact of the use of digital capability as a quality measurement. This chapter will provide an overview of the landscape and offer up some ideas about how librarians can contribute to their own and their colleagues' development of digital literacies.

A survey of UK heads of service undertaken by Society of College, National and University Libraries (SCONUL) considered and explored six main capabilities derived from the Jisc Seven Elements of Digital

Literacies model: ICT/computer literacy, information literacy, media literacy, communication and collaboration, digital scholarship and learning skills (SCONUL, 2012). The survey findings demonstrated various levels of current expertise in these literacies and identified priorities in their development (Inskip, 2016) and a high level of support within the workplace for staff development, particularly with a role or sector-specific focus. Wider contributions from professional associations and library schools were considered by the participants to be of less importance than workplace delivery. This chapter builds on the SCONUL findings by exploring how digital literacies are conceived and considering the role of the librarian as a developer of these literacies in others.

Digital literacies

First of all, we need to clarify where we stand on the meaning of 'digital literacy' (or 'literacies'). There has been much discussion on defining this multi-faceted terminology through the literature (e.g. Bawden, 2001; Pinto, Cordón, and Díaz, 2010; Webber and Johnston, 2017). While this discussion is essential, we will not be examining it in detail for now. Much of the literature highlights the relational and contextual nature of these literacies. In other words, if there is so much discussion and so many different interpretations, we need to recognise that there are multiple meanings depending on who is making that meaning, and what their context is. This constructivist approach to reality may be rather complex, and considered by some to be subjective, but if we understand the possibility of there being a kaleidoscopic view of truth then it makes inconsistencies easier to understand and accept. The use of the terms 'information literacy', 'digital literacy' and 'media literacy' appears to be converging: entering the three terms into Google Trends shows clearly that the use of 'digital literacy' as a search query is increasing, while the use of 'media literacy' is slowly declining and the use of 'information literacy' is declining more steeply (see Figure 10.1 opposite). According to Google Trends' data in January 2018 they were all being used with approximately equal frequency (Google Trends, 2018).

The following definition of digital literacy is aimed at primary and secondary school teachers. It focuses on the central importance of technology in the process of making and sharing meanings.

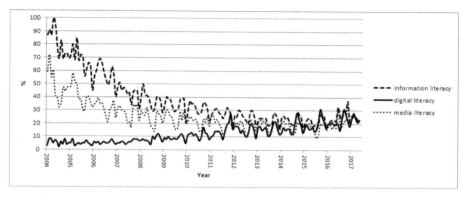

Figure 10.1 *Comparison of the frequency of use of 'information literacy', 'digital literacy' and 'media literacy' as search terms, 2004–2017*
Source: Google Trends (2018)

To be digitally literate is to have access to a broad range of practices and cultural resources that you are able to apply to digital tools. It is the ability to make and share meaning in different modes and formats; to create, collaborate and communicate effectively and to understand how and when digital technologies can best be used to support these processes.

Hague and Payton, 2010

The European Parliament (2006) recognises 'digital competence' as one of the eight key competences for lifelong learning:

Digital competence involves the confident and critical use of Information Society Technology (IST) for work, leisure and communication. It is underpinned by basic skills in ICT: the use of computers to retrieve, assess, store, produce, present and exchange information, and to communicate and participate in collaborative networks via the Internet.

In her analysis of 15 digital competence frameworks, Anusca Ferrari synthesises a definition:

Digital Competence is the set of knowledge, skills, attitudes, abilities, strategies and awareness that is required when using ICT and digital media to perform tasks; solve problems; communicate; manage information; behave in an ethical and responsible way; collaborate; create and share content and knowledge for work, leisure, participation, learning, socialising, empowerment and consumerism.   Ferrari, Punie and Redecker, 2012

The technologists' view is succinct; the British Computer Society (BCS), as part of its 'digital literacy for life' strategy, being quite specific: 'Digital literacy is about being able to make use of technologies to participate in and contribute to modern social, cultural, political and economic life' (BCS, 2017b).

This approach aligns with the other important technologist player in this arena, Jisc, whose definition directly informs the BCS approach (Jisc, 2014). Importantly, Jisc discusses the importance of going 'beyond functional IT skills to describe a richer set of digital behaviours, practices and identities. What it means to be digitally literate changes over time and across contexts, so digital literacies are essentially a set of academic and professional situated practices supported by diverse and changing technologies' (Jisc, 2014).

At the time, this definition referred to Jisc's Seven Elements of Digital Literacies Model, which identified media literacy, communications and collaboration, career and identity management, ICT literacy, learning skills, digital scholarship and information literacy as discrete elements of digital literacy. The model was subsequently revised to become the Digital Capability Framework (Jisc, 2017). ICT proficiency was situated at the heart of the model, linking together information, data and media literacies, digital creation and problem solving and innovation, digital communication, collaboration and participation, and digital learning and development, all encompassed by digital identity and wellbeing. In the proposed structure of the BCS's draft qualification, the Technical Award in Digital Literacy, the Jisc recommendation to go 'beyond the functional IT skills' seems to have been sidelined by BCS's technical mission, to close the digital skills gap. BCS aims to 'provide learners with the ability to use technology creatively, efficiently and safely to live, learn and work in a digital society' (BCS, 2017a). There is some tension between realising the Jisc vision of digital literacies becoming 'academic and professional situated practices' through BCS's focus on an 'ability to use technology'. However, this is not an issue if we remind ourselves of the relational and contextual nature of whatever 'digital literacy' may be, and if we recognise that all stakeholders have a part to play.

So, if 'digital literacy' is about people participating in a digital society, or learners developing their technology competences, what does this have to do with librarians?

Professional development

As digitisation has impacted on the information world, it has equally impacted on the role and skills of information professionals (Arif and Mahmood, 2012; Corrall, 2010; Cox and Corrall, 2013; Missingham, 2006; Shahbazi and Hedayati, 2016). Although library schools are rising to this challenge, particularly in relation to digital libraries (Bawden, Vilar and Zabukovec, 2005; Tammaro, 2007), a continuing developmental approach is needed if we are to address the issues caused by the dynamic changes in professional context and keep up to date successfully (Corcoran and McGuinness, 2014; Emanuel, 2013; Martzoukou and Elliott, 2016; Tattersall, 2017). Cooke asserts that 'librarians need to be as savvy as their clients' (2012) because the ethics of the profession demand it (Hurych, 2002) as the shifting nature of the information context means competences require constant development (Weingand, 2000).

When tackling digital literacy, there is also a need for librarians to address disintermediation through the wider use of internet technologies such as podcasts and social media (Brabazon, 2014). It has been suggested that continuing professional development (CPD) contributes to not only professional but also generic attributes such as confidence and communications (Hamid and Soroya, 2017). Although CPD is not globally formally required or mandated (Cooke and Teichmann, 2012; Thomas, Satpathi and Satpathi, 2010), in the UK it is strongly encouraged through the professional registration scheme of the Chartered Institute of Library and Information Professionals (CILIP, n.d.). This scheme, which is supported by an online learning programme and a mentored reflective portfolio, is designed to demonstrate participants' up-to-date skills and knowledge, and successful completion is required for inclusion in the professional Register of Practitioners, although exclusion from the register does not prevent one from practising (Cannon, 2017). Regular revalidation is encouraged but not mandated by the association, although employers may require evidence of CPD at annual appraisal. Registration is informed and assessed through application of the Professional Knowledge and Skills Base (PKSB), which is also used to accredit library school library and information studies programmes. This overarching application of criteria in the UK, linking learning providers' delivery with individual and employer-driven staff development, allows CILIP to guide a consistent view of competencies.

Through a digital lens

SCONUL's Seven Pillars model prioritises information literacy and encompasses digital and other literacies, attitudes and behaviours, many of which are also included in the more recent Jisc Digital Capability Framework. The SCONUL model was developed from the viewpoint of members of the professional association for UK national, university and college libraries and its 'informationist' (rather than 'technologist') approach here is clearly established through the set of pillars: identify, scope, plan, gather, evaluate, manage, present (SCONUL, 2011). An important recent development of the model was the addition of a digital lens (SCONUL, 2013). This not only demonstrated SCONUL's recognition of the role of librarians in supporting and developing digital literacies, but also met the revised core model aims, which were to make the seemingly inflexible 'pillars' more adaptable to local and professional contexts; other lenses were to follow, including health and graduate employability (SCONUL, 2017).

A brief comparison between the SCONUL digital lens and the BCS draft curriculum suggests that there is a link between the views of the informationists and the technologists. The SCONUL digital lens notes 'understanding' of various concepts and 'ability' to use, manage, identify or develop (for example) skills or tools related to each of the pillars. This approach sits more readily with the Jisc view although pragmatically recognising the importance of skills development within a wider framework, which includes understanding, behaviour and attitudes. While the Seven Pillars are predominantly designed (and widely used) to support students in UK higher education, a secondary purpose is to contribute to the development of librarian proficiencies, as a self-evaluative continuing development tool.

Jisc helpfully recently published a library and information professional profile aligned to its Digital Capability Framework, alongside other profiles (teacher, learning technologist, leader, researcher) (Beetham, 2017). The profile maps the framework to the CILIP PKSB and aims to act as an evaluative tool for staff development, almost as a digital literacy lens on the PKSB (CILIP, 2013). Each of the six elements are unpacked, looking at how librarians' practice would relate to the element and, importantly, how their practice would relate to the wider institution. This contextual analysis supports the potential use of the profile as a staff development tool and, particularly, an advocacy tool for evaluating impact. Although it is too early to tell how this is being received, case studies from the project development team suggest a 'whole organisation' approach is being readily adopted by some institutions (Jisc, 2017). The purpose of these two criteria links strongly to the strategic use of the Digital Capability Framework by the Quality Assurance Agency (QAA) in its recent assessment theme of digital literacy (QAA, 2014), which swiftly drew the attention of learning provider quality assurance offices to this concept. Through activities such as embedding their framework into the QAA, providing a mapping to the CILIP PKSB, and informing the development of BCS' proposed qualification Jisc is clearly engaging at a high level with a range of important stakeholders. This engagement suggests there is a continuing widespread adoption of their framework, which will continue to raise the profile of digital literacy in government, education and industry.

Jisc's examination of librarians' roles and competences through a digital literacy lens provides some useful guidance relating to these literacies, identifying skills relating to each element and how the library and information professional contributes to their organisation by applying them. For example, under 'digital learning and development', which maps to the PKSB's literacies and learning, we might:

- contribute to curriculum development, e.g. embedding of information literacies
- contribute to researcher development, e.g. around digital scholarship
- create digital learning materials independently or working with others (e.g. on information and library topics), ensuring they are fully accessible.

This means we are likely to:

- contribute to the development of online learning and online courses
- contribute to the use of learning and research technologies
- contribute to the development of the library as a space of (formal and informal) learning
- meet the information literacy learning needs of the whole organisation, e.g. for digital information searching, discovery, interpretation, critical evaluation, managing, sharing and disseminating.

This 'contributing' role recognises the reality of team-working across service and faculty departments, which is integral to academic librarianship. Breaking each element into skills and contributions helps to situate the guide, which may be helpful in the workplace as part of a toolkit, as a development and appraisal tool along with the PKSB.

For those outside further and higher education, the Society of Chief Librarians has introduced a sector-wide training programme for public library staff. The universal offers strategy, includes the information offer aims: 'To bring together government and non-government sources of information, which have been researched by information professionals in public libraries, giving the customer a level of quality assurance. To ensure that our staff and volunteers are continually developing their skills to provide the help some people need to access information and services online' (SCL, 2017b). And the digital offer states: 'As a baseline every public library service should provide: Free internet access (for a minimum period); Clear and accessible online information about library services; Staff trained to help customers access digital information' (SCL, 2017a)

The training programme, Digital Information Skills for Library Workforce (SCL, 2017c), notes key learning outcomes, such as the ability to 'fluently navigate and use national and local government information sites' through a set of online modules. Despite some technical problems in the delivery of this ambitious programme, it was reported that the nationally co-ordinated approach made a significant contribution in an increase of staff confidence, particularly in the use of government resources, and in staff feeling more able to help library users (Moorcroft and Myers, 2015).

These top-down initiatives are mirrored by numerous grassroots development opportunities such as TeachMeets, informal peer-to-peer networks within and between workplaces and other self- and community-motivated development approaches. Although it is not within the scope of this chapter to explore these in detail it is very important to recognise the value of the motivated practitioner in the self-development process. Bottom-up initiatives and those led by the supportive employer are widely used and engender involvement by the community through their participation in organising and running these as well as taking part in them. The UK professional association also supports CPD through its mentored Chartership scheme, where progress is evaluated within the framework of the PKSB (CILIP, 2013). 'Literacies and learning', which includes information literacy, is considered a professional competence within the PKSB. The CILIP Information Literacy Group plays an essential role in leading and encouraging staff development activities and advocating for information (and digital) literacies. It publishes the peer-reviewed *Journal of Information Literacy*, organises the international Librarians' Information Literacy Annual Conference (LILAC) and funds practitioner research in order to contribute to the development of good information literacy practice in the profession.

Conclusion

Recognition by CILIP's PKSB, Jisc's Digital Capability Framework and profile mapping, the BCS's draft curriculum and the Society of Chief Librarians' training programme demonstrates clearly that there are various offers available for CPD specifically relating to digital literacies for the profession. The value of these contributions in the delivery of quality-assurance-based interventions and guidance is in the raising of awareness at policy-maker level. Although the huge impact of grassroots efforts cannot be denied, without recognition at the top they are sustainable only because of the efforts of the communities and individuals concerned. Success is most likely to come from a combined approach, with high-level policy and grassroots efforts working together. If information literacy is recognised formally not only within the library and information studies curriculum but also in school, further and higher education curricula then the efforts of library and information professionals in developing their digital literacies to support and educate users effectively will not be in vain. It is recommended that individuals reflect on their digital (*and* information) literacies and capabilities and recognise that continuous development can be supported by peers as well as by employers and formal stakeholder communities, such as professional associations, special interest groups and library schools. A holistic approach, which encourages inter-disciplinary and multi-service conversations, would help to situate the profession within the wider context and reinforce the value and role of the librarian in a digitally capable world.

References

Abbott, A. D. (1988) *The System of Professions: an essay on the division of expert labor*, University of Chicago Press.

Arif, M. and Mahmood, K. (2012) The Changing Role of Librarians in the

Digital World Adoption of Web 2.0 Technologies by Pakistani Librarians, *Electronic Library*, **30** (4), 469–79.

Bawden, D. (2001) Information and Digital Literacies: a review of concepts, *Journal of Documentation*, **57** (2), 218–59.

Bawden, D., Vilar, P. and Zabukovec, V. (2005) Education and Training for Digital Librarians: a Slovenia/UK comparison, *Aslib Proceedings*, **57** (1), 85–98.

BCS (2017a) BCS Level 1/2 Technical Award in Digital Literacy, IT User Qualifications, Qualifications and Certifications, British Computer Society, www.bcs.org/category/19022.

BCS (2017b) Digital Literacy for Life, British Computer Society, www.bcs.org/category/17853.

Beetham, H. (2017) Digital Capability Profiles for Different Roles, Jisc Digital Capability Codesign Challenge Blog, https://digitalcapability.jiscinvolve.org/wp/2017/03/08/digital-capability-profiles-for-different-roles/.

Brabazon, T. (2014) The Disintermediated Librarian and a Reintermediated Future, *Australian Library Journal*, **63** (3), 191–205.

Cannon, P. (2017) A Review of Professionalism within LIS, *Library Management*, **38** (2/3), 142–52.

CILIP (2013) Using the Professional Knowledge and Skills Base, www.cilip.org.uk/careers/professional-knowledge-skills-base/using-professional-knowledge-skills-base.

CILIP (n.d.) Professional Registration, https://archive.cilip.org.uk/cilip/professional-registration.

Cooke, N. A. (2012) Professional Development 2.0 for Librarians: developing an online personal learning network, *Library Hi Tech News*, **29** (3), 1–9.

Cooke, N. A. and Teichmann, J. J. (2012) *Keeping Current: instructional strategies and techniques for information professionals*, Chandos Publishing.

Corcoran, M. and McGuinness, C. (2014) Keeping Ahead of the Curve: academic librarians and continuing professional development in Ireland, *Library Management*, **35** (3), 175–98.

Corrall, S. (2010) Educating the Academic Librarian as a Blended Professional: a review and case study, *Library Management*, **31** (8–9), 567–93.

Cox, A. M. and Corrall, S. (2013) Evolving Academic Library Specialties, *Journal of the American Society for Information Science and Technology*, **64** (8), 1526–42.

Emanuel, J. (2013) Digital Native Librarians, Technology Skills, and Their

Relationship with Technology, *Information Technology and Libraries*, **32** (3), 20–33.

European Parliament (2006) Recommendation of the European Parliament and of the Council of 18 December 2006 on key competences for lifelong learning, 2006/962/EC, http://eur-lex.europa.eu/legal-content/EN/TXT/HTML/?uri=CELEX:32006H0962&from=EN.

Ferrari, A., Punie, Y. and Redecker, C. (2012) Understanding Digital Competence in the 21st Century: an analysis of current frameworks. In Ravenscroft, A., Lindstaedt, S., Kloos, C. D. and Hernández-Leo, D. (eds), *Proceedings of the 21st Century Learning for 21st Century Skills: 7th European Conference of Technology Enhanced Learning*, Saarbrücken, Germany, Springer.

Google Trends (2018) Compare [the use of] Information Literacy, Digital Literacy and Media Literacy, 2004 to January 2018, https://trends.google.co.uk/trends/explore?date=all&q=information%20literacy,digital%20literacy,media%20literacy.

Hague, C. and Payton, S. (2010) *Digital Literacy Across the Curriculum*, Futurelab.

Hamid, A. and Soroya, M. S. (2017) Continuing Education for LIS Professionals: why, *Library Review*, **66** (1–2), 83–9.

Hurych, J. (2002) Continuing Professional Education as an Ethical Issue. In Ward, P. L. (ed.), *Continuing Professional Education for the Information Society: the Fifth World Conference of Continuing Professional Education for the Library and Information Science Professions*, International Federation of Library Associations and Institutions, 256–63.

Inskip, C. (2016) Novice to Expert: developing digitally capable librarians. In Mackenzie, A. and Martin, L. (eds.) *Developing Digital Scholarship: emerging practices in academic libraries*, Facet Publishing, 59–75.

Jisc (2014) *Developing Digital Literacies*, https://www.jisc.ac.uk/guides/developing-digital-literacies.

Jisc (2017) Building Digital Capability: building capability for new digital leadership, pedagogy and efficiency, Jisc, https://www.jisc.ac.uk/rd/projects/building-digital-capability.

Martzoukou, K. and Elliott, J. (2016) The Development of Digital Literacy and Inclusion Skills of Public Librarians, *Communications in Information Literacy*, **10** (1), 99–115.

Missingham, R. (2006) Library and Information Science: skills for twenty-first century professionals, *Library Management*, **27** (4/5), 257–68.

Moorcroft, S. and Myers, A. (2015) Evaluation of the Public Library Universal Information Offer Workforce Development Programme: supporting digital access to information and services, http://goscl.com/scl-continues-to-raise-digital-skills-and-leadership-standards/.

Pinto, M., Cordón, J. A. and Díaz, R. G. (2010) Thirty Years of Information Literacy (1977–2007): a terminological, conceptual and statistical analysis, *Journal of Librarianship and Information Science*, **42** (1), 3–19.

QAA (2014) *Higher Education Review: themes for 2015-16*, Quality Assurance Agency for Higher Education, www.qaa.ac.uk/publications/information-and-guidance/publication?PubID=2859#.WUV0g-vyvIU.

SCL (2017a) Universal Digital Offer, Society of Chief Librarians, http://goscl.com/universal-offers/digital-offer/.

SCL (2017b) Universal Information Offer, Society of Chief Librarians, http://goscl.com/universal-offers/information-offer/.

SCL (2017c) Workforce Development E-learning Modules, Society of Chief Librarians, http://goscl.com/training/.

SCONUL (2011) *The SCONUL Seven Pillars of Information Literacy: core model for higher education*, Society of College, National and University Libraries, https://www.sconul.ac.uk/sites/default/files/documents/coremodel.pdf.

SCONUL (2012) SCONUL Baseline Summary, Society of College, National and University Libraries, http://jiscdesignstudio.pbworks.com/w/page/50824902/SCONUL%20Baseline%20summary.

SCONUL (2013) *The SCONUL 7 Pillars of Information Literacy through a Digital Literacy 'Lens'*, Society of College, National and University Libraries, https://www.sconul.ac.uk/sites/default/files/documents/Digital_Lens.pdf.

SCONUL (2017) *Seven Pillars of Information Literacy Resources*, Society of College, National and University Libraries, https://www.sconul.ac.uk/page/seven-pillars-of-information-literacy.

Shahbazi, R. and Hedayati, A. (2016) Identifying Digital Librarian Competencies According to the Analysis of Newly Emerging IT-based LIS Jobs in 2013, *Journal of Academic Librarianship*, **42** (5), 542–50.

Tammaro, A. M. (2007) A Curriculum for Digital Librarians: a reflection on the European debate, *New Library World*, **108** (5/6), 229–46.

Tattersall, A. (2017) Supporting the Research Feedback Loop, *Performance Measurement and Metrics*, **18** (1), 28–37.

Thomas, V. K., Satpathi, C. and Satpathi, J. N. (2010) Emerging Challenges in Academic Librarianship and Role of Library Associations in Professional Updating, *Library Management*, **31** (8/9), 594–609.

Webber, S. and Johnston, B. (2017) Information Literacy: conceptions, context and the formation of a discipline, *Journal of Information Literacy*, **11** (1), 156–83.

Weingand, D. E. (2000) Describing the Elephant: what is continuing professional education?, *IFLA Journal*, **26** (3), 198–202.

Part IV
Digital citizens and workers

11
Digital literacy and open educational practice: DigiLit Leicester

Josie Fraser with Katharine Reedy

Introduction

Governments internationally are increasingly aware of the need to equip citizens with the skills and confidence necessary to benefit from and contribute to societies that can be characterised as 'digital'. The UK, along with many other countries, is facing challenges regarding digital literacy: understanding and sharing a definition of digital literacy; supporting people of all ages in the development of competencies considered to be beneficial or even essential; and addressing the risk that digital societies pose of exclusion and exacerbating social inequality.

The DigiLit Leicester project represents a novel and significant approach to addressing these wider issues in situ, locally and practically. The project was designed to enable schools to get the most out of their investment in technology and to support their aspirations to raise achievement, connect communities and open up opportunities to all. Fundamental to this was working with educators to develop their digital literacy knowledge, skills and practice, in order to enable the effective use of digital tools, environments and approaches with learners. Several of the approaches introduced by the project have gone on to influence and be adopted by government at national and international level. For example, the Digital Literacy Framework developed as part of the project directly informed the Welsh government's Digital Competence Framework (Learning Wales, 2016) and the European Schools Digital Competency Framework (Redecker and Punie, 2017).

Digital literacy

Mobile and web-based technologies are now mainstream, embedded into the fabric of our social, economic and cultural lives. Digital tools and environments play an important everyday role in how lives are lived – in how families, friends and communities come together, in the buying and selling of goods and services, and in political processes and protest. Access to or ownership of devices has become a marker for inclusion in mainstream life. Alongside the importance of access and connectivity, digital literacy is increasingly recognised as being as important to citizens as literacy and numeracy (House of Lords Select Committee on Digital Skills, 2015).

What digital literacy is, or how it can best be supported, is still a contested concept. The approach taken by the DigiLit Leicester project is that digital literacy is not best understood as either an abstract concept or a fixed set of skills, but makes most sense – and is best supported – in the context of practice and identity.

There is a broad range of additional basic requirements that are collectively characterised as digital literacy, by which we mean the confidence, knowledge and skills to make use of technology to participate in social, economic, cultural and political life: 'Digital literacy = digital tool knowledge + critical thinking + social engagement' (Fraser, 2012). This is in line with Helen Beetham's definition for Jisc of digital literacy as 'those capabilities which fit an individual for living, learning and working in a digital society' (Jisc, 2015).

Currently, we have a small but significant percentage of the population who have limited access to devices and connectivity, and are therefore socially disadvantaged and unable to develop the skills that come from frequent (and even habitual) use of technology for communication that many people now take for granted. We also have issues with literacy at its most basic level. However, even where these two conditions of 'digital inclusion' are met, it doesn't follow that people will have access to the knowledge and skills to make the most of the educational, social and economic opportunities technology presents.

While many of our young people (and indeed many adults) are confident and frequent users of social technologies, it cannot be assumed that they understand and can apply critical skills and thinking when using technologies. For example, they may be very confident users of search engines, but not understand how to evaluate the validity of online content, or how to check for and detect bias. Incidences of online bullying and harassment similarly indicate that policy, social and professional practice and education relating to appropriate behaviour online remains a critical area for discussion and action.

DigiLit Leicester

One of the key determinants of students' exposure to the use of technology in the classroom is the skills and confidence of educators, with investment in staff development being one of the main ways to develop the competencies required to make 'effective and efficient use of the available infrastructure' (European Commission, 2013a, 14).

The DigiLit Leicester project was developed in the context of Leicester City Council's Building Schools for the Future (BSF) Programme, a £340 million capital programme which rebuilt and refurbished 23 secondary and special educational needs schools across the city, between 2008 and 2015. The initial limitations of contracted professional development became apparent by 2010, providing the opportunity to renegotiate the council's approach to and investment in staff development in relation to ICT. The DigiLit Leicester project was designed to mitigate the risk of failing to realise the value of the investment in technologies in schools by prioritising staff and organisational development in the context of an ambitious, transformational approach to everyday practice across the entire estate.

The city of Leicester is home to a higher than national average number of children living in comparative poverty (estimated at 26,000 by Leicester Child Poverty Commission in 2013, or 32% of all children in the city) as well as lower than national average attainment results at GCSE, and higher than national average numbers of young people who have learning difficulties. Leicester is an international city, with high rates of school turbulence (pupils who attend for a short time and then leave) as well as many learners with English as a second language. In recognition of the significant challenges facing many young people across the city, including the practical limitations on mobility that poverty represents to many families, the principle of parity across educational provision was prioritised. That is the idea that young people should be able to benefit from the creative and effective use of technology to enhance their education regardless of disability or health, behavioural, social or emotional difficulties, or means, whichever secondary school they attended in the city. Underpinning this aspiration was the recognition that young people should not be leaving school at 16 without the basic skills and confidence to use technology critically and effectively in relation to further education, employment, or entrepreneurship. Significant work was carried out to rebalance the ICT budget across the city, which included ring-fencing funding to ensure that comparable support and opportunity was made available to every school in the programme. These were the three core project aims:

- to investigate and define digital literacy in the context of secondary school practice
- to identify school staff confidence levels, along with strengths and gaps across the building schools for the future schools, in relation to this definition.
- to support staff in developing their digital literacy skills and knowledge – raise baseline skills and confidence levels across the city, and promote existing effective and innovative practice.

The project was initiated by Leicester City Council, and developed in partnership with De Montfort University and the 23 BSF schools. A project lead was appointed as a knowledge transfer partnership (KTP), which serves to meet a core strategic need and to find innovative solutions to help that business (and social enterprises) grow. It was jointly supervised by the council and the university and part-funded by a successful bid to the Technology Strategy Board, with the balance of costs carried by the City Council. The core team consisted of Josie Fraser, Professor Richard Hall and Lucy Atkins.

The initial DigiLit Leicester project phase ran from September 2012 to September 2014 (the two years of the KTP contract) with additional work continuing until April 2016. Following completion of BSF school construction, all outstanding works were reallocated and dedicated BSF staff were made redundant, effectively ending the council's involvement in the project, although work continued across schools.

The BSF schools
Leicester's BSF school cohort is diverse, including 15 mainstream schools and eight special educational needs (SEN) and specialist provision schools. The mainstream schools support between 900 and 1570 pupils;

11 of the mainstream schools support learners aged 11–16, with four mainstream schools also supporting sixth form learners (typically aged 16–18). The eight SEN and specialist provision schools serve a wide range of learners, including pupils with moderate learning difficulties, learners with severe, multiple and life-limiting disabilities, learners with social, emotional and behavioural difficulties, and learners with mental and physical health difficulties. These specialist schools cater for between 80 and 160 pupils, with four schools supporting learners aged 11–16, and four supporting learners aged 4–19. The schools collectively support approximately 20,270 learners each year, most of whom are aged 11–16.

The project was necessarily designed to support schools and be relevant to school staff before and after the opening of new and refurbished buildings in order to realise the investment in ICT. While the project was designed to ensure staff would have the skills and confidence to take advantage of the new infrastructure, systems and equipment the building programme provided them with, it also aimed to support staff development during the building process, where they had significantly less flexibility in the use of and access to technology to support learners.

The project supported all staff who work with learners: senior leadership with a teaching role, teachers, classroom assistants, specialist provision and library staff – approximately 1780 school employees.

A pragmatic decision was taken to extend the project focus beyond teachers, recognising the range of staff who interact with and influence learners and the different roles that different categories of staff play across schools, as well as the need to develop and share practice across the organisation rather than within role-based silos.

Unsurprisingly, the group members had a wide range of confidence levels and experience of using technologies to support learning and learners, varying from newcomer to advanced practitioner. Additionally, the number of different working environments and the diversity of learners resulted in a range of priorities, interests and approaches to staff practice.

Developing a framework – identifying priorities

To understand what practice looked like across the city, a digital literacy framework was developed in consultation with schools and staff and mapped to classroom practice. The framework was designed through an iterative process, which included desk-based research, and consultation with school practitioners, academics, individuals, and staff of organisations with expertise in digital literacy.

The initial review of existing frameworks relating to digital literacy was carried out to identify likely priorities and, importantly, to review the use and success of existing frameworks in practice. The educational policy landscape was also accounted for – for example, teachers' standards (DfE, 2012), the Jisc further and higher education level Developing Digital Literacies Programme (Jisc, 2011), EU level work on digital competencies (Ferrari, 2012) and the US National Educational Technology Plan (US Department of Education, 2010).

Ongoing consultation with school staff shaped the final framework themes, the survey questions linking the themes to practice, the ordering of themes, the levels that define staff confidence and practices, and the approach to implementation.

In addition, the survey was piloted with staff working in different types of schools (mainstream and SEN) and with a range of confidence levels in their current use of technology to support learners. The pilot study consisted of survey completion, followed by qualitative interviews to understand user experience, including clarity of instructions and statements and overall relevance of content. The responses from the pilot further refined the final version of the framework and survey.

Six digital literacy areas were considered of most relevance to school staff across the cohort: finding, evaluating and organising; creating and sharing; assessment and feedback; communication, collaboration and participation; e-safety and online identity; technology-supported professional development (Fraser, Atkins and Hall, 2013) (see Figure 11.1 opposite).

Confidence levels within these six strands were assigned four level descriptors: entry, core, developer or pioneer.

This framework was then used to create an online survey, which was carried out across all BSF schools in 2013 and 2014 (Fraser, Atkins and Hall, 2013). All staff supporting learning in the 23 Leicester schools – senior leadership with a teaching role, teachers, classroom assistants, specialist provision and library staff – were invited to complete the survey. Completion rates increased from 24% in 2013 (Atkins, Fraser and Hall, 2013) to 39% in 2014 (Atkins, Fraser and Hall, 2014), recognising the increased familiarity with the survey across the cohort, the positive impact of the first year of the project across the city, and the usefulness of data to strategic planning within schools.

Recommendations for areas of focus and activity in work relating to the use of technology by school staff were developed in line with the strengths and gaps indicated by the 2013 and 2014 survey findings. These recommendations were used to drive and frame a range of opportunities for staff and schools. For example, between January 2013 and September 2014, the DigiLit team led on six events and projects, and 21 school-initiated projects were undertaken (Atkins, Fraser and Hall, 2014).

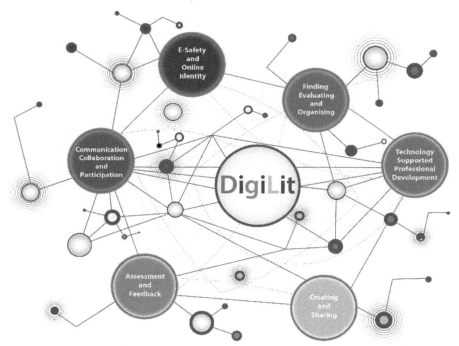

Figure 11.1 *DigiLit Framework Strands (DigiLit Leicester project, 2014, shared under Creative Commons Attribution 4.0 International License (CC by 4.0))*

For each of the six priority areas, staff undertaking the survey were presented with four statements relating to their use of technology in the classroom and asked to indicate how closely these statements represented their current practice, along a scale of none, some or all. On completion, aggregate scores generated individual feedback reports to staff members identifying their practice in each strand as entry, core, developer or pioneer. Each staff member's report included further resources and outlined what the next level to their current indicated level looked like.

162   PART IV   DIGITAL CITIZENS AND WORKERS

In addition, aggregated and anonymised profiles were produced and provided to individual BSF schools and at city-wide level. The results are shown in Figure 11.2.

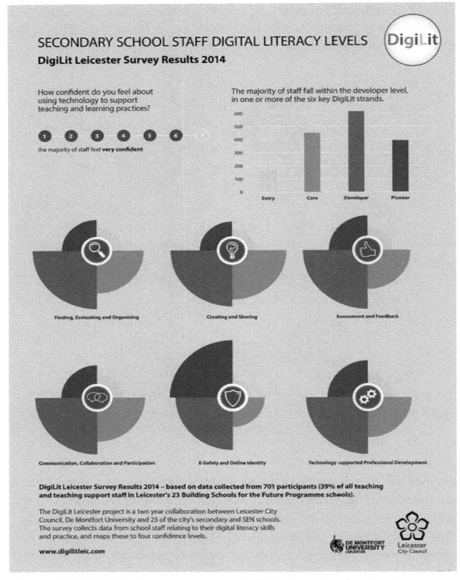

Figure 11.2 *DigiLit Leicester survey results 2014, shared under Creative Commons Attribution 4.0 International License (CC by 4.0)*

Centring open educational practice

Digital resources are largely integrated into teaching practice in the UK. School staff routinely search for, evaluate and organise digital content to support their practice, remix existing resources, and create and share original materials. The centrality of this practice is evidenced by the fact that finding, evaluating and organising, and creating and sharing were two of the six framework strands staff thought were priority areas (Fraser, Atkins and Hall, 2013). It calls for a basic knowledge of copyright to be considered as a fundamental professional competence for educators. However, the 2013 and 2014 surveys identified a significant lack of familiarity with open educational resources, and open licensing, and a lack of confidence in relation to intellectual property and copyright issues. These findings are in line with European Commission concerns that education and training providers are not taking advantage of the use and creation of open educational resources (European Commission, 2013b).

In response to the survey results, the project team identified the need to provide introductory level information and training in relation to finding, creating and using open educational resources and open licences, and information for school leaders on the benefits in terms of collaborative practice, public value, promoting professional practice across the school and showcasing and sharing high quality resources (Atkins et al, 2013).

The team also explored the legal position of school employees in relation to the production of materials within the line of their work. By default, the rights of work created in the line of employment are assigned to the employer, unless a specific agreement has been made. In response, Leicester City Council became the first European local authority to give blanket permission to its employees at 84 schools across the city to create open educational resources (OER), by sharing the learning materials they create under an open licence. This permission makes sharing resources simpler for everyone at these schools, and helps raise awareness of issues relating to intellectual property, including copyright and OER. Support and materials were also provided for the categories of school in the city (academies, foundation schools and voluntary aided schools) where the school governing body, rather than the local authority, is the employer (Leicester City Council, 2014).

In addition to identifying a lack of OER information and education for school staff, the project team committed from the outset to work in a way that modelled and supported open educational practice. This was immediately identifiable by the open licensing of all reports and resources created by activities associated with the DigiLit Leicester project produced by the central team, external contractors and school staff.

An open education approach was also evident in the attention paid to fostering partnership and collaborative working through project activities, and to supporting access to opportunity as widely as possible. For example, areas identified as priority action areas from 2013 onwards were addressed through central activities designed and managed by the DigiLit Leicester team, and school-led activities, proposed and delivered by the schools (Atkins, Fraser and Hall, 2014). This approach acknowledged the limited time available to some staff, and made it possible to differentiate training for staff depending on their level.

Similarly, when asking staff to fill in the survey, the number of priority areas and survey statements was limited, to acknowledge the practicalities of survey completion. The main concern was to identify and support staff priorities rather than produce an idealised framework. The number and scope of individual themes needed to be manageable and directly support key areas of practice. The length of time needed to complete the survey had to be reasonable in order to support completion rates.

Lessons learned
We learned the following lessons:

- *Use clear language and define terms.* The project team made sure the language used was understandable, came up with a definition of digital literacy and provided examples of what it looks and feels like in practice. This shared understanding made it possible to map the landscape.
- *Avoid box ticking by taking a nuanced approach.* This involved helping staff to identify their strengths and weaknesses, and provided a way of measuring improvement.
- *Prioritise.* Schools were encouraged to focus on one strand they wanted to develop and excel at. For example, assessment and feedback does not have the same priority for all SEN schools as it does in mainstream settings. The project focused on empowering school staff to develop relevant areas of practice.
- *Provide face-to-face support.* Staff who came in at entry level on the

self-evaluation required more intensive face-to-face support than others in order to increase their skills and confidence. Partnering with pioneers was one way of achieving this; however, more time was needed to enable these staff to move up the scale.
- *It is important to support individual and strategic development.* The project team worked with individuals in schools as well as at strategic and policy level.
- *The resource and development available can depend on national policy.* For example, e-safety scores were very high because of Ofsted requirements, so staff development in this area was prioritised. The OER policy that Leicester City Council introduced saved staff time and improved resource quality, but its impact was limited by a lack of activity and support for school staff nationally.
- *School staff lack confidence in basic copyright education* although they typically create, use and share digital resources daily. Providing staff with blanket permission to share their resources under open licence raised awareness of intellectual property laws and the terms of their employment, and enables them to access thousands of free and legal to use resources.
- *Technology-supported professional development is part of every professional's toolkit.* Being able to use technologies to connect and collaborate with other professionals locally and internationally is essential to high quality, personalised continuing professional development.

Conclusion

DigiLit Leicester provided an innovative and practical model to frame digital literacy in real-life contexts and make resources available. By encouraging educators to license and share resources under an open licence, it was possible to save time and avoid reinventing the wheel. By making resources openly available, access and inclusion could be promoted. Sharing resources openly helped staff promote the excellent work that they and their schools were doing, and encouraged everyone to 'raise their game'. The spirit of openness which characterised this project signals a way forward not just for digital literacy staff development, but for education more generally. Although no other UK cities have so far followed Leicester's example, the impact of the project has been hugely significant. Findings and outputs have informed other major strategic digital literacy developments at national and international level and continue to offer a practical model for professionals and support staff working in all stages of education.

References

Atkins, L., Fraser, J. and Hall, R. (2013) DigiLit Leicester: 2013 survey results, Leicester City Council, www.josiefraser.com/2015/10/digilit-leicester-project-roundup/.

Atkins, L., Fraser, J. and Hall, R. (2014) *DigiLit Leicester: project activities short report*, Leicester City Council, www.josiefraser.com/2015/10/digilit-leicester-project-roundup/.

DfE (2012) Teachers' Standards, Department for Education, https://www.gov.uk/government/publications/teachers-standards.

European Commission (2013a) *Survey of Schools: ICT in education – benchmarking access, use and attitudes to technology in Europe's schools*, European Commission and Directorate General for Communications Networks, Content & Technology, http://ec.europa.eu/information_society/newsroom/image/document/2016-20/surveyofschoolsictineducation_15585.pdf.

European Commission (2013b) *Analysis and Mapping of Innovative Teaching and Learning for all Through New Technologies and Open Educational Resources in Europe, Commission staff working document*.

Ferrari, A. (2012) *Digital Competence in Practice: an analysis of frameworks*, Institute for Prospective Technological Studies, European Commission.

Fraser, J. (2012) Developing Digital Literacies in Practice, blog, www.josiefraser.com/2012/03/digital-literacy-practice/.

Fraser, J., Atkins, L. and Hall, R. (2013) *DigiLit Leicester: initial project report*, Leicester City Council, www.josiefraser.com/2015/10/digilit-leicester-project-roundup/.

House of Lords Select Committee on Digital Skills (2015) *Make or Break: the UK's digital future*, HL Paper 111, https://www.publications.parliament.uk/pa/ld201415/ldselect/lddigital/111/111.pdf.

Jisc (2011) *Developing Digital Literacies: briefing paper in support of JISC grant funding 4/11*, http://digitalfuturesoer3.pbworks.com/w/file/fetch/51851938/Briefingpaper.pdf.

Jisc (2015) Developing Students' Digital Literacy, https://www.jisc.ac.uk/guides/developing-students-digital-literacy.

Learning Wales (2016) Digital Competence Framework, http://learning.gov.wales/resources/browse-all/digital-competence-framework/?lang=en.

Leicester Child Poverty Commission (2013) Recommendations, https://www.leicester.gov.uk/schools-and-learning/school-and-colleges/performance-inspections-and-reports/leicester-child-poverty-commission/.

Leicester City Council (2014) Open Education for Schools, https://schools.leicester.gov.uk/services/planning-and-property/building-schools-for-the-future-bsf/open-education-for-schools/.

Redecker, C. and Punie, Y. (2017) European Framework for the Digital Competence of Educators: DigCompEdu, Publications Office of the European Union, https://ec.europa.eu/jrc/en/publication/eur-scientific-and-technical-research-reports/european-framework-digital-competence-educators-digcompedu.

US Department of Education (2010) *Transforming American Education: learning powered by technology*, Office of Educational Technology.

12

Transforming the workplace through digital literacy

Bonnie Cheuk and Katharine Reedy

Introduction: technology, digital literacies and culture change

Computing power is growing at an exponential speed. In the consumer world, new digital tools appear every day. Keeping up with the new technologies can be exciting for some and exhausting for others. In the workplace context, while the pace of technology change tends to be slower than in our personal lives, unfamiliar and disruptive technologies that change the way people work are increasingly being introduced. As more and more technologies are being embedded in the workplace, what kind of digital literacies are required to be effective and productive at work in this ever-changing world?

In this chapter digital literacies are defined as the capabilities required to maximise the benefits that technology can bring to oneself as an individual employee, a team, across the company, the customers and even suppliers. This implies the ability to cope with and avoid stress caused by the prevalence of technologies.

In the next two sections we explore digital literacies from the perspective of two dimensions:

- What kind of digital literacies – aptitude, mindset, behaviours, leadership, skills and competencies – are required for employees to help to deliver company strategy in order to stay relevant in the market and achieve its strategic objectives?
- What kind of aptitude, mindset, behaviours, leadership, skills and

competencies are required to reap the full benefits of new digital technologies?

Dimension 1: the spectrum of workplace digital literacy

What kind of digital literacies are required for employees to get their work done to deliver company strategy? There is no 'one size fits all' requirement. Different levels of digital literacies are required depending on how employees see a situation at any particular time, the goals and outcomes they are trying to achieve, and the constraints imposed by the company and work environment. Digital literacy in the workplace is presented as different levels of digital aptitude, mindset, behaviours, skills and competencies:

1 At the most basic level, digital literacy is knowing what tools exist to do the current job.
2 Following from there, digital literacy is about knowing how to use the tools, and using them effectively to do the job.
3 The next level is knowing why you should use the tool, when to use it and for what purpose.
4 The next much more sophisticated level of digital literacy is about knowing if and how a digital tool may (or may not) help get work done in a better way. For example, what is the purpose of using e-mail to collaborate? Is it fit for purpose? If not, what are other digital solutions?
5 At a similar level, this includes knowing if and how a digital tool is fit for purpose in different business scenarios (for example, while normally communication may be delivered by e-mail and on the intranet, in a crisis, a conscious decision may be made to use SMS text messaging to reach all employees' work and personal mobile phones).
6 The next level of digital literacy is to explore, experiment with new digital tools, and see the connections with how digital tools used in personal lives or the consumer world can be applied in the workplace (for example, introducing social networking and collaboration platforms to change the operating model from a hierarchical one into a networked model, using social media to maintain relationships with clients in ways that transcend time and location).
7 The strategic level of digital literacy is to spot the opportunities (and

threats) to use digital tools in order to change existing business and operating models to achieve company strategy, thus challenging the status quo and gaining buy-in from decision makers to invest in the recommended digital services. At this level, one blends digital literacies with business acumen and digital is introduced for a purpose, recognising that 'there is no digital strategy, only company strategy'. One would also recognise any negative impact of digital technologies on employees and the company (for example, cyber threats, stress levels of staff, and automation leading to jobs reduction), and proactively consider the responses.
8 The final and transformation level of digital literacy is to turn the strategy intent into realities, introducing and embedding the new digital services into day-to-day work. This inevitably involves redefining business processes, roles and responsibilities, and ways of working. More importantly it requires the building of digital capabilities to reap the full benefits that the new technologies can offer.

It is important to point out that the level of digital literacy an employee exhibits in the workplace is influenced by job roles, team culture, function and level of seniority. Whether someone is considered digitally capable or not is not about which level one is at, but rather the appropriate level of digital literacies required for the function area or level of responsibility.

Dimension 2: digital literacies and culture change

What kind of leadership is required to reap the full benefits of new digital technologies? The key characteristic of digital is its fast-evolving nature. In the digital world, change is the new constant. In the workplace, operating at the 'transformation level' of digital literacies requires digital leadership: the ability to deal with paradoxes and uncertainty, and to be able to learn and unlearn fast to use digital technologies.

To embrace digital transformation a culture is needed where employees can admit they do not know the new landscape, are willing to try out new technologies, be vulnerable, have a go, make mistakes, learn and share the experience to move collectively to a better place. It is also about taking responsibility to learn, explore and be curious.

This means one has to be comfortable in recognising that one person's knowledge is limited and can be obsolete quickly. There is therefore a need to have the capabilities to draw on ideas from people in the network to seek advice, challenge status quo, inform decisions, offer support and explore possibilities together. This new culture is required at all levels when faced with technology disruption. The cultural change required is just as much about soft digital skills (for example, changing mindset) as it is about acquiring hard digital skills (for example, technical skills) (Capgemini, 2017).

An example: introducing a company social networking and collaboration platform

The first author of this chapter has had the experience of leading the strategy and the roll-out of a company-wide social-networking collaboration platform for various multinational companies. The new platform is opening up new ways of working unfamiliar to all (Cheuk, 2013), creating the space for employees to embrace the following behaviour (which was not possible before):

- *Lateral communication*: supports top-down, bottom-up and lateral communications
- *All staff* can participate if they want to – no specialised IT skills are required
- *Networking*: building business and social networking across teams and geographies
- *Expertise visualisation*: visualise the expertise in the network and trends and hot topics in the company from the ground up
- *Selfishness yet helpful to others*: focusing on satisfying the immediate needs of a user and as a by-product highlighting the collective intelligence which creates more value to all staff.

These are known as the LANES principles (Cheuk and Dervin, 2009).

Examples from the author's experience are drawn on to reflect on how the eight levels of digital literacies outlined above are exhibited and nurtured when these kinds of disruptive technologies are introduced into the workplace.

Eight levels of digital literacies in action
Any strategy for developing digital capabilities in a workplace has to start

with the company strategy, and not from the technology perspective. The first question to ask is always what the company objectives are, and how use of digital technologies will help to achieve these goals. There is no digital strategy, only company strategy.

In this case study, the senior executive team of the company identified the need to become more agile, innovative and responsive as a result of the changing market, new competition and regulatory requirements. Ideas and information should be allowed to flow in a lateral and networked way across hierarchies and geographical boundaries. With this intent, a strategic decision is made to bring in a new social networking and collaboration platform – together with a range of business change programmes – to enable the change. Digital literacies levels 6 and 7 are exhibited to spot the opportunities to adapt technologies that work in the consumer world into the company, and to put digital on the strategic radar.

Digital literacy at this level includes making responsible use of technology and the information stored or distributed via digital channels. Policies to handle confidential information and cybersecurity considerations are factored into the design of the solution.

As the new platform is introduced, the employees are taken through an on-boarding experience with the aim of:

- helping colleagues to be aware of the new platform, why it is being introduced, and what its strategic purpose is
- training colleagues to use a range of functionalities, and how to get started on the new platform
- understanding what the existing tools are inside the company, and with the new platform, what tools should be used for what purposes.

Existing staff can learn to use new tools at a time and place that suits them, whether via face-to-face training sessions or through videos posted on the intranet. Additional training is conducted in specific business contexts. For example:

- the sales team who need to better collaborate, in order to understand customers' needs and work together on sales materials, learn how to use the new platform to share insights and co-edit sales materials

- new hires who are learning about the company objectives are also trained on how to update their profiles, how to follow other colleagues relevant to their domain area, and how to set custom streams to receive relevant information
- the horizon-scanning and market intelligence team have a tailor-made session to learn how to set up alerts, monitoring what others in the company (or outside the company) are doing and how best to make connections and stay up to date with new developments.

These training sessions are conducted by the core team of digital coaches, and supported by a digital champions' network of around 40 active evangelists who are keen to use the new platform and show others the way, leading by example. By sharing their success stories – explaining how they become more effective when adopting new digital tools – they energise and help convince others to embrace the change. All these activities help to build digital literacies levels 1–3 across the organisation.

Once the basic levels are solidified, employees are invited to reflect on how they (or the team) should communicate and collaborate today, what tools to use today, consider whether those tools are still fit for purpose, and if not what they (the team) should stop doing and start doing using the new platform.

Digital literacies level 4 and 5 are introduced. These are some examples that a CEO might reflect on:

- How best to exercise leadership in a digital world. For example, how open should he or she be? Should the CEO reply to all comments posted on his or her blog? What is the new etiquette of communication online?
- Whether using e-mail to collaborate on documents is an effective practice, when it is difficult to manage version control, to consolidate changes made and to follow the e-mail chain discussion. A virtual collaborative group with document co-editing capabilities might be a more effective new way of working.
- Whether pushing an e-mail newsletter sent by the senior executive to all staff and/or publishing the message on a static intranet page meets the engagement objectives. He or she introduces an interactive forum named 'leaders in conversation' on the new platform to promote two-way dialogue and lateral sharing of ideas.

- What is the best approach to reach out to all staff when facing a crisis situation. He or she decides that while the new platform is good for promoting sharing and pull communication, it is not the most appropriate channel to contact all staff during a crisis. Instead, he decides to use text-based SMS to all mobile devices and push e-mail communications.

At these levels of digital literacies, it is expected that discussion around information literacy – what information is required to solve my problem or do my job, where the information resides on the new platform, how to judge the quality and popularity of the information, how to create and share information effectively, and the ethical use of information – is embedded in digital literacies training. In the LIS world, this is sometimes referred to as 'digital and information literacy', as the level of discussion goes beyond the tool itself into considerations about information search, use and sharing in an ethical way (Cheuk, 2017a and Cheuk, 2017b).

By bringing out the eight levels of digital literacies, the company help employees to become competent users of the new platform, to understand how to use it to serve specific goals, and to be inspired and empowered to discover more. The new social networking and collaboration platform, used by employees with eight levels of digital literacies, is enabling the company strategy to become more agile and responsive in times of change.

Culture change in action: digital leadership beyond 'digital'
As the new platform is introduced, in this case study, the company also realises there is a need to rethink the current ways of working, in order to cultivate the attitude to embrace change, challenge the status quo, experiment and venture into the unknown to fully embrace the disruptive nature of the new social networking and collaboration platform.

As digital technology disrupts existing work practices, to become digitally literate requires an a priori mindset – to be comfortable with change and navigating uncertainties, to accept change as the new constant.

In this example, the roll-out of the new social networking and collaboration is part of a broader programme to build the capability of the company to navigate change and uncertainty. A number of interventions are put in place, to name a few here:

- a leadership development programme focusing on developing a humanistic approach to connect and relate with one another, be willing to show vulnerabilities, and promote 'communicative' communication practices (active listening, facilitating dialogue, providing feedback etc.)
- a physical environment that promotes flexible working and collaboration
- an innovation programme to promote crowdsourcing of ideas, and turning ideas from conception into realities, drawing on energy and expertise from across the company.

These interventions all point to the need to think and act differently to cope with constant change. Informed by Dervin's Sense-Making Methodology (Dervin and Foreman-Wernet, 2013), the capabilities to navigate in a constantly changing environment require the leaders and employees at all levels to dig deeper, to understand and discover the hidden passion and unexpressed needs (which one cannot assume will surface in day-to-day spontaneous conversation). Digital leadership requires Leadership 2.0 (Cheuk and Dervin, 2009):

- *A re-set of communication protocol*: know what is appropriate (or not) at work; welcome dissent; invite staff to contradict seniors and experts and explain why.
- *Promote dialogue with disciplined communication*: invite hidden voices; learn from peers of all levels; understand the rationale for different views.
- *Be open to learning and unlearning*: see self-reflection as a learning process; listen and connect; learn to love surprises.
- *Be curious*: ask, search and discover.
- *Be human*: give support and help; share our feelings.

Digital leaders have to go beyond learning how to use digital to learning how to communicate in a communicative manner. Leadership 2.0 redefines what learning in the workplace means, and in this case, learning to become digitally capable at work. Learning goes beyond formal training and development programmes. Employees learn through self-reflection of good and emerging practices and even more from mistakes. Learning comes from listening to how employees experience digital in many different ways; that mistakes made when using a new digital platform are tolerated and encouraged; that hunches are invited and thus employees are encouraged to explore how to use the platform in a way that is meaningful to them. Through the learning process, experts, novices, senior executives and frontline staff learn and unlearn together. Learning also requires staff to pay attention to the power structure and be mindful of voices that are being suppressed.

In this example, the first author of this chapter has not only rolled out eight levels of digital literacies, she and her team have also practised Leadership 2.0, and encouraged others to do the same, to help the company go through the digital transformation journey (Cheuk and Mackenzie, in press).

Conclusion

Digital transformation takes place when employees have the digital environment, tools and services to empower them to bring out their full potential to deliver company strategy. Digital transformation requires employees' digital literacies to be upgraded to reap the benefits of digital investment. In this chapter, eight levels of digital literacies have been introduced. As the pace of digital change is fast, there is a priori requirement to develop digital leadership. Digital leadership in the workplace is about guiding employees' mindset and introducing culture change – especially to embrace Leadership 2.0 and to communicate 'communicatively' – in order to learn and unlearn. No doubt new digital technologies will continue to come and go in the workplace and our personal lives. When developing digital literacies, it is important that people go beyond just learning how to use digital tools and acquire the capabilities to stay digitally confident in times of constant digital disruption. Digital leadership in the workplace must go beyond 'digital'.

References

Capgemini (2017) *The Digital Talent Gap: are companies doing enough?*, https://www.capgemini.com/resources/digital-talent-gap/.

Cheuk, B. (2013) *Social Strategies in Action: driving business transformation*, Ark Group, https://www.ark-group.com/sites/default/files/product-pdf-download/ARK2497%20-%20Social%20Strategies%20in%20Action%20-%20Driving%20Business%20Transformation_Sample%20chapter.pdf.

Cheuk, B. (2017) The 'Hidden' Value of Information Literacy in the

Workplace Context: how to unlock and create value. In Foster, M. (ed.), *Information Literacy in the Workplace*.

Cheuk, B. (2017) Who Cares About Information Literacy in the Workplace? Keynote [speech] at European Conference of Information Literacy, https://www.slideshare.net/secret/vF3tdBP81DaZhl.

Cheuk, B. and McKenzie, J. (in press) Developing the Practice of Online Leadership: lessons from the field. In Kolbaek, D. (ed.), *Online Collaboration and Communication in Contemporary Organizations*, IGI Global.

Cheuk, W. Y. B. and Dervin, B. (2009) Leadership 2.0 and Web2.0 at ERM: a journey from knowledge management to 'knowledging'. In Chu, S., Ritter, W. and Hawamdeh, S. (eds), *Managing Knowledge for Global and Collaborative Innovations*, Series on Innovation and Knowledge Management, Volume 8, World Scientific.

Dervin, B. and Foreman-Wernet, L. (2013) *Sense-Making Methodology Reader: selected writings of Brenda Dervin*, Hampton Press.

13

Critical digital literacy education in the 'fake news' era

Philip Seargeant and Caroline Tagg

Introduction: panic and disaster

In the 1920s the political commentator Walter Lippmann famously wrote: 'Incompetence and aimlessness, corruption and disloyalty, panic and ultimate disaster must come to any people which is denied an assured access to the facts' (Lippmann, 1920). This seemed to sum up the mood for many in the last few months of 2016 and through into 2017. Following Donald Trump's victory in the US presidential election, and the result of the referendum about Brexit before that, the issue of 'fake news' has come to dominate the real news week. The idea of fake news has emerged as one of the defining concepts of our times, with its influence stretching around the globe (BBC, 2017), and being blamed for everything from a rise in xenophobia (Solomon, 2017) to the all-out undermining of Western democracy (Cheshire, 2016). The issue has become of such public concern that it has led to parliamentary enquiries in the UK (Commons Select Committee, 2017), and the establishment of 'collaborative journalism verification projects' (CrossCheck, 2017), as well as major soul-searching by the large technology firms. In this chapter we examine the role that communications technology – and specifically social media – plays in the phenomenon of, and discourse around, fake news, drawing on findings from a research project we conducted into the way people interact on Facebook. Based on the implications of this research we then look at how critical digital literacy education – which combines an understanding of the affordances and implications of digital media with an awareness and sensitivity to the role the media play in everyday social politics – can assist in providing people with the knowledge and resources to make informed decisions about their consumption of information circulated online.

Filter bubbles and fake news

In the immediate aftermath of Trump's election it was social media companies such as Facebook which came in for particular and persistent criticism for their role in the way that fake news was being spread. Trotter (2016), for instance, wrote, 'Throughout [2016's] presidential campaign, journalists have focused, correctly, on the power of Facebook to shape, distort, and ultimately control the news and information that inform and educate voters.' And Read (2016) argued that 'whether through a failure of resources, of ideology, or of imagination, Facebook has seemed uninterested in and incapable of even acknowledging that it has become the most efficient distributor of misinformation in human history'.

Most of the solutions that were proposed in the media for tackling the perceived problem therefore focused on what Facebook should do to change its service. The main argument was as follows: the personalisation algorithm that shapes the way people experience the site is responsible for creating 'filter bubbles', which shield users from views they disagree with, and allow fake news and highly partisan opinions to circulate unchecked. The term 'filter bubble' was coined by Eli Pariser (2011, 9), who explains it in the following terms:

> The new generation of internet filters looks at the things you seem to like – the actual things you've done, or the things people like you like – and tries to extrapolate. They are prediction engines, constantly creating and refining a theory of who you are and what you'll do and want next. Together, these engines create a unique universe of information for each of us . . . which fundamentally alters the way we encounter ideas and information.

In other words, the algorithm works in interaction with users' actions, reading the content that people post and predicting or anticipating their future actions, constantly responding to what people are doing on the site, even as it shapes people's likely future actions. One of the problems with this, according to Jones (2015), is the fact that users themselves are not always fully aware of either the role that the technology is playing in shaping their behaviour, nor how their responses to the technology contribute to the effect it has on their communication.

Yet blaming it all on the technology (and thus the technology companies) runs the risk of implying that people themselves are helplessly naïve. It casts users of the technology as being prey to how the machines are mediating our understanding of reality. It also suggests a clear dividing line between good and bad media, and between truth and falsehood. In doing so it ignores the fact that all media has an agenda: it always constructs its own particular version of events.

Research that we conducted into online communication via social media shows that people's own actions are a key factor in the way stories and opinions are shared, and that often they themselves create a filter bubble effect through these actions. By carrying out a large survey of 140 Facebook users as part of an ongoing project, Creating Facebook (Tagg, Seargeant and Brown, 2017), which aimed to illuminate users' ideas about the social network site, we were able to unearth some of the complex decisions behind people's interactions on Facebook, and in this way map how user agency is an important complementary factor in the types of opinions and information people access online.

User agency and the bubble effect

There are a number of dynamics in people's behaviour which are relevant here. First, our survey participants expressed awareness of the fact that they were speaking in front of an audience made up of friends and acquaintances from all parts of their lives, who often have very different values and political views – and voiced concern over managing these diverse and complex relationships. They also reported experiencing little control over the ways in which their posts might be reposted or shared, making it more difficult to predict who would read them in the future, and how they might be interpreted. As a result our participants 'designed' their online contributions more carefully than they might have spoken in a face-to-face interaction.

At the same time, our survey participants acknowledged that they were also concerned with constructing a particular image of themselves through what they say and do, overwhelmingly seeking to create a positive persona which avoids offending or challenging others. Although people responded in different ways to the content of their news feeds – some finding it overly trivial and others objecting to the use of Facebook as a space for discussion of more serious political topics – there was a general concern with creating a friendly or convivial communicative space. Rather than engaging others in debate, people more often reported quietly 'unfriending' people who offended them or blocking their posts from appearing in their news feed – in effect, helping to contribute to the filter bubble effect by filtering out opposing views (Seargeant and Tagg, 2016). All of these considerations about self-image, relationship-building and conviviality intersect in complex ways with the decisions that people are simultaneously making about the validity of different news stories and how to respond to them. Also crucial to our argument is the fact that the strategies people were developing for managing their social lives on Facebook were ad hoc and often the result of a trial-and-error process, as people unwittingly offended others and then sought to change their behaviour. In other words, people do not approach social media with a fixed or shared understanding of appropriate communicative norms; instead, these are co-constructed, negotiated and contested during online interactions – and the typical process involves people learning from their own (and others') mistakes.

Technological solutions
The media landscape today is starkly different from the one that existed even a few years ago and is changing constantly. Because of this, people's ability to make informed decisions about how they communicate depends on understanding not just how the technology works, but how it works *socially*. For example, it is not just a matter of knowing how to keep on top of your privacy settings, it also involves knowing the implications of what can happen as a result of choosing one setting over another. It is not just a matter of understanding how to flag something you find suspect, it is also a matter of evaluating its provenance and purpose in the first place, bearing in mind that you may have received the news via someone you trust or whose views you share – or simply from someone you know well and do not wish to offend.

In response to the criticisms levelled at the company about being responsible for the spread of false news, Facebook has taken a number of steps to address the apparent problem, focusing on three particular areas (Mosseri, 2017a). The first is to remove the economic incentives that advertising revenue provides to fake news mills (sites which purposefully post fabricated and sensational articles as a means of generating advertising revenue from high levels of clicks). Second is the creation of software solutions and collaborations with external organisations, aimed at tackling the circulation of fabricated news (CUNY J-School, 2017). For example, in December 2016 Facebook announced a set of measures including getting readers to flag stories for fact-checking, marking dubious stories as being 'disputed' and dropping them down the news feed (Mosseri, 2016). Finally there is the creation of tools which it hopes will allow people to make 'more informed' decisions about the content they encounter – educational initiatives. To this end, in April 2017 the company launched what it refers to as an 'educational tool' intended to help users identify suspect stories, and flag them as unreliable (Gibbs, 2017).

Working in association with the non-profit journalism coalition First Draft (Shorenstin Center, 2017), Facebook came up with a list of bullet points which it hopes will help guide users through their online news consumption. These include things such as being sceptical of headlines, checking the URL and source of an article, examining the genre (formatting, use of images, whether it is meant as satire, etc.), looking at the evidence cited, and cross-referencing with other articles on the same topic. The list ends with the advice to 'think critically about the stories you read, and only share news that you know to be credible' (Facebook, 2018).

This is all highly sensible guidance, and standard content for critical literacy education (Open University, n.d.). But it will only really have any impact if people bother to follow it. And this is the problem. As an effective educational tool, such guidance lacks any in-built motivational incentive, relying instead on the assumption that users of the site feel this to be an important issue, and will take the time to follow up on these precepts (Huitt, 2011). In other words, there is no discussion or illustration of *why* false news is an issue or the effects it can have on society. In a press release, Adam Mosseri, vice-president for Facebook's news feed, asserts that 'false news and hoaxes are harmful to our community and make the world less informed' and that we all 'have a responsibility to curb' its spread (Mosseri, 2017b). But without persuading people in concrete terms as to why it is a problem they are simply asking people to believe in the authority of their assertions rather than those of others.

From false to fake news

The central questions, then, are why fake news has become an issue and for whom, and who should be held responsible for it. At the moment the answers to these questions are assumed rather than explicitly laid out, and there is no particularly strong evidence that the assumptions about them are always correct.

For example, recent research suggests that social media has less influence on the polarisation of civic debate than other factors, such as 'traditional' media outlets. A paper for the National Bureau of Economic Research, which examined statistics from the American National Election Survey, suggests that polarisation of political views is much greater in older voters, who are less likely to use social media (Boxell, Gentzkow and Shapiro, 2017). For these voters, the influence of cable television and talk radio – much of which takes a very partisan perspective on news events – is liable to have more of an effect.

As important as *how* the news is circulated, therefore, is the issue of *what* it consists of – what the balance is between opinion and fact – and how this is influenced by the aims of those writing, publishing and citing it. As an interesting side note to Facebook's initiative, in introducing its educational tool the company pointedly spoke of 'false news' rather than 'fake news'. This distinction reflects just how contested the concept has become in public debate, and specifically how the latter term has been co-opted by populist politicians as a cover-all insult for their rivals (Seargeant, 2017), as well as something with which to mock the 'mainstream media' (@DonaldJTrumpJR, 2017). By using 'false news', Facebook was trying to return to the original concerns about intentionally misleading content, and stories with extreme bias (Constine, 2017). 'False news', in other words, is a specific notion of evidence-free or purposefully fabricated stories, disseminated for profit or political manipulation; while 'fake news' refers to a broad state of anxiety about the role and identity of journalism in an era of social media and populist politics.

Given this context, the ethics of journalism, publishing and politics all need to be part of the debate. Pushing the responsibility back onto the consumer of news does not place enough stress on the ethical responsibilities of those producing and disseminating it, and those citing it for political influence. Instead it gives these institutions free licence to pursue a partisan stance, while arguing that the onus lies on readers to understand the implications of the way news is produced by these institutions and evaluate it accordingly. At this point, the category of 'false news' becomes subsumed under that of 'fake news'. Although it is possible to give readers a roadmap with which to navigate the shades of bias and fabrication that are circulated, if the centres of power are themselves citing and defending these stories, flagging up factually dubious content on Facebook feels somewhat futile.

This broader discourse of fake news is proving to have unexpected and unintended consequences in society. At around the same time that Facebook was launching its tool, for example, it was argued in the press that the antagonistic attitude that the Trump administration has taken towards what he calls the 'fake news media' had led to foreign presses being able to take the lead in shaping the public narrative for any international relations disputes (Borchers, 2017). In other words, by undermining his national press, Trump loses a valuable mouthpiece for expressing his country's perspective on issues on the world stage.

Conclusion: educational solutions

The research reported on in this chapter offers significant evidence that the way people use the technology is as important as how it is designed, and that their use depends on their understanding of the affordances and implications for online communication. The interface between user behaviour and algorithmic personalisation is crucial in shaping people's online experiences. Personalisation from an algorithmic point of view reacts to data generated, in part, by an individual's actions on the site: how they create and react to the content that constitutes their news feed. In this respect it is possible to say that each user 'designs' the experience they have of the site by means of their communicative actions, as these are then interpreted by the algorithm and converted into the ordering and selection of the news feed. But the click signals that the algorithm picks up on are not the only way in which the context of the communicative space that users experience is designed by their behaviour. There are a host of other factors involved, which range from their cognitive engagement with information, decisions about how to react (which can result in an absence of action – deciding to do nothing), awareness of and agency over the affordances, and the subtle manipulation of style and content.

Modifying the algorithm, therefore, or otherwise policing people's use of the site with fact-checkers and facilities to flag controversial content, will not address the fact that sharing information on Facebook is fundamentally a social activity, nor the impact this has on the way people consume and evaluate information. Instead, what is important, we would suggest, is a form of critical digital literacy education which can focus on not simply how the technology works, but how it works socially – and what the implications of this are for the way society functions. In the same way that projects on internet safety awareness are important at primary and secondary school for understanding the possible dangers of the online world (e.g. UK Safer Internet Centre; https://www.saferinternet.org.uk/), so education about how people share, process and consume information on social media is important in preparing university students to become critically engaged citizens. Navigating online information is not something people simply intuit; it is something that is learnt. Education can help raise awareness of how the flow of information in society is managed, and what this means for how people engage with each other's opinions and values.

There are two aspects to such education. The first is to develop skills which assist with the sifting, evaluating and authenticating of information. This is an area of critical digital literacy, which has been explored and theorised in the research literature (e.g. Dudeney, Hockly and Pegrum, 2013), and is incorporated to varying extents in existing school and higher education digital literacy programmes (e.g. Johnston and Webber, 2010; Webber and Johnston, 2017). The second part – which is less well incorporated into such programmes, and in fact represents a shift (at least in higher education) from seeing digital literacy as a study skill to recognising its role in civil society – involves raising awareness of how the flow of information in society as a whole is managed in the era of social media, and the implications this can have for the maintenance of an effective society. One could refer to these aspects of education as digital media literacy and social digital literacy respectively. At a fundamental level they involve an understanding of how technology mediates communication and the flow of information, and how this shapes, and is shaped by, user actions and media ideologies. The latter, however, enables us to acknowledge the increasingly complex role that social media plays as a social network site and media institution, and to enable citizens to recognise the extent of their own agency in the sharing and dissemination of information in the 'fake news' era.

Ultimately, though, an awareness of how information is circulated and discursively shaped, and how it is mediated and used to persuade, is something that comes from inquisitiveness and an immersion in civic debate. It is likely to be a product of an environment as much as a specifically targeted curriculum. As we saw in our research, online norms and practices emerge from a complex interplay between people's evolving ideas about the site and about their own agency on it, their past experiences and their future expectations. Therefore a skills-oriented pedagogy is only part of the solution. What is also needed is a critical approach to the nature of information and debate more generally, which seeks to build on and enhance people's understanding of the complexities of social media interaction.

References

@DonaldJTrumpJR (2017) I'm going to have to buy 5–10,000 of these to pass around to our buddies in the #MSM, Twitter, 15 April, https://twitter.com/DonaldJTrumpJr/status/853341481175789571.

BBC (2017) How Fake News and Hoaxes Have Tried to Derail Jakarta's Election, BBC News, 18 April, www.bbc.co.uk/news/world-asia-39176350.

Borchers, C. (2017) The Real Cost of Trump's 'Fake News' Accusations, *The Fix*, 8 April, https://www.washingtonpost.com/news/the-fix/wp/2017/04/18/the-real-cost-of-trumps-fake-news-accusations/?utm_term=.b9392a35f975.

Boxell, L., M. Gentzkow and J. M. Shapiro (2017) *Is the Internet Causing Political Polarisation?: evidence from demographics*, NBER Working Paper 23258, National Bureau of Economic Research.

Cheshire (2016) Sky Views: Facebook's fake news threatens democracy, Sky News, http://news.sky.com/story/sky-views-democracy-burns-as-facebook-lets-fake-news-thrive-10652711.

Commons Select Committee (2017) 'Fake News' Inquiry Launched, 30 January, https://www.parliament.uk/business/committees/committees-a-z/commons-select/culture-media-and-sport-committee/news-parliament-2015/fake-news-launch-16-17/.

Constine, J. (2017) Facebook Puts Link to 10 tips for Spotting 'False' News, TechCrunch, 6 April, https://techcrunch.com/2017/04/06/facebook-puts-link-to-10-tips-for-spotting-false-news-atop-feed/.

CrossCheck (2017) Emmanuel Macron avait-il une oreillette pendant le débat du 3 mai?, https://crosscheck.firstdraftnews.com/france-fr/.

CUNY J-School (2017) Announcing the News Integrity Initiative to Increase Trust in Journalism, 3 April, City University of New York Graduate School of Journalism, https://www.journalism.cuny.edu/2017/04/announcing-the-new-integrity-initiative/.

Dudeney G., N. Hockly and M. Pegrum (2013) *Digital Literacies*, Pearson.

Facebook (2018) Tips to Spot False News, Facebook Help Centre, https://www.facebook.com/help/188118808357379.

Gibbs, S. (2017) Google to Display Fact-checking Label to Show if News Is True or False, *Guardian*, 7 April, https://www.theguardian.com/technology/2017/apr/07/google-to-display-fact-checking-labels-to-show-if-news-is-true-or-false.

Huitt, W. (2011) Motivation to Learn: an overview, *Educational Psychology Interactive*, Valdosta State University.

Johnston, B. and Webber, S. (2010) Information Literacy in Higher Education: a review and case study, *Studies in Higher Education*, **28** (3), 335–52.

Jones, R. H. (2015) Surveillance. In Georgakopoulou, A. and Spilioti, T. (eds) *The Routledge Handbook of Language and Digital Communication*, Routledge.

Walter Lippmann, (1920). Liberty and the News. Princeton, Oxford: Princeton University Press, 2008.Mosseri, A. (2016) News Feed FYI: addressing hoaxes and fake news, Facebook Newsroom, 15 December, https://newsroom.fb.com/news/2016/12/news-feed-fyi-addressing-hoaxes-and-fake-news/.

Mosseri, A. (2017a) Working to Stop Misinformation and False News, Facebook Newsroom, 6 April, https://newsroom.fb.com/news/2017/04/working-to-stop-misinformation-and-false-news/.

Mosseri, A. (2017b) A New Educational Tool Against Misinformation, Facebook Newsroom, 6 April, https://newsroom.fb.com/news/2017/04/a-new-educational-tool-against-misinformation/.

Open University (n.d.) Evaluating Information: knowing what to trust, Open University Library Services, www.open.ac.uk/library/library-videos/evaluating-information-knowing-what-to-trust.

Pariser, E. (2011) *The Filter Bubble: what the internet is hiding from you*, Penguin.

Read, M. (2016) Donald Trump Won Because of Facebook, *New York Magazine*, 9 November, http://nymag.com/selectall/2016/11/donald-trump-won-because-of-facebook.html.

Seargeant, P. (2017) How 'Fake News' Became Trump's Favourite Insult, *Huffington Post*, 1 March, www.huffingtonpost.co.uk/politics/.

Seargeant, P. and Tagg, C. (2016) The Filter Bubble Isn't Just Facebook's Fault – It's Yours, The Conversation, 5 December, https://theconversation.com/the-filter-bubble-isnt-just-facebooks-fault-its-yours-69664.

Shorenstein Center (2017) First Draft: about, Shorenstein Center on Media, Politics and Public Policy, Harvard Kennedy School, https://firstdraftnews.org/about/.

Solomon, S. (2017) Fake News, False Info Stoke Xenophobia in South Africa, Voice of America, 1 March, https://www.voanews.com/a/fake-news-flase-info-stokesw-xenophobia-in-south-africa/3745228.html.

Tagg, C., Seargeant, P. and Brown, A. A. (2017) *Taking Offence on Social Media: communication and conviviality on Facebook*, Palgrave.

Trotter, J. K. (2016) How Much is Facebook to Blame?, *Gizmodo*, 10 November, https://gizmodo.com/how-much-is-facebook-to-blame-1788773278.

Webber, S. and B. Johnston (2017) Information Literacy: conceptions, context and the formation of a discipline, *Journal of Information Literacy*, **11** (1), 156–83.

14

Onwards! Why the movement for digital inclusion has never been more important

Adam Micklethwaite

Introduction

This chapter shows how we still live in a digitally divided world, with levels of digital exclusion remaining unacceptable despite the seeming ubiquity of technology and access to smart devices. It surveys the main drivers of digital exclusion and the substantial benefits of investing in digital inclusion: the process of helping people engage with digital for the first time and develop basic digital skills.

Noting that as a body of practice digital inclusion is changing, driven by the evolution of technology and the ways in which it is becoming increasingly integrated with human life, it goes on to describe the effective features of digital inclusion from a UK and public policy perspective. From there, it notes the strong 'movement' effect arising as a consequence of effective digital inclusion, and argues that this movement is required now and into the future, not only to close the digital divide but also to continue building our human relationship with technology as it continues to evolve.

The digitally divided world

We live in a digital world. Or do we? Digital exclusion – lacking basic digital skills or being entirely offline – is still remarkably prevalent. In 2017, research by Lloyds Banking Group (Lloyds Bank, 2017) showed that 4.8 million adults in the UK said they had never been online, and 11.5 million adults lack all of the basic digital skills considered essential to participate in the digital world, from internet searching to carrying out basic online transactions. Globally, although more people now say they use the internet than those who do not, 3.9 billion people (more than half the world's population) do not have internet access.

Being digitally excluded correlates strongly with social exclusion in all its many forms. If you are unemployed, living in poverty, living with a disability, or have low skills you are much more likely to be offline, and lacking internet access or digital skills has a significant impact on your ability to take advantage of routes to opportunity and wellbeing. According to the same Lloyds research (Lloyds Bank, 2017), 97% of those in the UK earning above £75,000 per annum have all five of the basic digital skills considered essential today, compared with 63% of those earning less than £9499 per annum.

Contrary to what many people believe this remains a digitally divided world: and the digital divide reinforces – and is reinforced by – social inequality in all its dimensions.

People who are offline and lack basic digital skills are unable to realise benefits that most of us take for granted: from saving money through online shopping to communicating online with friends and relatives. In a real sense they are excluded from full participation in society, and will fall further behind as technology, already embedded into most areas of life, continues to evolve and change. Furthermore, digital exclusion presents wider risks to society: for example, a lack of digital skills might prevent the modernisation of public transport systems in rural areas because people don't know how to use a responsive Uber-style service; and people who are only able to access the internet through Facebook may be more susceptible to the 'echo chamber' effect sometimes created by social media.

Digital exclusion is personal and frequently motivational

There is no single story on digital exclusion and no single route to digital inclusion. Digital exclusion can be driven primarily by motivational factors rather than access to technology. Every person's situation is different: both their reasons for being offline or having low digital skills, and the journey they take in moving online. Digital exclusion may be hard to spot, and recent research by Nominet Trust (2016) highlighted the barriers to digital inclusion among disadvantaged 15–24-year-olds in the UK, despite being heavy users of social media. Nor is digital inclusion a linear process:

people drop in and out of engagement as they build their confidence, learn new skills or refresh existing ones.

Access to digital technology has risen dramatically in recent years, and mobile device ownership is increasingly common. In the UK, studies show that the single biggest reason for being offline is motivational, rather than because of lack of access. In 2016, the UK digital and communications market regulator Ofcom found that 1 in 10 adults in the UK said they had no intention of going online, of whom over 50% cited lack of motivation (in its different forms) as the main reason (Ofcom, 2017a, 2017b) The Lloyds Consumer Digital Index (Lloyds Bank, 2017) showed that over half (51%) of those offline say their primary reason for being offline is lack of interest. The same study revealed a marked lack of awareness of the benefits of being online. Levels of trust in digital technology are also a significant issue for this group.

Because of this motivational barrier, compounded by the range of social exclusion disadvantages frequently faced by those offline, effective digital inclusion is built on personal relationships. This idea is discussed further below.

The benefits of digital inclusion

As well as the obvious moral case for helping people join the digital world, there is a wealth of evidence about its benefits for individuals and society. The Future Digital Inclusion programme, funded by the UK Department for Education, which is helping one million adults get online over five years, has had a strong and positive impact: the confidence and wellbeing of 60–70% of people who become digitally capable improves, 90% progress to further learning, 80% have positive employment outcomes and 60–70% show social and personal benefits, from increases in self-confidence to reduced social isolation (Good Things Foundation, 2017a).

There is also a strong positive economic return on investment in digital inclusion. A UK study by the Centre for Economics and Business Research commissioned by Tinder Foundation and Go ON UK estimated this return as approaching £10 per £1 invested, comprising cost and time savings to the individual, higher earnings, greater likelihood of being in employment, and savings across public services as more services are delivered digitally (Hogan et al., 2015). The same study calculated that the economic cost of equipping every adult in the UK with basic digital skills and a digital device would be around £1.65 billion, and the corresponding economic return as much as £14.3 billion over the subsequent ten years.

Digital inclusion is changing as technology changes

As a body of practice digital inclusion is changing. There is a strengthening focus on digital skills for the future of work, driven by the current global debate about artificial intelligence, machine learning and robots; this may lead to new models of digital inclusion that focus more strongly on working productively alongside technology as well as learning how to use it. In the UK there is also continuing debate about trust and safety in digital, centred on children's use of social media but spanning the whole of society. This debate is moving rapidly, and it was interesting to see the first admission from Facebook in December 2017 that its platform can pose a mental health risk (Levin, 2017).

As well as focusing on digital skills, governments and organisations active in digital inclusion will need to turn more of their attention to the relationship between digital and society, as the UK organisation doteveryone has started to do through its work on digital understanding (Doteveryone, n.d.), focusing on the individual's awareness of how digital affects their agency and rights, and the treatment of their personal data. As technology becomes easier and easier to use – witness the growth of speech recognition devices such as Alexa, Siri, Amazon Echo and Google Home – 'how do I use this?' becomes a less important question than 'how am I being used?'

Ultimately, we will need to understand how digital interfaces with human beings at the cognitive level, exploring how we take in or generate information about digital and how that information is used to drive how we 'act digitally' – so that as humans we can maximise our wellbeing as technology becomes an ever more dominant and (physically) integrated part of our lives. Just as children develop adaptive behaviours that allow them to function well in the world and with others, young people and adults may be able to develop digitally adaptive behaviours that allow them to act well in the digital world. This could range from knowing when to stop scrolling through social media posts, to taking better breaks from a screen and using the automation of processes to free up more human time to be creative.

A range of evidence suggests that models of digital inclusion – particularly those based on personal relationships, delivered informally and in community locations – could be an effective way of developing digitally adaptive behaviours. For example, it seems evident that taking the plunge into digital for the first time requires an 'adaptive leap', and this could start a positive chain reaction that supports other adaptive behaviours to develop. At Good Things Foundation we are starting work on this, working with digital inclusion practitioners, think tanks, scientists and others to investigate the relationship between technology and behaviour and how it can be influenced.

These and other 'big conversations' about humans and technology will inevitably affect the process of helping people to build digital confidence and skills, so we cannot assume the current benchmarks for what constitutes being digitally included will stay the same. Nevertheless, there is strong evidence that – irrespective of the status of technology – effective digital inclusion displays some core characteristics.

The principles of effective digital inclusion

Governments, the private sector and civil society should collaborate
The first critical principle of effective digital inclusion is that governments, the private sector and civil society should collaborate. As an intervention with clear public as well as personal benefit, and a strong moral justification, digital inclusion is rightly the business of government. However, the private sector can benefit substantially from this investment and arguably has its own moral obligation to act. Public and private sectors need to work with civil society, because the most effective delivery models for digital inclusion (see below) are those which operate in communities, frequently outside the ambit of public services and formal education and training systems. Collaboration in the delivery of digital inclusion draws on the strengths of and contributions of each sector: government with its convening power and public profile, the private sector with its resources and innovation, and civil society with its reach.

In the UK, the government recently launched a digital strategy (DCMS, 2017), putting digital skills and inclusion at the heart of a policy package designed to ensure the country is making the most of the digital economy. A significant number of large corporates with UK interests – including global names such as Google and IBM – pledged direct support. Following the publication of the strategy, the UK government has now formed a digital skills partnership (Hancock, 2017) with industry and civil society, bringing together representatives from all sectors and facilitating action on digital skills and inclusion at the national and local level.

Personal relationships are key
The second principle is about how digital inclusion is delivered with the people who need support, and reflects that at the heart of digital inclusion is a simple idea. As noted above, the primary barrier for those offline is motivational – whether this is a lack of interest in the internet, a lack of confidence in using computers and other digital devices, or lack of trust in digital – and this is frequently compounded by a range of social exclusion factors, from unemployment and low skills to poverty, disability, poor health and wellbeing. As well as being excluded from the digital world, those offline tend to be excluded from other aspects of society and participation, not least the formal education and training system. There is a range of evidence to suggest that, on balance, the most effective way of delivering digital inclusion is through developing and maintaining personal relationships.

Within this idea, there are two clear priorities. First, to establish trust. As we have seen, the reasons for being offline can be very personal, and in many cases digital exclusion is associated with shame. 'Opening up' in order to start the process of digital inclusion can be a significant step. Although the rules of placing trust are complex, in most cases people find it easier to build trust with a person they know well (friend or family) or someone in a nearby organisation, one which feels part of the digitally excluded person's immediate community and not part of 'the big system'. In the Online Centres Network we have seen many examples of practitioners spending a lot of time at the start of an intervention working to build trust, before digital is even discussed.

The second priority is to identify a practical application – based around life or work – that will enable the person to 'hook' into the idea of digital so they can see why they should engage and commit, and how it can benefit them. For example, I may find out that John would like to get a job, in which case helping him learn how to search for work online may be an effective first step in engaging him. Once the 'hook' is established, the process of digital inclusion can start to move forward. Recognising – as above – that no individual's situation is the same, the journey to digital inclusion can take differing amounts of time: from days for those with some confidence and few barriers, to months and even years for those facing fundamental barriers. In 2017 Good Things Foundation published Routes to Inclusion (2017b), a longitudinal study of digitally excluded learners that bears out this model, focusing on their relationship with the people and organisations supporting them and following their personal journeys.

The relationship-based model of digital inclusion is particularly important where the idea of digital meets with strong resistance. The 2017 Lloyds Banking Group research suggested that in the UK the views of adults offline may be becoming more entrenched, with 68% saying nothing would motivate them to go online compared with 44% having this view the previous year (Lloyds Bank, 2017). More recently evidence from 'Getting the Most Out of Digital', a study of older people carried out by Centre for Ageing Better and Good Things Foundation (Centre for Ageing Better, 2017), underlined how even the word 'digital' can strengthen rather than remove motivational barriers to getting online.

So effective digital inclusion isn't about digital, but about people: about how building and sustaining personal relationships is key in helping those offline, who frequently face various forms of social exclusion, to engage with digital and use it to improve their lives.

The movement is important

The third principle – and the overriding focus of this chapter – builds on the first two, combining the importance of collaboration with the centrality of personal relationships in building digital confidence and skills. This is the principle of the movement, where people and organisations have appraised and internalised the benefits of helping others to build digital confidence and skills. As one volunteer digital champion put it at a recent launch of one of Good Things Foundation's programmes: 'It means I can put something back, open up a whole new world for the people I help, and develop my confidence.'

People realise their own benefits from helping others to cross the digital divide. And from a civil society perspective, embedding digital inclusion into social purpose and mission – together with the use of suitable tools and resources – can help increase the social impact of a charity or non-governmental organisation (NGO). It also opens a new channel through which community-based organisations can recruit volunteers, and provides a route for the charity or NGO to streamline and improve its processes and ways of working.

But, critically, when there is a movement effect a 'cascade' starts through which people who benefit from digital pass their confidence and skills on to others, whether by helping family and friends or by volunteering in a local community-based organisation. Digital inclusion provides a powerful fuel for individual opportunity and social cohesion.

It is the principle of the movement that has most strongly guided the work of Good Things Foundation in the UK since 2010, during which time the organisation has reached over 2.3 million people. The Foundation has grown the movement through the Online Centres Network, a 'big club with a shared vision', comprising more than 5000 community-based organisations in every part of the UK: job clubs, healthy eating classes, community learning projects, library learning groups, housing association residents' clubs, and others. The Foundation's model has two core parts:

- a free membership offer to any organisation wishing to join (telephone advice and support through a network team, training, events, collateral, campaigns and a learning platform designed for people with low digital confidence and skills that enables community organisations to manage and use outcome data).
- the design and delivery of funded programmes, using partnership with government (national and local), private sector organisations and grant-making organisations to channel grant funding to the network to deliver a range of different social outcomes through digital.

Over time, the strength of the movement has grown: across the UK there are online centres delivering digital inclusion as a part of their day-to-day operation, not because they are being funded to do so but because they recognise the moral, social and economic case for doing so and understand how digital inclusion can help them pursue their social mission. There are also over 30,000 volunteers across the Online Centres Network, all of whom want to help others and pass on their digital skills. Overall, the online centres help more than 300,000 people each year across the UK.

In the UK, Good Things Foundation and its partners have created a movement at grassroots level (working with community organisations and volunteers) and at stakeholder level (working with government and other large organisations), operating simultaneously. Nether movement can thrive without the other. In many ways, it is a 'movement squared'.

Conclusion: why the movement needs to continue
In this chapter the range of arguments for prioritising and investing in digital inclusion, and the key features of effective digital inclusion delivery, have been presented. But there are three reasons why the 'movement squared' is so important right now, and why it needs to continue:

- Public funding is under unprecedented strain, while demand for public services continues to rise, including in areas such as health and ageing, poverty reduction and support for children. So digital transformation among public services is at a premium, requiring digital inclusion to ensure everyone can benefit: and the movement is the most effective way of resourcing this activity, working across sectors.
- Digital itself provides an increasingly important tool for co-ordinating the movement. Social media is just the beginning: as our society becomes even more connected through the internet of things, artificial intelligence and big data, new opportunities for the movement will be created together with new structures to support them.
- The whole of (global) society is discussing and debating our human relationship with digital, and we will need to continue to think together as the challenges inevitably keep coming. From data privacy to robot co-workers, technology is changing too rapidly for humans to adapt through anything less than continuous conversation, and by its nature this is something the movement can support. If we are all talking, all sharing, we will make better decisions and be able to do more to drive collective wellbeing.

No one organisation has a premium on the right model for digital inclusion, including Good Things Foundation. We know that relationships work as the basis for effective digital inclusion, but we're driven by a desire to innovate – testing new approaches, learning and improving – and this is critical as our human relationship with technology continues to change.

Digital skills are fundamental – for individuals, for communities and for economies – and will remain so as technology continues to evolve. Digital inclusion is a moral and economic imperative, but also underpins the development of digital skills among a significant proportion of the world's population. But beyond this, there is a strong argument that the movement for digital inclusion is something we need across the whole span of digital skills, now and into the future, not only as individuals but as the whole of humanity.

References

Centre for Ageing Better (2017) Getting the Most Out of Digital, https://www.ageing-better.org.uk/our-work/digital.

DCMS (2017) *UK Digital Strategy*, Department for Digital, Culture Media and Sport, https://www.gov.uk/government/publications/uk-digital-strategy.

Doteveryone (n.d.) *Defining Digital Understanding*, https://doteveryone.org.uk/our-work/defining-digital-understanding/.

Good Things Foundation (2017a) Future Digital Inclusion, https://www.goodthingsfoundation.org/projects/future-digital-inclusion.

Good Things Foundation (2017b) Routes to Inclusion, https://www.goodthingsfoundation.org/projects/routes-to-inclusion.

Hancock, M. (2017) Working Together to Increase Digital Skills, DCMS blog, Department for Digital, Culture, Media and Sport, https://dcmsblog.uk/2017/11/3345/.

Hogan, O., Sheehy, C., Uppala, S. and Jayasuriya, R. (2015) *The Economic Impact of Digital Skills and Inclusion in the UK: a report for Tinder Foundation and Go ON UK*, Centre for Economics and Business Research, https://www.goodthingsfoundation.org/sites/default/files/research-publications/the_economic_impact_of_digital_skills_and_inclusion_in_the_uk_final_v2.pdf.

Levin, S. (2017) Facebook Admits it Poses Mental Health Risk – But Says Using Site More Can Help, *Guardian*, 15 December, https://www.theguardian.com/technology/2017/dec/15/facebook-mental-health-psychology-social-media.

Lloyds Bank (2017) *Consumer Digital Index*, https://www.lloydsbank.com/assets/media/pdfs/lloyds-bank-consumer-digital-index-2017.pdf.

Nominet Trust (2016) *Digital Reach: digital skills for the hardest-to-reach young people*, https://www.nominettrust.org.uk/wp-content/uploads/2017/07/Online_NT_Digital_Reach_Prospectus_Final.pdf.

Ofcom (2017a) *Adults' Media Use and Attitudes*, https://www.ofcom.org.uk/__data/assets/pdf_file/0020/102755/

adults-media-use-attitudes-2017.pdf.

Ofcom (2017b) *Communications Market Report*, https://www.ofcom.org.uk/research-and-data/multi-sector-research/cmr/cmr-2017/uk.

Conclusion

The chapters in this book have broadly addressed the question of what it means to live, learn, work, play, interact and exercise leadership in the contemporary world. Through the wide-ranging perspectives presented here we have seen that digital literacy is a collective, collaborative and creative endeavour spanning all stages of life. In this final section we draw together some of the threads which run throughout the whole volume.

An important insight is the way in which digital literacy is not just or even primarily about technical expertise, but rather involves a shift in mindset. This is about an openness to doing things differently. It is also about the capacity to draw on a range of skills and practices in situ. Context is crucial, and a number of our contributors (Secker, Nicholls, Bennett and Folley, Fraser with Reedy, Micklethwaite) highlight the need for digital practices to be relevant and embedded in authentic and meaningful ways. The motivation to get online and develop digital skills and capabilities comes from having a clear purpose, whether that is getting a job, creating excellent learning experiences or achieving company goals.

Developing digital literacy is a personal learning journey and a collaborative project. Many of our contributors highlight the need for partnership between different stakeholders. This results in the blurring of traditional boundaries – between formal and informal learning, between students and their teachers, between staff hierarchies and across geographical zones. Learners and teachers are in it together, with teachers adopting a more facilitative role. Playful learning and games are being used to good effect (Walton et al). Digital leaders must be human, vulnerable and willing to admit and learn from their mistakes. Building relationships and trust is key (Killen, Secker, Nerantzi and Jackson, Fraser with Reedy, Cheuk and Reedy, Micklethwaite). Community-building, peer coaching and individual support all have a role to play.

Alongside this there is a clear message about the importance of high-level backing from stakeholders at organisational or national level to provide the necessary strategic direction and resource for grassroots initiatives to flourish. In this way, pockets of innovation and good practice can be scaled up and put on a sustainable footing.

The first step in agreeing an institutional or national approach is to come to a clear shared understanding about what digital literacy means in a given context and a number of our contributors (Secker, Nicholls, Inskip, Fraser with Reedy, Cheuk and Reedy, Micklethwaite) have helpfully addressed this question. It entails focusing on who your stakeholders are, and what they need to be able to do. Frameworks and models can be useful in identifying the appropriate skills and attributes in order to audit current provision, pinpoint gaps and determine what needs to happen.

While information literacy as a term may be less widespread outside the library community than digital literacy, the skills and attributes it promotes have never been more important. A number of contributors (Fraser with Reedy, Cheuk and Reedy, Seargeant and Tagg, and Secker) emphasise the crucial role of critical thinking in relation to digital content and social interaction. Copyright literacy (Morrison, Fraser with Reedy) emerges as a key competence, not only to protect the rights of creators, but also to promote the proactive sharing of open educational content.

Digital literacy has the potential to transform lives, whether in gaining access to opportunities in the first place, or being empowered to do things differently in educational and workplace settings. The social mission is clearly set out in chapters by Fraser with Reedy and Micklethwaite. By equipping people to participate fully in a digital world, they are able to develop the confidence, resilience and skills to take their place as engaged digital citizens.

We encourage you to reflect on what you have read and to consider which elements relate best to your own situation. Once you have come up with your shortlist of ideas, look for opportunities to put them into practice. It may be easiest to start small and build on that, seeking to collaborate and work in partnership with others. If you are a manager, consider how digital literacy initiatives can be encouraged and rewarded. We aim through our blog https://diglitunpacked.wordpress.com/ to share examples of where people are making a difference in their workplace, community or educational setting. We would love to feature your stories.

Index

#creativeHE Google Plus
   community platform 123–32
   changes to thinking and practice 128–9
   collaborative social learning 123–4
   Creative Academic Magazine 132
   culture of trust 126
   evaluation 128–31
   illustration 126–8
   impact on thinking 134–7
   lessons learned 131–2
   pedagogical thinking and practices 124–5
   playground pedagogy 125–6
   scaffolded social learning 124–5
   suggestions for improvements 130–1
   valuing #creativeHE design characteristics 129–30

A New Curriculum of Information Literacy (ANCIL) 9
academic practices
   digital literacy 10–11
   reading and research, Student

Ambassadors for Digital Literacy (SADL) 89
Age of Empires, digital game 73
All Aboard Project, digital capabilities 30–2
AMORES project 47–61
   activities 53–4, 56–7
   collaborative learning 50–3
   digital technologies 58–9
   example learning scenario 53–4
   facilitating student learning 57–8
   findings 54–5
   limitations 60
   models for learning 49–51
   motivation for 48–9
   recommendations 55–60
   reflecting on learning 50
   social media 59
   staff perspectives 55
   student perspective 54–5
   teaching methodology 49–54
   tools 56–7
   videoconferencing 59–60
Appreciative Inquiry Model 114–15, 117, 118
Association of College and Research Libraries (ACRL) 9

Beetham and Sharpe Learning Literacies Development Framework 19–22, 112–13
Beetham and Sharp's model of digital literacies 6, 112–13
Birmingham Digital Student, partnerships 36
Breakout EDU, digital game 72
British Computer Society (BCS) 142
bubble effect, fake news 181–2
Building Schools for the Future (BSF) Programme, DigiLit Leicester project 157, 158–9

case study
 digital literacy development 25–6
 presentations 26
central services 17–27
 case study 25–6
 conversations 22–3
 core curriculum 25
 design for learning 23–6
 digital literacy development 17–27
 IT skills 19–21
 knowledge curation 23, 25
 learning literacies 18–22
 way forward 26–7
Change Agents' Network, partnerships 36
ChangeMakers programme, University College London (UCL) 35
children *see* AMORES project; digital games
CILIP (Chartered Institute of Library and Information Professionals), Professional Knowledge and Skills Base (PKSB) 143, 144–7
Civilization, digital game 73
collaboration
 see also partnerships
 digital capabilities 33–6, 38–40
 digital inclusion 195–7
 digital literacy 203–4
 Salford City College 34–5
 social networking, company 172–7
 University College London (UCL) 35
 University of Lincoln 35–6
collaborative learning, AMORES project 50–3
collaborative social learning, #creativeHE Google Plus community platform 123–4
company social networking and collaboration platform 172–7
context importance, digital literacy 203
conversations, central services' role 22–3
copyright 97–106
 'communication to the public' 102–3
 compliance 102
 copyright education 104–5
 copyright literacy 97–8, 99, 105–6
 Copyright the Card Game 104–5
 Creative Commons 103
 definitions 97–8

digital technologies 98–101
  fair dealing 101–2
  fair use 101–2
  history 98–101
  open licensed content 103–4
  open practice 102–4
  playful approaches 104–5
  risk 101–2
  rules 102
core curriculum, central services'
  role 25
Creative Academic Magazine,
  #creativeHE Google Plus
  community platform 132
Creative Commons 103
culture change, workplace digital
  literacy 171–2, 175–7

D4 Curriculum Design Model
  111–20
  Appreciative Inquiry Model
    114–15, 117, 118
  developments 119–20
  digital practices 112–13
  digital skills 112–13
  Jisc ViewPoint cards 115, 116
Derby Adult Learning Service,
  peer coaching 39–40
design for learning, central
  services' role 23–6
DigiLit Leicester project 155–66
  aims 157–8
  approach 156–8
  Building Schools for the Future
    (BSF) Programme 157,
    158–9
  centring open educational
    practice 163–5

  confidence levels 160, 163
  digital inclusion 156
  digital literacy areas 160–2
  framework 159–62
  funding 158
  knowledge transfer partnership
    (KTP) 158
  lessons learned 164–5
  open educational practice
    163–5
  priorities 159–62
  special educational needs
    (SEN) schools 157, 158–9
  staff development 158
  survey 160–4
digital capabilities
  see also IT skills
  All Aboard Project 30–2
  collaboration 33–6, 38–40
  developing 29–41
  European Commission's Digital
    Competence Framework
    (2017) 30
  frameworks 30–2
  Go ON UK's Basic Digital
    Skills Framework (2015) 30
  Jisc Digital Capabilities
    Framework for Individuals
    30, 31
  partnerships 33–6
  peer coaching 38–40
  South East Regional College 40
  terminology 4–5, 29–32
  value 32–3
digital competence 141
digital games 63–76
  Age of Empires 73
  Breakout EDU 72

Civilization 73
digital childhoods 64–5
digital player identity 70
engagement 67–71
Escape the Guillotine! 72–3
examples 66–8, 71–4
Foundation of the Hellenic World of Athens 73
Game 1910: 73
gaming literacies 68–9
Minecraft 71–2
new literacies 65–6
next steps 74–5
online environments, learning in 65–6
player engagement 67–71
player participation 67–8
Playhist project 73
Quest Atlantis 71
Rome: Total War 73
Scratch 71
'screen time' 64–5
social relationships 70
Transmedia storytelling 72
Unity 72
digital identity management, Student Ambassadors for Digital Literacy (SADL) 90
digital inclusion 191–200
  benefits 193–4
  changing with technology 194–5
  collaboration 195–7
  continuation reasons 199–200
  DigiLit Leicester project 156
  Good Things Foundation 195, 197–200
  motivational barrier 192–3, 197
  personal relationships 196–8
  principles 195–8
  social exclusion/inequality 191–2
digital literacy
  defining 5, 48, 140–2, 156, 169
  vs information literacy 8–10
  digital native debate 11–12
  digital practice example, presentations 20
digital practices
  D4 Curriculum Design Model 112–13
  higher education curriculum 112–13
digital skills
  D4 Curriculum Design Model 112–13
  higher education curriculum 112–13
  terminology 4, 5
digital technologies
  AMORES project 58–9
  copyright 98–101

educational solutions, fake news 185–7
Escape the Guillotine!, digital game 72–3
European Commission's Digital Competence Framework (2017), digital capabilities 30
evaluating and finding information, Student Ambassadors for Digital Literacy (SADL) 88–9

Facebook, fake news 180–7

fake news 179–87
  bubble effect 181–2
  educational solutions 185–7
  Facebook 180–7
  false news 183–5
  filter bubbles 180–1
  social media 180–7
  technological solutions 182–3
  user agency 181–2
false news, fake news 183–5
filter bubbles, fake news 180–1
finding and evaluating
    information, Student
    Ambassadors for Digital
    Literacy (SADL) 88–9
Foundation of the Hellenic World
    of Athens, digital game 73

Game 1910:, digital game 73
games, digital *see* digital games
Go ON UK's Basic Digital Skills
    Framework (2015), digital
    capabilities 30
Good Things Foundation, digital
    inclusion 195, 197–200

higher education curriculum,
    digital skills and practices
    112–13
holistic approach to student
    learning 12–14
holistic understanding, digital
    literacies 19

information literacy
  vs digital literacy 8–10
  literacies landscape 6–7
IT skills

  see also digital capabilities
  case study 25–6
  central services 19–21
  Learning Literacies
    Development Framework
    19–21

Jisc Digital Capabilities
    Framework for Individuals
    30, 31
Jisc Digital Capability Framework
    142
Jisc Seven Elements of Digital
    Literacies Model 139–40,
    142
Jisc ViewPoint cards, D4
    Curriculum Design Model
    115, 116

knowledge curation, central
    services' role 23, 25
knowledge transfer partnership
    (KTP), DigiLit Leicester
    project 158
Kozbial, Sebastian 136–7

Lancaster University
  Digital Lancaster 37
  organizational digital capability
    37
LANES principles, workplace
    digital literacy 172
Leadership 2.0, workplace digital
    literacy 176–7
learning literacies
  Beetham and Sharpe Learning
    Literacies Development
    Framework 19–22, 112–13

central services 18–22
Leicestershire Adult Learning
    Service
    peer coaching 40
    staff development 40
levels of digital literacy, workplace
    172–5
library staff digital literacies
    139–47
    see also staff development;
    staff–student partnerships
    defining digital literacy 140–2
    Digital Information Skills for
        Library Workforce 146
    Jisc Digital Capability
        Framework 142
    Jisc Seven Elements of Digital
        Literacies Model 139–40,
        142
    professional development 143
    Professional Knowledge and
        Skills Base (PKSB) 143,
        144–7
    SCONUL survey 139–40
London School of Economics and
    Political Science (LSE) *see*
    Student Ambassadors for
    Digital Literacy (SADL)

managing and sharing information,
    Student Ambassadors for
    Digital Literacy (SADL)
    89–90
Minecraft, digital game 71–2
motivational barrier, digital
    inclusion 192–3, 197
Mozelius, P. 75

new literacies 65–6

online environments, learning in
    65–6
open educational practice, DigiLit
    Leicester project 163–5
organizational digital capability
    Lancaster University 37
    transformative approaches 36–8
    University of Hertfordshire
        37–8

partnerships
    see also collaboration
    Birmingham Digital Student 36
    Change Agents' Network 36
    digital capabilities 33–6
    Student Ambassadors for
        Digital Literacy (SADL)
        85, 91–4
    student–staff partnerships 85,
        91–4
    University of Southampton 34
pedagogical thinking and
    practices, #creativeHE
    Google Plus community
    platform 124–5
peer coaching
    Derby Adult Learning Service
        39–40
    digital capabilities 38–40
    Leicestershire Adult Learning
        Service 40
    South East Regional College 40
personal relationships, digital
    inclusion 196–8
playground pedagogy,
    #creativeHE Google Plus

community platform 125–6
Playhist project, digital game 73
presentations
  case study 26
  digital practice example 20
professional development 143
  see also library staff digital literacies
Professional Knowledge and Skills Base (PKSB), CILIP (Chartered Institute of Library and Information Professionals) 143, 144–7

Quest Atlantis, digital game 71

reflecting on learning, AMORES project 50
Rome: Total War, digital game 73

Salford City College, collaboration 34–5
scaffolded social learning, #creativeHE Google Plus community platform 124–5
schools projects *see* AMORES project; DigiLit Leicester project
SCONUL Seven Pillars model 144
SCONUL survey, library staff digital literacies 139–40
Scratch, digital game 71
'screen time', digital games 64–5
sharing and managing information, Student Ambassadors for Digital Literacy (SADL) 89–90
social exclusion/inequality, digital inclusion 191–2
social media
  AMORES project 59
  Facebook 180–7
  fake news 180–7
social networking and collaboration platform 172–7
social relationships, digital games 70
Society of Chief Librarians (SCL), Digital Information Skills for Library Workforce 146
South East Regional College
  digital capabilities 40
  peer coaching 40
special educational needs (SEN) schools, DigiLit Leicester project 157, 158–9
spectrum of workplace digital literacy 170–1
staff development
  see also library staff digital literacies
  DigiLit Leicester project 158
  Leicestershire Adult Learning Service 40
staff–student partnerships 85, 91–4
  see also library staff digital literacies
Student Ambassadors for Digital Literacy (SADL) 83–96
  academic practices: reading and research 89
  aims 85
  benefits 92–3
  challenges 93–4

digital identity management 90
evaluation 92–3
finding and evaluating
    information 88–9
funding 85–6, 93–4
future 95–6
guidance and support 94
impact 92–3
institutional context 84
key points 94–5
lessons learned 94–5
managing and sharing
    information 89–90
motivation 94–5
operation 86
partnerships 85, 91–4
recruitment 86
resource–intensive nature 93–4
senior ambassadors 87
set–up 85–6
student research practices 93
students' capabilities
    development 87–90
student–staff partnerships 85,
    91–4
success measures 94
teaching team 90–1
workshops 87–90

teaching methodology, AMORES
    project 49–54
terminology
    digital capabilities 4–5
    digital literacy 3–14
    digital skills 4, 5

transformative approaches,
    organizational digital
    capability 36–8
Transmedia storytelling, digital
    game 72

UK network for Researching,
    Advancing and Inspiring
    Student Engagement 36
Unity, digital game 72
University College London (UCL)
    ChangeMakers programme 35
    collaboration 35
University of Hertfordshire,
    organizational digital
    capability 37–8
University of Lincoln,
    collaboration 35–6
University of Southampton,
    digital capabilities
    partnerships 34
user agency, fake news 181–2

workplace digital literacy
    company social networking and
        collaboration platform 172–7
    culture change 171–2, 175–7
    LANES principles 172
    Leadership 2.0 176–7
    levels of digital literacy 172–5
    spectrum of workplace digital
        literacy 170–1